SOA Made Simple

Discover the true meaning behind the buzzword that is 'Service Oriented Architecture'

Lonneke Dikmans

Ronald van Luttikhuizen

BIRMINGHAM - MUMBAI

SOA Made Simple

Copyright © 2012 Packt Publishing

All rights reserved. No part of this book may be reproduced, stored in a retrieval system, or transmitted in any form or by any means, without the prior written permission of the publisher, except in the case of brief quotations embedded in critical articles or reviews.

Every effort has been made in the preparation of this book to ensure the accuracy of the information presented. However, the information contained in this book is sold without warranty, either express or implied. Neither the authors, nor Packt Publishing, and its dealers and distributors will be held liable for any damages caused or alleged to be caused directly or indirectly by this book.

Packt Publishing has endeavored to provide trademark information about all of the companies and products mentioned in this book by the appropriate use of capitals. However, Packt Publishing cannot guarantee the accuracy of this information.

First published: December 2012

Production Reference: 1131212

Published by Packt Publishing Ltd.

Livery Place

35 Livery Street

Birmingham B3 2PB, UK.

ISBN 978-1-849684-16-3

www.packtpub.com

Cover Image by David Gimenez (bilbaorocker@yahoo.co.uk)

Credits

Authors
Lonneke Dikmans
Ronald van Luttikhuizen

Reviewers
Howard S. Edidin, MCTS
Anant Kadiyala
Derkjan Zweers

Acquisition Editor
Robin De Jongh
Stephanie Moss

Lead Technical Editor
Arun Nadar

Technical Editors
Brandt D'Mello
Worrell Lewis

Project Coordinator
Shraddha Vora

Proofreader
Mario Cecere

Indexer
Monica Ajmera

Graphics
Sheetal Aute
Valentina D'silva
Aditi Gajjar

Production Coordinator
Conidon Miranda

Cover Work
Conidon Miranda

About the Authors

Lonneke Dikmans lives in the Netherlands with her husband and two children. She graduated with a degree in cognitive science from the University of Nijmegen in the Netherlands. She started her career as a usability specialist but went back to school when she lived in California to pursue a more technical career. She started as a JEE developer on different platforms such as Oracle and IBM, and specialized in integration. She now works as an architect, both on projects and as an enterprise architect. She has experience in different industries such as financial services, government, and utilities. She advises companies that want to set up Service Oriented Architecture and Business Process Management. Lonneke was one of the first five technical experts to be recognized as an Oracle Fusion Middleware Regional Director in 2005. In 2007, the program was renamed and is now known as the Oracle ACE program. Lonneke is a BPMN certified professional and was awarded the title of Oracle Fusion Middleware developer of the year by Oracle Magazine in 2007.

Lonneke is the managing partner of Vennster with Ronald van Luttikhuizen. Vennster is a knowledge-driven organization. Vennster's single most important ambition is to help her customers improve their products and services by improving the quality of the information flow. This is accomplished by offering services in the areas of User Experience, Business Process Management, and Service Oriented Architecture.

Lonneke has contributed to the *Oracle SOA Suite 11g Handbook*, *Oracle Press* by Lucas Jellema that was published in 2011. She publishes on a regular basis in magazines and on the internet, participates in podcasts, and speaks at international conferences about Service Oriented Architecture and Business Process Management.

> I would like to thank the people that I have worked with over the years that helped shape my thoughts about Service Oriented Architecture. It would take too much space to list them all. Everyone contributed in different ways and were from different fields: technical people, enterprise architects, project managers, departmental managers, product managers, and so on. I would like to thank the reviewers Derkjan Zweers, Anant Kadiyala, and Howard Edidin for their valuable input. Their perspective, remarks, questions, and suggestions were very valuable. Last but not least I would like to thank my husband Hans and our children Mathijs and Anne for their support, encouragement and patience. My final thoughts are for our neighbor Dafnis, who died earlier this year at the age of 13. His courage and determination have become an example for me. We miss him!

Ronald van Luttikhuizen lives in Nijmegen, the Netherlands with his partner Susanne. He has over 10 years of experience in IT. Ronald studied Computer Science at the University of Utrecht and University of Wisconsin – Madison and received his MSc degree in 2003. Ronald creates valuable solutions for the business using a structured approach to Service Oriented Architecture. He takes into account both technical and functional aspects of a process to come up with a feasible solution. Ronald worked in projects for government, financials, energy, logistics, and services.

Ronald has experience in various roles such as architect, project lead, information analyst, software developer/designer, coach, trainer, team lead, and consultant in a wide variety of enterprise applications. He started his career as a specialist in analysis and design, application development, and application and process integration. The main technology focus in these projects were UML, Java, and XML. In later years, Ronald focused on architecture within service-oriented environments and other types of EAI environments, describing the to-be architecture, defining roadmaps, guiding implementation, and building parts of the solution.

Ronald is a speaker at (international) conferences and regularly publishes articles on Oracle Technology Network, his blog, Java Magazine, Optimize, and participates in OTN ArchBeat Podcasts. In 2008, Ronald was named Oracle ACE for SOA and middleware. Ronald was promoted to Oracle ACE Director in 2010. Ronald wrote several chapters for the *Oracle SOA Suite 11g Handbook*, *Oracle Press* by Lucas Jellema and served as a technical reviewer for the book. The book was published in 2011.

I would like to thank everyone that helped me in my professional career and my personal life. Without them I wouldn't be able to do the job I do today! A big thanks to my friends and family for supporting me and putting up with all the time I spent on the book and not with them; especially Susanne.

Last but certainly not least I would like to thank the reviewers Derkjan Zweers, Anant Kadiyala, and Howard Edidin and the people at Packt for their valuable input, suggestions, improvements, help, and patience! Without them this book wouldn't exist.

About the Reviewers

Derkjan Zweers is an Information Architect in the province of Overijssel, a regional government in the Netherlands. His primary responsibility is to advise the management on IT-related solutions. His roots in education—he holds a Bachelor of Education degree—have equipped him to communicate about his field of work in common, understandable language.

Previously, Derkjan worked several years for a governance agency as an IT Architect and for a multinational as a Desktop Manager responsible for the branches in the Netherlands.

Derkjan strongly believes in the necessity of one IT agency for the entire Dutch government. He is one of the initiators of the government platform of architects (PPA-Provinciaal Platform Architecten). The platform strives for standardization across the regional governments as a stepping stone to standardization across all government agencies. Service Oriented Architecture is one of the fundamental principles.

During the years 2009 – 2011 Derkjan participated, with the authors, in a major SOA implementation and experienced at firsthand how the theory worked out in practice. His experiences have reinforced his belief that SOA is not primarily a technical issue but rather an organizational one. It is concerned with questions such as the following: what are the objectives of the business and is SOA the means to deliver them? What has to change in the IT-governance? Do vendors deliver solutions that fit an SOA? These are just some of the important questions that are addressed in this book.

Apart from information architecture, Derkjan likes gardening and watching sci-fi movies, and he has an interest in everything that is out of the ordinary and does not fit our established patterns.

Howard S. Edidin is an independent BizTalk architect/consultant specializing in providing guidance and training for companies implementing BizTalk. He was first exposed to BizTalk about the time when "Soap on a Rope" was introduced by Microsoft. He didn't get a chance to use it, until BizTalk 2002 came along. Most of Howard's BizTalk career has been in contract work, which has allowed him to utilize almost all of BizTalk's capabilities. Last year Howard established his own consulting company, the Edidin Group Inc., in order to expand the services he provides. Howard has been very active in the BizTalk community. He has contributed several articles to the TechNet Wiki, provided answers to questions on the LinkedIn BizTalk Groups, contributes to several BizTalk Administration blogs, and maintains his own blog http://biztalkin-howard.blogspot.com/.

Howard is certified MCTS in BizTalk 2010 and has been an MCP for over fourteen years.

Howard is also the co-author of *Microsoft BizTalk 2010 Administration Essentials*, *Packt Publishing*.

www.PacktPub.com

Support files, eBooks, discount offers and more

You might want to visit www.PacktPub.com for support files and downloads related to your book.

Did you know that Packt offers eBook versions of every book published, with PDF and ePub files available? You can upgrade to the eBook version at www.PacktPub.com and as a print book customer, you are entitled to a discount on the eBook copy. Get in touch with us at service@packtpub.com for more details.

At www.PacktPub.com, you can also read a collection of free technical articles, sign up for a range of free newsletters and receive exclusive discounts and offers on Packt books and eBooks.

http://PacktLib.PacktPub.com

Do you need instant solutions to your IT questions? PacktLib is Packt's online digital book library. Here, you can access, read and search across Packt's entire library of books.

Why Subscribe?

- Fully searchable across every book published by Packt
- Copy and paste, print and bookmark content
- On demand and accessible via web browser

Free Access for Packt account holders

If you have an account with Packt at www.PacktPub.com, you can use this to access PacktLib today and view nine entirely free books. Simply use your login credentials for immediate access.

Instant Updates on New Packt Books

Get notified! Find out when new books are published by following @PacktEnterprise on Twitter, or the *Packt Enterprise* Facebook page.

Table of Contents

Preface	**1**
Chapter 1: Understanding the Problem	**7**
The importance of information	**8**
Example – insurance company	8
Mismatch between business and IT	9
Duplication of functionality and data	10
Example – insurance company	11
Process silos	13
Example – utility companies	14
Example – international software company	15
Example – insurance company	17
Strategies to stay ahead	17
Example – a software company	18
Architecture as a tool	**19**
Layering of architecture	22
Models	23
Requirements	24
Architecture ontology	24
Enterprise architecture	25
Reference architecture	27
Solution architecture	28
Project architecture	29
Software architecture	29
Service Oriented Architecture	30
Summary	**30**

Chapter 2: The Solution — 31
What is a service? — 32
Elements of a service – contract, interface, and implementation — 32
- Example – let's have breakfast — 33
- Example – ordering a passport — 35
- Consumer and provider — 35

From sunny-side-up eggs to IT — 36
- Example – international software company revisited — 38
- Consumer and provider — 43

Drivers for services — 45
Common myths — 45
- Every service has to be automated by software — 46
- Every service is a web service — 46
- Consumers of services are always IT systems — 46

Putting it together – what is SOA? — 46
Solutions — 47
Example – utility company — 47
International software company – changing existing processes — 49
Functional duplication – rationalizing application landscapes — 51
Standardization – enabling change — 53

Summary — 54

Chapter 3: Service Identification and Design — 55
Service identification — 56
Top-down — 56
- Example of top-down service identification — 59
Bottom-up — 60
Meet in the middle — 60
I have identified my services, now what? — 61

Service design — 61
Provide value — 62
Meaningful — 62
Implementation hiding — 63
Trust — 63
Idempotent — 63
Isolated — 63
Interoperable — 64
Isolation — 65
- Example: print service — 65
Trust — 66
- Security — 66
- Fault-prevention and handling — 67

Idempotency	69
Idempotency and statefulness	70
Granularity	73
How big should my lasagna be?	75
Classification	76
Reusability	76
Example – reusability	78
Example – good or bad service?	**82**
Service definition revisited	**87**
Summary	**88**
Chapter 4: Classification of Services	**89**
Service classification revisited	**89**
Example – insurance company	90
Other classifications	92
Actor type	93
Channel	93
Organizational boundaries	93
Security level	94
Architectural layer	94
Combining classifications	95
Why classify your services?	96
Composability	**97**
Aggregation versus orchestration	97
Example – DocumentService as a composite service	98
Elementary services	**98**
Realization	98
Composite services	**99**
Where to put the composition logic?	99
Implementation	100
Example 1 – database link	100
Example 2 – service invocation	102
Process services	**103**
Implementation	104
Isolation and composition – a contradiction?	**104**
Passing information from smaller to larger services	**105**
Summary	**109**
Chapter 5: The SOA Platform	**111**
Overview	**112**
Services	**113**
Implementation	114
Using existing software	114
Build the implementation	114

Interfaces	115
Proprietary interfaces	115
Web services	115
Contracts and Policies	117
Events	**118**
Interfaces for events	119
Service composition	**120**
Enterprise Service Bus	120
Business Process Management	122
Case Management	123
Business rules	**125**
User interface	**127**
Integrated user interfaces	129
Information mismatch	130
Security	**131**
Applying security in your SOA	133
Service registry and service repository	**134**
Canonical Data Model	134
Design tooling	**136**
Development tooling	**137**
Example – Order-to-cash revisited	**139**
Designing the solution	139
Developing the solution	140
Running the solution	141
Summary	**141**
Chapter 6: Solution Architectures	**143**
Comprehensive suite or best of breed	**143**
Comparison	**145**
Oracle	**149**
Services	149
Events	149
Oracle Event Processing (OEP)	150
Business Activity Monitoring (BAM)	150
Service composition	150
Oracle Service Bus	150
Oracle SOA Suite	151
Oracle BPM Suite	152
Business rules	153
User interface	153
Security	154
Registry and repository	154

Design tooling	154
Design tooling for developers	154
Design tooling for business analysts	154
Development tooling	155
Test tooling	155
Testing transformations	155
SCA testing framework	156
Testing from the console	156
Deployment tooling	156
Deployment from the IDE	156
Deployment from the console	157
Deployment using scripting	157
Monitoring	157
Error handling	158
IBM	**158**
Services	158
Events	158
WebSphere Operational Decision Management	159
IBM Business Monitor	159
Service composition	159
IBM WebSphere Enterprise Service Bus	159
IBM Business Process Manager	160
Business rules	161
User interface	161
Security	161
Registry and repository	162
Design tooling	162
Services	163
Composite services	163
Development tooling	163
Test tooling	163
Deployment tooling	163
Deployment from the IDE	163
Deployment from the web interface of the server	164
Deployment scripts	164
Monitoring	164
Error handling	164
Microsoft	**165**
Services	165
Events	165
Message-oriented middleware	165
Complex Event Processing (CEP)	165
Business Activity Monitoring	165

Service composition	166
BizTalk Server	166
Windows Server AppFabric	166
Business rules	167
User interface	167
Security	168
Registry and repository	168
Design tooling	168
Development tooling	168
Test tooling	168
Deployment tooling	168
BizTalk Server	169
Monitoring	169
Error handling	169
Summary	**170**
Chapter 7: Creating a Roadmap, How to Spend Your Money and When?	**171**
Organize the SOA effort	**171**
Business case – benefits for different stakeholders	**175**
Business case explained	175
Company as a whole	177
Example 1 – insurance company WATB needs shorter time to market	177
Example 2 – insurance company TPIR needs to decrease operational cost	180
IT	182
Example – insurance company TMS needs to consolidate systems	182
Departmental benefits	185
Example – insurance company X wants to cut cost	185
Analysis of the scenarios	188
Approaches	**190**
Example – Document Management Service	190
Top-down identification	191
Bottom-up identification	192
Meet in the middle	192
Roadmap	**193**
Work packages	193
Service by service	194
Process by process	194
Feature by feature	194
System by system	195
Comparison	195
Maturity and stages	**197**
Stage 0: Starting with SOA	198
Stage 1: Newlyweds	198

Stage 2: Live	198
Stage 3: Growing up	198
Stage 4: Experience	199
Stage 5: Maintenance	199
Summary	**201**
Chapter 8: Life Cycle Management	**203**
Service stages	**203**
Versioning of services	**205**
Type of change – contract, interface, and implementation	206
Changing the contract	206
Changing the interface	207
Changing the implementation	207
Versioning schemes	208
Versioning and life cycle stages	209
Making the version explicit for service consumers	210
Communicating change	212
Tooling	**213**
Standards	215
Information needed	216
Find services	216
Troubleshooting	216
Change process	217
Registries and repositories in your IT landscape	218
Enterprise architecture tools	218
Business Process Management tool	219
Configuration Management Database	219
Bug and issue tracker system	220
ESB	220
Business Activity Monitoring	221
Infrastructure monitoring	221
Summary	**221**
Chapter 9: Pick your Battles	**223**
Governance	**223**
Architecture process	**225**
Ad hoc business need	225
Define the solution	226
Deviations	227
Integration in the solution architecture	227
Planned feature	228
Pick your battles	229
Development process	**230**
Pick your battles	232

Operations	**233**
Pick your battles	235
Change management	**237**
Pick your battles	238
Summary	**239**
Chapter 10: Methodologies and SOA	**241**
Demand management	**242**
Methodology	243
Impact of SOA	244
Project management	**246**
Methodology	246
Impact of SOA	248
Software development	**249**
Methodology	250
Impact of SOA	251
Application management	**251**
Methodology	252
Impact of SOA	253
IT service and operations management	**254**
Methodology	254
Impact of SOA	255
Summary	**257**
Index	**259**

Preface

A lot of organizations are implementing, or want to implement, Service Oriented Architecture to support their goals. Service Oriented Architecture is a natural step in the evolution of Information Technology; we started out with big systems in universities and banks, and moved to desktop computers in the workplace and at home. We are now moving to solutions in the cloud, offering services to consumers and businesses alike, adding mobile computing to the mix. So what is a service? A service is something that has value. Service orientation is not a difficult concept to grasp, everyone knows services and uses them daily; think of a hotel that offers a shuttle service to the nearest airport. Or the hairdresser that cuts your hair. This book describes how you can accomplish service orientation successfully in your organization and in IT, using a practical and simple approach. It is done without overly complex abstractions, but with examples from different industries and hands-on experience of the authors. The approach is independent of the specific technology or programming language you apply in your organization.

What this book covers

Chapter 1, Understanding the problem?, discusses the challenges that organizations face with respect to information technology and is illustrated with examples. Architecture is explained as a means to solve these problems structurally and in compliance with your organization's goals.

Chapter 2, The Solution, explains how applying SOA can help your organization to solve the problems that were discussed in the previous chapter. In this chapter, the concept of services is explained as well as Service Oriented Architecture.

Chapter 3, Service Identification and Design, describes how services are the base of a Service Oriented Architecture. The process of identifying services and designing their interface, contract, and implementation are important activities when realizing a Service Oriented Architecture.

Preface

Chapter 4, Classification of Services, covers the different types of services. You learn in this chapter how classification can help you in your SOA effort. The chapter explains different ways of classifying your services and the reason to choose a particular classification. Classification based on service composition is discussed in detail.

Chapter 5, The SOA Platform, identifies the different components of an SOA platform and explains the use of these components, keeping in mind that to realize an SOA in your organization, you need a platform to build it with

Chapter 6, Solution Architectures, tells us about how you can go for a best-of-breed solution to realize your SOA, or use a product suite. The solution of the big software vendors Oracle, IBM, and Microsoft are discussed in terms of the components you need for an SOA platform.

Chapter 7, Creating a Roadmap, How to Spend Your Money and When?, explains how to plan your endeavor. In this chapter, creating a roadmap for the realization of your SOA is discussed.

Chapter 8, Life Cycle Management, explains how to maintain services. Requirements may change, services may become outdated, and new services may be needed. This chapter discusses life cycle management of services, and tooling that supports registries and repositories.

Chapter 9, Pick your Battles, talks about how during the realization and operation of an SOA you will run into issues with stakeholders. A common pitfall for architects is to be too strict and unrealistic about what can be achieved. This chapter discusses some common issues you will run into and discusses how to handle them.

Chapter 10, Methodologies and SOA, talks about how there are existing methodologies in IT that you are probably using right now in your organization for project management, demand management, and so on. This chapter discusses the impact of using SOA on these existing methodologies.

What you need for this book

To create the code samples given in this book, you need tooling that can display XML. You can view the samples with any XML viewer, text editor, or integrated development environment (IDE) or browser.

Who this book is for

This book is for anyone (architect, designer, developer, administrator, team lead) who is implementing or is about to implement an SOA in an IT-related environment. This guide tells you everything you need to know about an SOA in a clear and easy way. Knowledge or experience with software architecture and information architecture is helpful but not a strict requirement.

Conventions

In this book, you will find a number of styles of text that distinguish between different kinds of information. Here are some examples of these styles, and an explanation of their meaning.

Code words in text are shown as follows: " Both offer `showMenuItems` as an interface to `BreakfastService`."

A block of code is set as follows:

```
<xsd:element name="OrderProductRequest">
  <xsd:complexType>
    <xsd:sequence>
      <xsd:element name="ProductId" type="xsd:string"/>
      <xsd:element name="Quantity" type="xsd:nonNegativeInteger"/>
      <xsd:element name="CustomerId" type="xsd:string"/>
    </xsd:sequence>
  </xsd:complexType>
</xsd:element>
```

When we wish to draw your attention to a particular part of a code block, the relevant lines or items are set in bold:

```
<wsdl:documentation>
   The Order will create an order for multiple orders
   Version history
          V1.0.0 Initial service description
</wsdl:documentation>
```

New terms and **important words** are shown in bold.

> Warnings or important notes appear in a box like this.

> Tips and tricks appear like this.

Reader feedback

Feedback from our readers is always welcome. Let us know what you think about this book—what you liked or may have disliked. Reader feedback is important for us to develop titles that you really get the most out of.

To send us general feedback, simply send an e-mail to feedback@packtpub.com, and mention the book title via the subject of your message.

If there is a topic that you have expertise in and you are interested in either writing or contributing to a book, see our author guide on www.packtpub.com/authors.

Customer support

Now that you are the proud owner of a Packt book, we have a number of things to help you to get the most from your purchase.

Downloading the example code

You can download the example code files for all Packt books you have purchased from your account at http://www.PacktPub.com. If you purchased this book elsewhere, you can visit http://www.PacktPub.com/support and register to have the files e-mailed directly to you.

Errata

Although we have taken every care to ensure the accuracy of our content, mistakes do happen. If you find a mistake in one of our books—maybe a mistake in the text or the code—we would be grateful if you would report this to us. By doing so, you can save other readers from frustration and help us improve subsequent versions of this book. If you find any errata, please report them by visiting http://www.packtpub.com/support, selecting your book, clicking on the **errata submission form** link, and entering the details of your errata. Once your errata are verified, your submission will be accepted and the errata will be uploaded on our website, or added to any list of existing errata, under the Errata section of that title. Any existing errata can be viewed by selecting your title from http://www.packtpub.com/support.

Piracy

Piracy of copyright material on the Internet is an ongoing problem across all media. At Packt, we take the protection of our copyright and licenses very seriously. If you come across any illegal copies of our works, in any form, on the Internet, please provide us with the location address or website name immediately so that we can pursue a remedy.

Please contact us at copyright@packtpub.com with a link to the suspected pirated material.

We appreciate your help in protecting our authors, and our ability to bring you valuable content.

Questions

You can contact us at questions@packtpub.com if you are having a problem with any aspect of the book, and we will do our best to address it.

Understanding the Problem

This chapter investigates what problems people who apply **Service Oriented Architecture (SOA)** are trying to solve. The problems can be categorized into two major areas:

- The mismatch between the business and IT
- Duplication of functionality and process silos

One discipline that can help solve these issues is the application of architecture in an organization and in projects. As the term Service Oriented Architecture indicates, SOA is about architecture. In this chapter you will learn about different types of architecture, like reference architectures and solution architectures, and common layering concepts that can be applied on different levels within the organization to make sure that the strategy of the company is in line with the developments and projects that are executed. But first, let's dive into the problems that modern companies face and look at the increasing importance of (electronic) information in companies.

The importance of information

When **Information Technology** (IT) had its entrance in businesses, it was used primarily by specialist people. The data entry professionals and other users were trained to use the systems all day. Other people were busy doing their job without using the computer, but instead using information on paper. Now the computer is everywhere in the business—from the front office to the back office, from the manager to the concierge.

Modern organizations rely on IT for their day-to-day operations. On top of that, information technology is used in management and supporting processes. The dependency on information technology is even bigger in organizations that deliver services, rather than physical products. For example, a bakery depends on information technology to do accounting, order supplies, and so on. But the core process of baking bread is more dependent on the quality of the ingredients, the physical machines in the factory, and the procedure than on information technology.

Example – insurance company

Now think about a services organization like an insurance company. The operational or core processes of an insurance company consist of policy administration, claims processing, underwriting and acquisition, and reinsuring. These processes are illustrated in the following example:

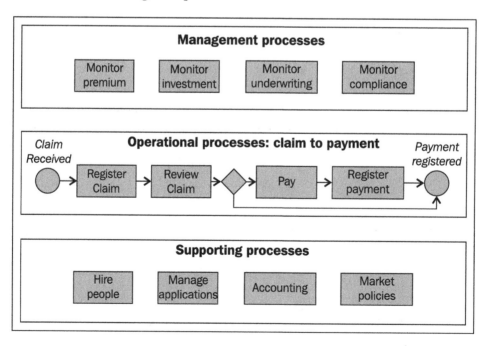

The figure consists of three types of processes:

- **Management processes**: These consist of monitor premium, monitor investment, monitor underwriting, and monitor compliance.
- **Operational processes: claim to payment**: When a claim is received, it is reviewed against the policy of the insured. If the claim is valid, it is paid. The payment is registered in the file of the customer (the insured).
- **Supporting processes**: To support this primary process and the management process, a number of supporting processes are shown in the lower part: **Hire people**, **Manage applications**, **Accounting**, and **Market policies**.

All these processes are information intensive – the insurance company stores information about the different products they insure, the combinations they offer in a policy, the customers they insure, the claims that are processed, the money that is invested, and so on. This information is used across all the processes, both the operational processes and the management and supporting processes. On top of that, information needs to be accumulated to manage the organization. For example, the profit of an insurance company is determined by the earned premium, the investment income minus the incurred loss and underwriting expenses. So management of the company needs information about the earnings, the operational cost, and return on investment to increase their profit. Compare this to the factory that bakes bread; for them, information technology is obviously also very important for the management and supporting processes, but for insurance companies information is what determines for a large part the quality of the service. Information is the main ingredient for this process.

Mismatch between business and IT

As organizations are so dependent on information, it is very important that the technology that provides this information and is used to support these processes is in line with the needs of the organization. This is what we call business and IT alignment. *Henderson and Venkatraman* can be seen as the founding fathers of business/IT alignment and published an article called *Strategic Alignment: Leveraging Information Technology for Transforming Organizations*, IBM Systems Journal, vol32, No1. In their model, the objective of business and IT alignment is to manage three separate risks associated with IT projects:

- **Technical risk**: will the system function, as it should?
- **Organizational risk**: will individuals within the organization use the system as they should?
- **Business risk**: will the implementation and adoption of the system translate into business value?

Business value is jeopardized unless all three risks are managed successfully.

When you talk to people in different organizations, they often complain about IT performance. This technical misalignment of business and IT manifests in two ways:

- IT is not able to change fast enough along with the business
- IT is not able to deliver the functionality the business needs correctly

The first item, IT not being able to change fast enough, is becoming more and more important in today's market. It is one of the problems that SOA can help you solve, if applied correctly. In general, organizations that are in one of the following situations need to be able to change fast:

- Organizations that have to deal with changing rules and regulations, like health insurance companies, financial institutions, and the public sector.
- Organizations that are in fast changing markets, like the telecommunication industry.
- Organizations that are merging, splitting up, or outsourcing part of the operational processes. These organizations need to be able to change their IT according to the changes in the organization and processes. Examples are the financial services industry, product oriented companies with multiple suppliers, and utility companies.

Duplication of functionality and data

Apart from the misalignment of business and IT, there is another problem that becomes more and more important because of the dependency on information—*duplication of data and functionality*. Traditionally, companies are organized functionally. This means that there are different departments for different functions in a company; a customer service department to service the customers, a claims department that assesses the claims, the human resources department for the workforce. All these departments use their own IT systems that keep track of the data that is needed. Because all the departments use their own IT systems, and these systems are not connected to each other, information is duplicated within an organization. This can lead to differences between departments, because the information is not only stored, but also changed in these systems. This leads to inconsistencies across the organization, unless the information is synchronized between all the systems.

Example – insurance company

Let's investigate the impact of duplication of functionality and data with an example from an insurance company again. The marketing department stores information about the products they want to sell to prospects in the **Content Management System (CMS)**.

> A CMS is a system that allows publishing, editing, and modifying content of a website. Often these systems offer procedures to manage workflow. There are two types of content management systems: **enterprise content management systems** and **web content management systems**. The first is used to organize the content of your organization. The latter is used to organize the content for web pages (intranet or internet). Content can be defined as documents, movies, text, pictures, phone numbers, and so on.

An example of such a product is health insurance for students. The Customer Service department also needs this product information, because they need to answer questions they receive from prospects and customers about the product. They often use a **Customer Contact System (CSS)** to support interaction with customers. The product information that is stored in the **Customer Contact System (CCS)** needs to be the same as the product information that is stored in the CMS, to be able to answer questions that customers have about the product. A student might call for example, to ask if he or she is eligible for the student health insurance. Apart from product information, the Customer Service employees need access to policies, the customer data, and claims for a particular customer that is calling. If the marketing department changes something in the product description, this should also be changed in the CSS. The same applies to the Insurance Administration system and the Enterprise Resource Planning system, information should be consistent and both departments—the claims department and the finance department—need the claim, policy, and customer data in their process. The claims department handles claims and the finance department pays claims and collect premiums. If one department changes something, the other department needs to change the data the same way. Often this does not happen, because the departments are not always aware what data is stored redundantly or what changes impact other departments. The next figure shows an example of duplication of data in an insurance company. As you can see, there are several systems storing and maintaining the same type of data and functionality:

Understanding the Problem

- **Product** information is stored and maintained in the CMS by the Marketing department and in the CCS by the Customer Service department;
- **Customer** information is stored and maintained in the CCS by the Customer Service department and in the IAS by the Claims department, and in the ERP by the Accounting department;
- **Call** information is stored and maintained in the CCS and in the IAS
- **Policy** information is stored and maintained in the CCS, in the IAS, and in the ERP system
- **Claim** information is stored and maintained in the CSS, the IAS, and the ERP system

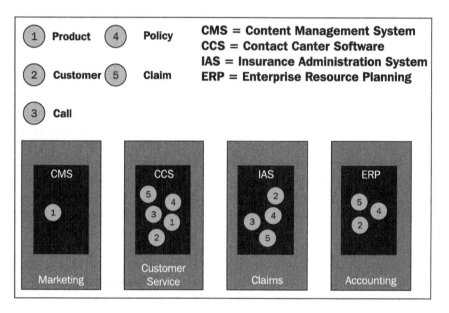

Apart from inconsistencies because of the data duplication, functionality is also duplicated. Take for example adding a product to the portfolio; rules are associated with adding products. These rules are implemented in the IT systems where products are added. When the rules associated with adding a product are changed, this needs to be changed in all the systems where products can be added. This is costly and error prone.

Process silos

Departments that are self sufficient and isolated from the other departments are called **organizational silos**. These silos not only lead to duplication of functionality and data, but also to suboptimal process execution. The processes are divided based on organizational structure, not based on the most efficient end-to-end process. These processes are often referred to as **process silos**. Within a department, there is often not a clear picture what the impact of the output is on a different department. This leads to rework and bottlenecks in other business processes, and eventually to unhappy customers because of delay and mistakes. Take for example the situation in the following figure, where an organization tells the employees in the front office to minimize the time they spend on each phone call, so they can handle as many customers as possible. They minimize the time to complete a phone call, but unfortunately they forget to ask questions and register information that is important for the department that needs to fulfill the order. So even though the front office optimized its processing time, the total end-to-end client process has become slower because of the organizational silos.

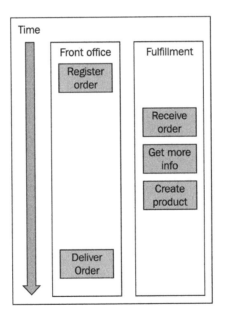

Now that we have seen the general problems that modern companies face with regards to information technology, let's look at some concrete examples from different industries and see what types of problems arise because of this duplication of information and functionality and because of the misalignment between business and IT.

Example – utility companies

To keep energy costs low for consumers and to guarantee the energy delivery, a law in the Netherlands requires utility companies to split into two different entities—the network operator that is responsible for the infrastructure of the gas and electricity grid(s) and the supplier that deals with the consumers (both business and private consumers).

All the utility companies had both activities in their portfolio before this law came into place. Some also generate energy, and offer services to end users regarding the equipment on location (meters, central heating system). The utility companies all started as government agencies, owned by municipalities. Customers did not choose what energy company to get the service from; it was determined by their location. A lot of these companies built big IT systems to keep track of the energy connections, the consumers, the usage, and so on. The IT systems or applications span multiple domains and multiple roles. These systems were built using relational databases; all the data is interconnected. A change in one part of the system will have an impact on another part of the system. Splitting the company is extremely difficult as the entire IT is intertwined, and only all or nothing scenarios can be applied as a solution.

An example of such an IT landscape is shown in the following figure.

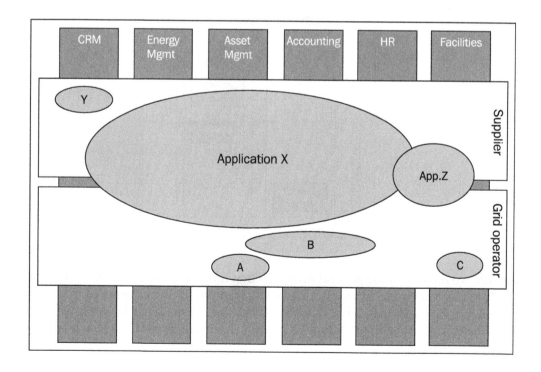

Application X spans multiple domains—CRM, Energy management, asset management, and accounting. It spans two roles—the role of the utility company as a supplier and the role of the utility company as a grid operator. It contains information about the customers from an energy supplier perspective, and information about the energy that is needed in the organization to service all customers, about the assets that the company owns and uses to service the customers and last but not least, the application is used to send invoices to customers. Application **Y** is an off-the-shelf Customer Contact System (CCS) that serves a specific purpose that supports the supplier role of the utility company. The same is true for applications **A**, **B**, and **C**; they service well-defined functionality in a specific domain. When the company has to split into a grid operator and a supplier **A**, **B**, and **C** will go with the grid operator and **Y** will stay with the supplier. For application **X** and **Y** there is a problem as they are used by both and because of their architecture, it is difficult to split the application into a supplier and a grid operator part. They have run into this problem before, when the company bought an off-the-shelf ERP system. They wanted to use the invoice module of this ERP system but couldn't because they could not take out the invoice part of application **X** without breaking other functionality that they wanted to keep. Other smaller changes also cause problems for the IT department; they are not able to implement them fast enough in application **X** to satisfy the business.

This is a typical example of the misalignment between business and IT. The organization needs to change before the date that is set by law, but the IT is built in such a way that it takes years to realize the changes. Sometimes this type of problem is referred to as a **legacy** problem, because difficulty to change tends to arise in systems that have been around for a while. The architecture and technology are out-dated and it is becoming harder and harder to change the system. In this example, the problem is not the age of the technology, but the fact that everything is connected with everything in this huge system.

 Organizations can't be changed fast enough because there is one big IT system with a lot of relationships between different entities.

Example – international software company

An international software company wants to change the way the order-to-cash process is executed. The company has started to sell their products online, and the customer can download the product after paying for it online. This means that the process *order-to-cash* needs to be adjusted—in this case the customer has to pay upfront, instead of after receiving the product.

The **process logic** (the order of the steps) is coded into the custom application that the organization uses for this process. Therefore, changing the process impacts the entire application. This is expensive and very disruptive for day-to-day operations because it is one of the core processes of the company.

Rather than changing the existing process for online purchases, the company decides to create a whole new application, thus creating a problem with data synchronization, customer service, and management information. This is shown in the following figure: there are two applications that handle orders. Depending on the origin of the order, different systems handle it. There is no clear separation in the application between process logic, and the components cannot easily be taken out or replaced. Both functionality and data are duplicated.

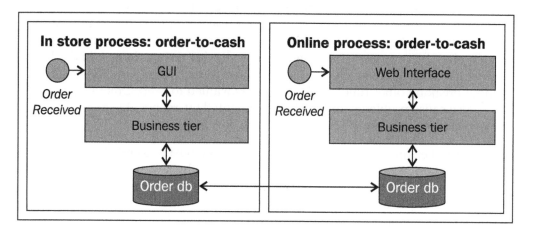

This example covers both misalignment of business and IT, and duplication of functionality and data.

IT can't keep up with process changes because of the way the applications are structured and solves this with data duplication and functional duplication, thus creating more problems for the future.

Example – insurance company

In the Netherlands, people can choose new health insurance every year in December. For insurance companies this means a lot of work; they need to market their new policies, determine prices, and entice people to either switch to their company or stay there if they are already a customer. The competition is fierce, everybody is switching at the same time, there are sites comparing different brands, and whoever publishes a price first sets a trend or loses to the competition. Most insurance companies carry more than one brand and different policy types for different target groups. On top of that, health insurance has a lot of political visibility, both from the perspective of care and from an income perspective. This means that laws and regulation change frequently. Insurance companies often have different systems in the back office and the front office, as you have seen in the previous insurance company example. This means that adding a product needs to be handled both in the back office application and in the content management system of the company. It is difficult to keep track of both systems and every year errors are made with the processing of the new customers and products.

This example shows the problems that occur because of functional duplication and data duplication. This leads to misalignment between business and IT as IT can't deliver fast enough.

 Companies lose out in the competition because IT can't deliver solutions fast enough.

Strategies to stay ahead

The previous sections showed that companies struggle to change fast enough. Companies need to be able to change fast, to be able to compete with each other. Markets are changing fast, so it is very important to be able to change quickly. Depending on the strategy of the company, it might even be necessary to be ahead of everybody else and change to set trends and be proactive in the market. Other companies don't compete by being the first, but by being the cheapest. The strategy that a company uses is important when creating your architecture. If cutting cost is important, reuse of existing assets is important. If changing fast is more important, replacing parts of your IT fast is more important.

You learned in this chapter that it is important for IT to be aligned to the business goals of an organization. There are different strategies that an organization can use such as operational excellence, customer intimacy, and product leadership. These strategies lead to different requirements for the IT systems in your organization.

- **Operational excellence**: Companies that apply operational excellence, focus on operations and execution. This means that efficiency is a very important goal; volume and low cost are important factors. Data and functional duplication are a problem for these companies, because it increases cost in the operation. Companies that focus on operational excellence have a keen eye for waste and redundancy. These kinds of companies strive to optimize their business processes by automation, tracking, and benchmarking the KPIs.

- **Product leadership**: When a company strives for product leadership, innovation and marketing are important. These companies usually operate in dynamic markets. Focus is on innovation, time to market, and design. Business and IT alignment are very important for companies like this.

- **Customer intimacy**: The third strategy means that a company strives to excel in customer service. Products and services are not standardized, but tailored to the needs of the specific customer. There is a focus on CRM, delivery on time, and reliability. The IT systems and processes of companies like this should be highly customizable and flexible; there is less need for standardization than in companies that use operational excellence as a strategy.

Example – a software company

Let's compare the three strategies and the impact on software and processes with an example. Consider an independent software vendor who offers software for customers to support their purchase-to-pay process. They have a number of competitors in the market, with whom they can compete in three ways:

- **Operational Excellence**: If the company wants to compete based on price, it can use operational excellence as a strategy. This means that the software realization process is very much automated and executed like a factory. Every customer gets the same software. If a change is requested, it will be built into the standard software that is delivered to everyone. Customers will have to change their process a little to fit the software. The company will target customers that don't want to spend a lot of money on this process, because supplier management is not an important strategic process for them. The software development process is standardized, but also the supporting processes, like customer service and HR processes like training.

- **Product leadership**: If the company competes based on product leadership, it will invest money in becoming the best. This means spending time and money in a research and development center, training employees, evaluate the user experience of the software and last but not least, keep track of the latest developments in the field of purchase-to-pay. The company will be the first to support functionality like self-billing or other trends in the market. Standardization and reuse are important, but only as far as it does not hinder product development and improvement.
- **Customer intimacy**: If customer intimacy is the strategy of the company, it will invest a great deal in making sure the software can be customized exactly to the wishes of the customer. The customer can determine the exact requirements and design of the application. Every customer gets his or her custom application, and service level. Reuse and standardization are important, but only as long as it does not hinder the customization options in the software and the possibilities to treat every customer differently, according to their needs.

Architecture as a tool

You learned in the previous paragraphs that organizations become more and more dependent on information and information technology, and that organizations have different strategies to compete in their markets. This puts demands on IT planning. This is how Service Oriented Architecture emerged, to cater for these needs. Before we dive into Service Oriented Architecture, it is important to define architecture.

Architecture is a discipline that helps organizations to align the IT with the business and the strategy of the organization. In the construction world, architecture is a well-defined discipline. The profession is protected; not everybody can call him or herself an architect. But in IT, we lack clear definitions of roles and capabilities. In different countries, industries, and communities we use different definitions. Although we will define architecture in this paragraph, and adhere to de-facto definitions and standards, there is no consensus in the world of IT. So if in your company, you employ different names and titles for the activities described as follows, that is fine. It is important that activities are executed, not what you call them or who executes them.

Time for a definition, ISO/IEC 42010:2007 (http://www.iso-architecture.org/42010/cm/) defines *architecture* as:

> *The fundamental organization of a system, embodied in its components, their relationships to each other and the environment, and the principles governing its design and evolution.*

Understanding the Problem

The Standard takes no position on the question, *What is a system?* In the Standard, the term *system* is used as a placeholder. For example, it could refer to an enterprise, a system of systems, a product line, a service, a subsystem, or software. Systems can be man-made or natural.

What is important in this definition is the scope of a **system**. In the following paragraphs, we describe different types of architecture, defined by the scope of the project or the system. For example, if we are describing the architecture of a municipality, the system is everything within the municipality. If we are describing or designing the IT landscape for the front office, the scope of the system is the front office IT. But if a project is about implementing a new regulation, then the scope of the system we are describing is everything that is impacted by the new regulation.

It is important to note that architecture does *NOT* equal standardization. It depends on your company's strategy or operational model, how much integration and standardization you need and in what processes and systems and organizational parts you need it. The goal of architecture is to translate the business strategy into appropriate guidelines for standardization and integration. Architecture is a means to an end; making sure that IT can fulfill the business requirements is the goal, not standardization, or documentation.

To make sure that the architecture meets the demands of the business, Zachman (`http://www.zachman.com/about-the-zachman-framework`) defined a number of questions that need to be answered when creating the architecture of the system. They are: *Why, how, what, who, where, when,* and *what-if?* Consider a company that sells printers, faxes, and other peripherals and wants to redesign their outdated front office architecture. To make sure the front office architecture is aligned with the goals of the company, the following questions need to be answered:

- *Why*: What are the goals of the organization with regards to the front office? Do we want to encourage customers to use the phone or the website? Do we cross-sell or up-sell on the phone? Do we want to minimize the time spent per customer or maximize customer satisfaction?

- *How*: What type of functionality should the IT systems support in the front office? Do the users need to look up payment history? Do we need to see previous purchases from this customer? Do we need to change data directly or just put in requests to be handled in the back office?

- *What*: What types of data do we use and store in the front office? Do we have all customer related data in the front office? Do we store the same data the customer can see, or more, including everything that is known in the back office?

- *Who*: Who is using the systems in the front office? What is the education level and experience of the target users? How many users are working in the front office, are they working with the systems all day?
- *Where*: Where are the systems of the front office, what does the network look like? Are the systems located on-site, or does a remote provider host them? Are the users on-site, or using the systems remotely from home?
- *When*: What type of availability do we expect of the front office systems, 24/7 or office hours? The systems that support the call centers and website probably need more availability than the systems that are used by the employees at the office.
- *What-if*: Is there an alternative way to deliver the solution? What if we outsource the front-office activities?

The answers to these questions depend very much on the perspective or stakeholder. If we are talking about the IT landscape of the front office from a security perspective, we have different interpretations and focus for the *why, what, how, who, where*, and *when* questions compared to the perspective of the controller, who is paying for the new system. For example, from a security perspective it is important to differentiate roles that have different permissions and responsibilities. The *who* question will focus around that. From a financial perspective, it is more important how many users there are, not what they do exactly. The answer to the *who* question from a financial perspective will be focused more on actual *number* of users, and less on the roles and types of users.

Because of these different perspectives, there are several ways of breaking up the organization of a system or architecture. Systems can be divided into **logical layers**, **tiers**, or **viewpoints/views**:

- When we divide *everything in a municipality* in business, information, and technical topics, we are talking about *layering* of the architecture
- When we divide software in the front office in presentation, business logic, and data parts, we are talking about logical tiers in the software
- When we describe the system differently depending on the perspective of the stakeholder, we say we are describing a view of the architecture from a specified viewpoint

While viewpoints, layers, and views refer to logical concepts, tiers often refer to physical division.

Layering of architecture

There are different layering schemes used by different architecture frameworks. A common layering in architecture is dividing it in three main layers: the business layer, information systems layer, and technology layer. This is the layering applied by **The Open Group Architecture Framework (TOGAF)**. In this framework, the information systems layer is divided in services or applications and data. Other layers can be divided into several layers too. Whether a layer is a first-class citizen or part of another layer can be cause for great debate within organizations. To keep things manageable we use the three layers (**Business**, **Information**, and **Technology**) of architecture throughout the book, with different parts within the layers as shown in the next figure. **Security** and **Administration** cut across the three layers, so they are positioned next to these layers.

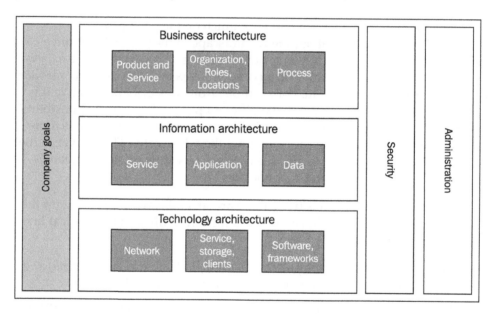

Layers and aspects within these layers can be described from different perspectives: strategic, tactical, or operational. The security view is written from the viewpoint of the security officer. The administration view is described from the viewpoint of the system administrator. The other layers are not written from a specific perspective, but are divided according to the type of information that is captured from the system. For example in the business architecture, one typically finds information about the business processes. This can be described from different perspectives, for example from the perspective of the operation, or from the perspective of a controller. The same is true for information in the other layers.

Models

Architecture is often expressed using diagrams and models, apart from text. There are different (formal) modeling languages available to model. All models target different stakeholders and have a different scope. The following table shows modeling languages that can be used in the different layers together with their target architecture. Apart from these formal modeling techniques, diagrams can be created that are free format. Depending on your target audience and your own modeling skills you can pick any of these languages to communicate the architecture of your system.

Modeling language	Scope	Standard/ Proprietary	Target audience
Archimate	Business, information, and technology layer	Standard (The open group)	Architects, developers
UML (Unified Modeling Language)	Business, information and technology layer	Standard (Object management group)	Developers, architects
BPMN (Business Process Modeling Notation)	Process models	Standard (Object management group)	Process analysts, business consultants
EPC (Event driven Process Chain)	Process models	Proprietary	Process analysts, business consultants
ERM (Entity Relationship Model)	Information (Data) layer	De-facto standard (There is no official standardization body that maintains ERM)	Developers, architects
Not applicable (Free format)	Business, information, and technology layer	Proprietary	Entire organization

Note that in this book, we will use mainly UML diagrams, BPMN diagrams, and free format to describe the various concepts and architecture examples.

Requirements

Architecture is not a means to an end, but a way to assure that organizations can change and meet market demands, and that they operate efficiently. To accomplish this, the following architectural requirements are imposed on the architecture by the organization:

- It is understandable to the *stakeholders* involved.
- It is well known and visible in the organization.
- It is useable. When a project is started or the organization has to take decisions, the architecture will help make this decision or scope the number of possible solutions for a problem. This means that it should have clear principles and guidelines, and use terms and layering that are valuable for the organization.
- It can be changed. Because organizations change, the architecture needs to change as well. It is not a cookie cutter that keeps its shape; it is a plan that will have multiple versions as time passes.

This list applies to any architectural style or reference architecture you choose for your organization. When you notice that architecture is described in your organization, but not used in projects or within the decision making process, one of these requirements is not met. Instead of continuing to describe the architecture, it is important to investigate which of these requirements is not met. Common pitfalls are that the architecture is too detailed, out-dated or too complex.

Architecture ontology

In this paragraph you will learn about the different types of architecture that you can apply or use for your organization to ensure business and IT alignment. This will put Service Oriented Architecture in perspective and helps you chose the right scope for your efforts. There are two different axes on which you plot architecture; one is scope of the system, the other one is generalization. Scope can be really big, or specific and small. As you recall from the definition of architecture, the scope of the system it describes can be anything. In this paragraph we discuss enterprise architecture, project architecture, and software architecture, as examples for scope of the system. Apart from scope, there are also grades of generalization that you can put in architecture. You will also learn about reference architecture and solution architecture. Last but not least you will learn about a specific type of solution architecture—Service Oriented Architecture—as an introduction to the rest of this book.

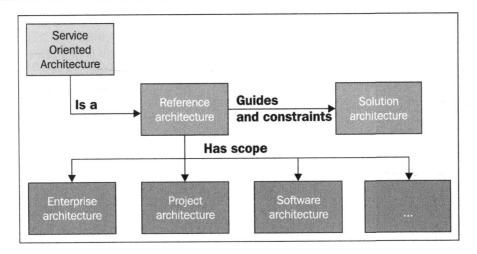

The figure shows the relationship between the different architecture types. As you can see, Service Oriented Architecture is a reference architecture that guides and constraints solution architectures. The reference architecture can have different scopes such as Enterprise architecture, Project architecture, Software architecture, and so on.

Enterprise architecture

If the scope of the architecture consists of the entire company or organization (enterprise), or the architecture scope spans multiple organizations, we practice **enterprise architecture**. Enterprise architecture as defined in *Enterprise Architecture As Strategy: Creating a Foundation for Business Execution*, *Ross*, *Weill*, and *Robertson*, *Harvard Business Review Press*:

> *Enterprise Architecture is the organizing logic for business processes and IT infrastructure, reflecting the integration and standardization requirements of the company's operating model. The enterprise architecture provides a long term view of a company's processes, systems, and technologies so that individual projects can build capabilities, not just fulfill immediate needs.*

Understanding the Problem

There are several frameworks and methodologies available for enterprise architecture. One of the first frameworks that became a basis for other frameworks is the Zachman framework. It is a framework for structuring the enterprise architecture and consists of a matrix of 6 x 6. The columns consist of questions we mentioned earlier. The rows are organized from high level to more detailed as can be seen in the following screenshot from Wikipedia (http://en.wikipedia.org/wiki/Zachman_Framework):

	Why	How	What	Who	Where	When
Contextual	Goal List	Process List	Material List	Organizational Unit & Role List	Geographical Locations List	Event list
Conceptual	Goal Relationship	Process Model	Entity Relationship Model	Organizational Unit & Role Model	Locations Model	Event Model
Logical	Rules Diagram	Process Diagram	Data Model Diagram	Role Relationship Diagram	Locations Diagram	Event Diagram
Physical	Rules Specification	Process Function Specification	Data Entity Specification	Role Specification	Location Specification	Event Specification
Detailed	Rules Details	Process Details	Data Details	Role Details	Location Details	Event Details

An architect describing the enterprise architecture using this framework needs to decide what columns and rows need to be described for the organization/enterprise. Not every cell needs to be filled. For example, if the focus is on introducing Business Process Management into an organization in order to get rid of functional silos, the *How* column needs to be filled with process models, diagrams, and execution details. If the different locations of a company are critical the *Where* column needs to be described. The same applies to the rows, depending on the needs of the organization more or less rows can be described.

Open Group offers another comprehensive framework—TOGAF. It consists of several parts:

- **Architecture Development Method (ADM)**: It describes the methodology.
- **Content framework**: It contains deliverables, artifacts, and building blocks.

- **Enterprise continuum and tools**: This is a view of all the different types of solutions and architectures, ranging from detailed to abstract, for different types of stakeholders.
- **Reference models**: TOGAF offers generic reference models that can be used as a starting point for organizations to structure their own enterprise architecture.
- **Architecture Capability Framework**: This framework explains the capabilities an organization needs, or the roles and responsibilities, to maintain the architecture.

There are several other frameworks that can be used. When you choose a framework, pick one that fits your purpose best. Some frameworks are more elaborate than others; some frameworks focus on both the organization of the system and on the process of designing it. Others focus only on the process, or the system. After choosing a framework, you will have to adapt it to the needs of your organization.

Reference architecture

There are a lot of similarities between different organizations in the same industry. For this reason, **reference architectures** are developed. Wikipedia (http://en.wikipedia.org/wiki/Reference_architecture) defines it as:

> *A reference architecture in the field of software architecture or enterprise architecture provides a template solution for an architecture for a particular domain. It also provides a common vocabulary with which to discuss implementations, often with the aim to stress commonality.*

Using reference architecture has several advantages:

- Standardization of terminology, taxonomy, and services eases working with suppliers and partners
- It reduces the cost of developing enterprise architecture; the organization can focus on what sets it apart from the reference architecture and other organizations in the industry instead of reinventing the wheel
- It makes it easier to implement commercial off-the-shelf (COTS) software, because common terminology and processes are used

Obviously, it also has some disadvantages:

- It takes some time to learn industry reference architecture; they are often (over) complete
- The reference architecture is typically written by a group of people from different organizations and so is the result of a compromise

Understanding the Problem

As we saw in the previous image, and in the definition of reference architecture, the scope of the reference architecture can differ.

Examples of (enterprise) reference architectures are the Dutch Government reference architecture—NORA (http://e-overheid.nl/images/stories/architectuur/nora_maart%202010-eng.pdf), TM Forum Frameworx and eTOM for telecommunications (http://www.tmforum.org/), and the US reference architecture for federal government, Federal Enterprise architecture—FEA(http://www.whitehouse.gov/omb/e-gov/fea).

Solution architecture

Solution architecture is a detailed (technology) specification of building blocks to realize a business need.

Open Group recognizes different types of solutions in the solution continuum:

- **Foundation solutions**: This can be a programming language, a process or other highly generic concepts, tools, products, and services; an example of a process is **Business Information Services Library (BISL)**.
- **Common systems solutions**: For example CRM systems, ERP systems as we have seen in the previous examples, and also security solutions.
- **Industry solutions**: These are solutions for a specific industry. They are built from foundation solutions and common systems solutions, and are augmented with industry-specific components.
- **Organization-specific solutions**: An example of this is the solution for the health insurance companies that want to offer self-service to prospective clients. The solution architecture describes the multi-channel solution for the organization, the tools and products that are used to implement it, and the relationship between the different layers.

The difference between reference architecture and solution architecture is that reference architecture is a *generic* reference where common problems are described together with principles and constraints on how to solve these. Solution architectures describe a *specific* solution to solve a specific problem or problems. For example, the Dutch reference architecture NORA is used as a reference for the solution architecture in a municipality.

Project architecture

Project architecture defines what part of a solution architecture will be realized by the project, or is in scope. This can overlap with a solution architecture if there is only one project needed to realize the solution architecture. If the solution is too big for one project, or there are different parts that are assigned to different projects, the project architecture describes what part of the solution architecture will be realized in the project.

Project architecture serves two purposes:

- **Guarding the enterprise or solution architecture**: A project is typically focused on short-term goals. The project architecture explicitly describes what part of the project is supposed to satisfy long-term strategic goals, what deviations from the target architecture are going to occur and how these will be resolved in the future.
- **Provide input for, or change the enterprise or solution architecture**: Enterprise architecture and solution architectures need to be adjusted based on experiences from projects and the current situation. Valuable feedback about the usability and understandability of the architecture is gathered from projects.

Reference architecture can also have the scope of a project. The project architecture is then less specific than solution architecture and contains guidelines, principles, and constraints for projects in the organization in general.

Software architecture

Software architecture is focused on the structure of the software. It can be viewed as a special type of solution architecture, project architecture, or part of the technology architecture. The target audience of these types of architectures are developers. Often these are not referred to as architecture, but rather as **software design**.

Service Oriented Architecture

We saw earlier on in the chapter that for companies that apply product leadership or customer intimacy as a strategy, flexibility is key. One of the possible solutions to make sure that IT is flexible and can be easily changed is by applying a solution architecture based on Service Oriented Architecture (SOA). Service Oriented Architecture is a reference architecture that can be applied in organizations that are part of a (supply-) chain or network, and organizations that have to deal with a lot of regulatory changes, or fast-changing markets. It makes it possible to change parts of the IT landscape, and processes, without affecting other parts. Reusing existing functionality (services) makes sure that it can be changed quickly because you don't have to start from scratch every time, and also makes it cheaper. Reuse is also important for companies that aim for operational excellence. Finally, the quality of the data is easier to control, because we can appoint specific services with the responsibility of maintaining the data and enforcing the business rules.

Summary

In this chapter, we addressed the problem that a lot of companies face today, their organization and their IT are organized in silos. This leads to duplication of functionality and information and makes it hard and expensive to change and to adapt to changing markets, rules, and regulations. The IT department is not able to deliver solutions and changes fast enough and the business people are not able to communicate their needs well enough. This results in IT that is lagging behind and frustrated people in the organization on both sides.

To solve this problem, we need to design our organization in a way that fits the long-term business goals of an organization. The IT solutions need to be aligned with our organization and with these same goals. To make this possible, architecture should be applied whenever a change is implemented in the organization that involves information (systems). There are different types of architecture that can be applied such as enterprise architecture, solution architecture, and project architecture.

Service Oriented Architecture is a specific reference architecture that helps solve the data and functionality duplication, thus making the companies that apply this more flexible, and operate more efficiently.

In the next chapter, we explain in detail exactly what services and Service Oriented Architecture mean, and how this type of architecture is a solution to the misalignment of business and IT, and for functional and data duplications in the situations that we've mentioned in this chapter.

2
The Solution

In the previous chapter, you read about the challenges that organizations face in today's fast moving, demanding, and competitive economy. Organizations need to adapt and respond rapidly to customer demands, put new products and services in the market before competitors do, adhere to changing rules and regulations in time, and need to work together with other organizations in changing partnerships. In short, organizations need to be *agile*. These challenges are hard to solve, even more so because of the frequent misunderstanding between businesses and IT and the problems shared by business and IT such as duplication of data and functionality.

This chapter explains why SOA makes it easier to bridge this gap, making sure IT can deliver what the business needs to be successful by creating a more flexible architecture. The chapter is divided into the following sections:

- *What is a service?*: The first part explains what services are and discusses some of the important concepts of SOA; is SOA a collection of web services, is it a team of architects united in an SOA center of excellence, is it about purchasing a middleware stack, or is it Superman?

- *Drivers for services*: The middle part continues this explanation by listing the main drivers for using services, discussing common myths that you can encounter in SOA-related projects, and concludes by providing a definition of SOA.

- *Solutions*: Now you have an overview of what SOA is and the solutions it offers to the common challenges an organization and its IT faces, as explained in the previous chapter. For every challenge here is an explanation of the solution SOA offers to solve these challenges.

The Solution

What is a service?

SOA is about services. So, let us start there. What is a service? Informally, and in the broadest sense of the word, a **service** is *something useful a provider does for a consumer*. **Products** can be considered a service too. Services can be paid for since the producer has created added value during their production. A service can be something tangible like a carton of milk, a car, a new house but also something intangible such as travel insurance or medical treatment. Services can be simple like fixing a bike. However, there are also more complex services such as purchasing a new smartphone together with a flexible phone plan including 300 free text messages a month, and the accompanying advice from a provider's sales representative. These more complex services are thus composed of various other services.

In short, a service is an economic term to describe the goods and services that organizations and people produce, sell to one another, and buy from each other. Services are nothing new and have been around as long as mankind has been. Consider a land worker in medieval England who harvests crops (the service) in exchange for a place to live.

Let's dive into a more modern example of a service.

Elements of a service – contract, interface, and implementation

For every service you need to define certain characteristics in order for the services to be well defined and usable. If the service is not well defined it might not be clear for all consumers what value the service exactly offers, how much it costs to use it, or how to use the service at all. This will lead to customer confusion and can even cause consumers to not use the service at all. The three components of a service are:

- Contract
- Interface
- Implementation

The following diagram shows the components of a service:

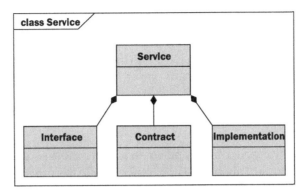

A **contract** specifies what consumers can expect from a service based on their predicted needs, and what a service provider needs to offer. The **interface** defines how you can make use of the service and access it, while the **implementation** is about the realization of the service. The contract and interface are visible to the outside world. The implementation is more a *hidden feature* or a *black box* to consumers. Consumers generally don't care about its implementation.

Example – let's have breakfast

You can think of it in the following way. Suppose you go to a diner to have breakfast. The diner offers a menu that lists all their services. One of the services offered by the diner is the diner's famous classic breakfast consisting of toast with eggs and some side dishes.

The following figure shows the contract for the breakfast, the interface (English Menu and waitress Jane) and the implementation:

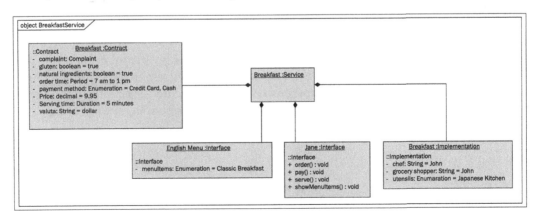

The Solution

Let's take a closer look at all three components for this example.

Contract

When entering the diner, a waiter explains the breakfast contains only local products and natural ingredients, but has gluten in it. The breakfast is *available from 7 a.m. to 1 p.m.* and it *costs $9.95*. You can *pay by credit card or cash*, but *only in dollars, not in Euros*. The waitress informs you that breakfast *will be served in five to ten minutes*. In case you are not happy with the breakfast *you can contact the manager at a given telephone number to complain.*

Quality, price, availability, order time, and so on are all examples of important aspects of the breakfast that you care about as a consumer. While the diner will probably not define a formal contract that both the diner and you sign, it can be considered as the contract of the breakfast service nonetheless.

Interface

The interface is the way you interact with a service. To order breakfast you interact with:

- Jane, our waitress
- The menu that is in English and Spanish

These are two channels of the interface. A **channel** is a route of communication or access. As you can see, there are different ways to communicate the items on the menu to the customer. To know what items you can order, you can ask for menu items. This can be accessed using the menu, or a different channel such as asking the waitress Jane. Both offer `showMenuItems` as an interface to `BreakfastService`. You could think of other channels as well: the diner could also open a self-service buffet.

Implementation

You are very interested in the contract and interface of the breakfast. If the breakfast costs $25.99 or did not have natural and high-quality ingredients, you might have decided to get breakfast in the hotel next door or go to a 7-Eleven and get some breakfast there. The same is true for the interface; if the waitress is rude or the menu is in a language you do not understand, you could also decide to go to the hotel next door. So, *contract and interface highly determine if you as a customer are willing to order the breakfast.*

On the other hand, you are not that interested in the implementation; you probably do not need to know how the diner prepares their meals. What you care about is that the breakfast is according to your expectations, is there on time, and costs no more than indicated on the menu. Whether the chef is named John, who bought all the ingredients himself and uses a Japanese stainless-steel knife, or whether the ingredients were delivered by a wholesaler, the chef is named Maria and she uses a German knife does not really matter to you, as long as the quality is as expected.

If consumers *do* care about certain aspects of the implementation these aspects will usually be stated in the contract; for example, that there is no child labor involved in creating a particular service or goods.

Example – ordering a passport

Another quick example illustrating the difference between interface, contract, and implementation is the scenario in which your passport expires and you want to get a new one. You care about how much a new passport costs, where you need to go to get it, and how long it takes to get one. You are probably not that interested in how the government actually creates the passport (implementation).

Consumer and provider

Returning to the example of the breakfast you can clearly identity the two main parties of interest: you as a person ordering and enjoying the breakfast, and the diner providing the breakfast to us. Hopefully you are not the only one ordering breakfast there. Dozens of people visit the diner every morning to have pancakes, toast, cereals, and what not. In this case, the breakfast service is offered to several customers.

Note that there is a distinct, but maybe not immediately clear difference between provider and producer (or **implementer**). The diner offers the breakfast to us, thereby designating it as the service provider. It could however be that the diner buys the breakfast in the hotel next door for a cheaper price and offers it to us. In this case, the hotel produces or implements the service, while the diner provides it to us.

Strictly speaking, what you do with the result of the breakfast service is not part of the service and not of interest to the provider. You might eat the breakfast in five minutes, take an hour, throw the breakfast out of the window, take it with you, give it to somebody else, sell it, sit at the table and look at it, freeze it, and so on.

The Solution

Dealing with lots of service providers – service registry

If you want to have breakfast in an unknown city when you are on holiday you might ask the hotel clerk or look in Yellow Pages that lists all the breakfast places in the neighborhood. Such a listing of services where consumers can look and discover the services that are provided is usually called a **service registry**. This might come in quite handy if there are lots of providers for the same service.

How can you make sure that people use a service?

Lots of people have breakfast at the diner. A service is **reused** if a service has several consumers. An important condition for achieving reuse is that (future) consumers put trust in the quality of the service and agree with the conditions under which it is provided. So basically, contract and interface. If consumers are not convinced of the quality of service or do not agree with the terms it is provided with, they are more likely to use services from another provider.

> A service that is only used by one consumer for one particular use case can still be reusable, meaning it has the *potential* for reuse. This could for example be the case when introducing a new organization-wide Shared Service Center for IT, billing, and HRM. Suppose that in its first month of existence its services are only used by the Marketing department and only for billing purposes. You can still call the services offered by the Shared Service Center reusable. Later on, other departments such as Sales and Customer Care can also use the services offered by the Shared Service Center, or the Marketing department starts using other capabilities of the service, making the services reused.

From sunny-side-up eggs to IT

Services are nothing new. What is new nowadays is using the notion of services in the domain of (enterprise) architecture and IT.

According to OASIS:

> *A service is a mechanism to enable access to one or more capabilities, where the access is provided using a prescribed interface and is exercised consistent with constraints and policies as specified by the service description.*

Organization for the Advancement of Structured Information Standards (OASIS) is a not-for-profit consortium that drives the development, convergence, and adoption of open standards for the global information society. See http://www.oasis-open.org/org.

An oversimplified example of an order-to-cash business process can clarify the meaning of this definition. Order-to-cash refers to a process spanning the ordering of products by customers to their delivery and payment by the customer. All shops, for example, need to implement this process in order to make money by selling products like books, music, clothes, and so on.

Services are *mechanisms to access* **capabilities**, you can realize the order-to-cash business process by orchestrating the use of services (capabilities) in a particular order.

Of course this service-oriented approach is not the only possible implementation. The key here is that if you want our business process to be flexible, to be able to make changes quickly or to reuse existing functionality and data, the use of services has several benefits.

The following figure displays the order-to-cash business process and its process steps on one hand (top), the services that are orchestrated to realize the business process on the other hand (bottom), and the usage of services by the process (dotted lines).

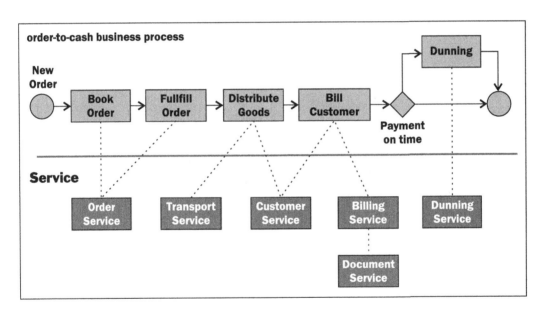

The Solution

The following steps are executed:

1. A new order is received. This event starts the process.
2. The order is booked using `OrderService`.
3. The order is fulfilled using `OrderService`.
4. The goods are distributed using `TransportService` and the `CustomerService`.
5. The customer is billed using `CustomerService`, `BillingService`, and `DocumentService`.
6. If the customer does not pay, dunning is started using the `DunningService`.

Example – international software company revisited

You learned in the previous chapter how the international software company created functional and data duplication by creating a new application for their online order process. The following figure shows the resulting two applications:

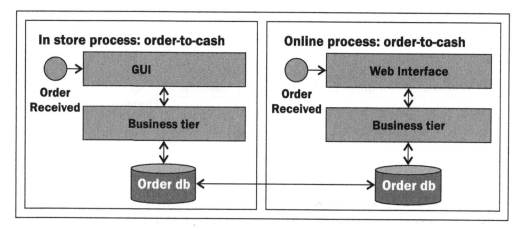

The company is not happy with the solution and decides to buy a standard off-the-shelf CRM application from a supplier. The company decides to use `OrderService` offered by the packaged application. This service can be used to create order entries, retrieve order information, cancel orders, and so on. Both the company's online web application and the Customer Care Portal will start to use `OrderService`.

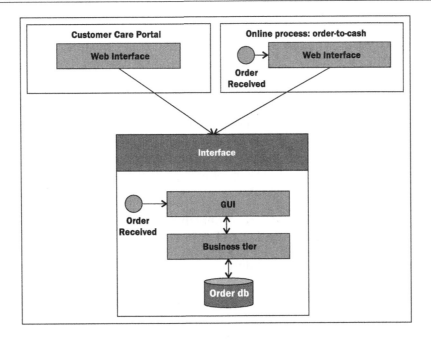

As you can see in the figure, the Order System offers the interface to the web application and to the customer portal. These systems don't need to duplicate the logic or the data of the Order System, as was the case in the old days. Both systems use the implementation of OrderService (the Order System) by accessing the interface that the Order System offers.

Let's have a closer look at the contract, interface, and implementation of the OrderService.

Contract

The contract specifies the conditions under which the Order System offers OrderService to its consumers (Online Web Application and Customer Care Portal). This contract should answer questions such as "What is the uptime of the OrderService? and "How expensive is it to invoke the web service?".

An oversimplified contract could contain the following information:

- OrderService will be capable of handling up to 2,000 orders an hour
- OrderService will have an uptime of 99.95% and an outage will take no more than 90 minutes
- Usage of OrderService is free of charge

The Solution

Interface

Interfaces are the *points of contact* between services and their consumers. It is the way consumers can interact with services. In terms of technical services it concerns message payloads, operations, endpoint of services, and so on.

Interfaces can be described from both a functional and a technical perspective. A **functional interface** can be seen as a free-format summary of the service and its capabilities. Such a summary should at least list the capabilities offered by the service (operations), the information that the service operation needs (input), and the information it returns (output). In case of unexpected operation or invalid input, the service may return a **business fault**.

The Order Service can be used to create orders in the Order System, retrieve order information including its status, and cancel orders.

Let's look at a simplified functional interface description for the Order Service:

Operation	Description	Input	Output	Business fault
Order product	Creates a new order in the Order System and returns the calculated price and new identification for the order. All inputs are required. If the customer ID is invalid, a `customer not found` fault is returned. If the product is not in stock, a `product not in stock` fault will be returned.	Product identification, Quantity, Customer identification	Order identification, total price	Customer not found, product not in stock
Retrieve order information	Retrieves the order information from the Order System. All inputs are required. If the order is not found based on the order ID, an `order not found` fault would be returned.	Order identification	Order date, product identification, quantity, customer id, total price	Order not found

Operation	Description	Input	Output	Business fault
Cancel order	Cancels an order in the Order System. All inputs are required. If the order has already been delivered to the customer (based on order status), an `order already delivered` fault will be returned.	Order identification	N.A.	Order already delivered

In order for the customer web application and Customer Care Portal to actually use `OrderService`, you will need more technical details for the interface. This is provided using a technical interface. Remember that `OrderService` is implemented in a packaged application that was bought from a supplier. The supplier chose to expose the service using web services instead of a more proprietary technology since it doesn't want to lose potential customers due to interoperability issues.

As part of the web service standards, **Web Service Description Language (WSDL)** and **XML Schema (XSD)** can be used for describing SOAP-based web service contracts. A WSDL is an XML document describing the functionality offered by a web service in terms of its operations, the input, output, and business faults of these operations, and possibly some other details such as the endpoint location where the web service is located, and (security) policies for invoking the web service.

The following code fragment shows some of the operations offered by `OrderService`: `orderProduct`, `retrieveOrder`, and `cancelOrder`. For each operation an input and output is specified. You can further see that the `orderProduct` operation might reply with a business fault instead of a normal response, indicating that the product is not in stock or the customer is not found.

```
<wsdl:operation name="orderProduct">
    <wsdl:input message="ord:OrderProductRequestMessage"/>
    <wsdl:output message="ord:OrderProductResponseMessage"/>
    <wsdl:fault message="ord:ProductNotInStockFaultMessage"
            name="ProductNotInStockFault"/>
    <wsdl:fault message="ord:CustomerNotFoundFaultMessage"
            name="CustomerNotFound"/>
```

The Solution

```
  </wsdl:operation>
  <wsdl:operation name="cancelOrder">
    <wsdl:input message="ord:CancelOrderRequestMessage"/>
    <wsdl:output message="ord:CancelOrderResponseMessage"/>
  </wsdl:operation>
```

>
> **Downloading the example code**
> You can download the example code files for all Packt books you have purchased from your account at http://www.PacktPub.com . If you purchased this book elsewhere, you can visit http://www.PacktPub.com/support and register to have the files e-mailed directly to you.

The WSDL can internally define the request, response, and fault messages or as a cleaner option, can refer to an external XML Schema for this. The input of the request message for the `OrderService.orderProduct` operation is defined in the following code fragment. This fragment shows that the `orderProduct` operation expects a product identifier, the number of products to order (quantity), and the identifier of the customer that ordered the goods. It also shows the data types of the request parameters.

```xml
<xsd:element name="OrderProductRequest">
  <xsd:complexType>
    <xsd:sequence>
      <xsd:element name="ProductId" type="xsd:string"/>
      <xsd:element name="Quantity" type="xsd:nonNegativeInteger"/>
      <xsd:element name="CustomerId" type="xsd:string"/>
    </xsd:sequence>
  </xsd:complexType>
</xsd:element>
```

The response may be defined as the identifier of the newly created order and the calculated total price of the order:

```xml
<xsd:element name="OrderProductResponse">
  <xsd:complexType>
    <xsd:sequence>
      <xsd:element name="OrderId" type="xsd:string"/>
      <xsd:element name="TotalPrice" type="xsd:double"/>
    </xsd:sequence>
  </xsd:complexType>
</xsd:element>
```

Note that technical interfaces can also be formally described in another language or protocol such as Java or .NET. Using a proprietary language can even result in a more strongly typed interface that provides more information to consumers.

> Using proprietary protocols and technologies for *interface descriptions* can reduce interoperability. For example; a Java interface containing Javadoc (documentation), using inheritance, generics, and annotations provides a very rich interface, but puts a constraint on the consumer: it has to communicate using Java. You cannot generate a .NET client to invoke the service based on the native technical Java interface, because they are two different programming languages. You can however, generate a .NET client based on WSDL, even if the implementation of the service is written in Java, or vice versa.

Implementation

Since a web service is a set of standards and protocols and not a programming language, a web service needs to be implemented in some concrete language. So, for example you can have an Order System that is implemented in Java and exposes a web service on top of it. Most programming languages and vendors such as Microsoft, IBM, and Oracle offer frameworks to easily create and consume web services.

As you saw earlier in this chapter for the breakfast example, consumers do not really care about the implementation. The web application and Customer Service Portal will not care if the Order Service is implemented using Java, .NET, C++, or some other framework or programming language. As long as the service operates as specified by the contract and is accessible according to the interface.

For the provider of the service, the choice of implementation is of course very important. This will depend on the knowledge and skills of the developers, organizational policies, and so on.

Consumer and provider

The Order System implements `OrderService`, while the Online Web Application and Customer Care Service Portal consume it. The Sales department provides `OrderService`. They got a license from the organization that developed the software, to use it for their sales activities.

Note that the provider does not necessarily need to be the same as the organization that hosts the service. In this case, the Order System is developed by a third-party packaged applications supplier and is hosted by the company's IT department.

The Solution

The different stakeholders are illustrated in the following diagram:

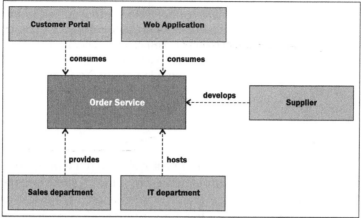

Reuse

There are two consumers of `OrderService` as you can see in the previous diagram: the Online Web Application and the Customer Care Portal. This means that the service is reused. The customer care department that is responsible for Customer Care Portal and Online Order Application, will only be willing to use `OrderService` if it is performing well, reliable, secure, and so on.

The importance of quality of service is illustrated in the following cartoon from Geek and Poke; see: `http://geekandpoke.typepad.com`.

Drivers for services

The international insurance company wanted to re-use `OrderService`. Reuse is not the goal here, but the means to an end: cost-reduction or faster time-to-market. The following are drivers for SOA and services:

- **Flexibility**: Services are small building blocks with a limited and clear set of capabilities. That means it is easier to support the changing requirements of your organization. Your IT landscape is more modular, preventing *domino* effects for changes in software.
- **Standardization**: Services are frequently provided using open standards thereby hiding the underlying technical complexity and details. This makes the consumers and the organization as whole more vendor-independent. A consumer can still use a service, even if it is provided by another system as long as it uses the same interface. Almost all large vendors support open standards such as REST, SOAP, WSDL, WS-*, XML, and so on.
- **Cost reduction**: Reusing a service is cheaper than building, maintaining, and hosting duplicate functionality.
- **Shorter time to market**: By reusing services, functionality can be realized faster, thus diminishing the time to market.
- **Increase in quality**: Because more consumers use a service, it is better tested. There is no data duplication, so the data quality increases as well.

Common myths

A side-effect of the popularity of SOA is that the term "service" has become quite overloaded. It can have different meanings depending on who you talk to. For example, a developer thinks of a service as a technical specification: an SOAP-based web service or a REST service. An architect thinks of a service as a logical way of organizing the architecture of the organization. A product manager thinks of a service as something that the company sells. By looking at some common misunderstandings or service myths you will learn to recognize the different perspective that people use when talking about SOA and services. The myths are exaggerated statements that you might or might not encounter literally when reading or talking about SOA and services.

The Solution

Every service has to be automated by software

This is a myth. Not every service has to be automated. A service can also be rendered entirely or partially through human activities. Everyone that likes coffee will consider a traditionally brewed Italian espresso by Luigi a service. Another example is `TransportService` that was used in the order-to-cash business process example.

Every service is a web service

While a service can be implemented as a web service, it can also be a PL/SQL procedure or a .NET class containing methods. That said, the use of web services and web service standards does help to achieve interoperability.

Consumers of services are always IT systems

Not all services are accessed by a system. An automated service can have a graphical user interface accessed by humans (employees, customers, and so on). Think of portlets or gadgets like calendars you can use in mash-ups such as Enterprise portals, Wikis, iGoogle, and so on.

By now you have a grasp of what services are. Next up is the A in SOA, the architecture.

Putting it together – what is SOA?

Service Oriented Architecture is a reference architecture that is based on services. This means that SOA is a specific structured approach, based on services.

If architecture is defined from the perspective of services, it is called "service-oriented" or SOA in short.

Service-orientation can be applied on all levels: business level (the breakfast example), information level (applications delivering services to realize business processes), and technology level (web services such as `OrderService`, services provided by infrastructure such as storage or high-availability, and so on).

According to The Open Group, a global consortium that enables the achievement of business objectives through IT standards, SOA has a set of distinctive features:

> It (SOA) is based on the design of the services – which mirrors real-world business activities – comprising the enterprise (or inter-enterprise) business processes.

Service representation utilizes business descriptions to provide context (i.e. business process, goal, rule, policy, service interface, and service component) and implements services using service orchestration.

It places unique requirements on the infrastructure – it is recommended that implementations use open standards to realize interoperability and location transparency.

Implementations are environment-specific – they are constrained or enabled by context and must be described within that context.

It requires strong governance of service representation and implementation.

It requires a "Litmus Test", which determines a 'good service'.

A service-oriented architecture is centered around services. Services are small building blocks that provide clear access to a limited set of capabilities that belong together. The same service is responsible for the business logic and data consistency of that particular set of capabilities. If the data belonging to a service needs to be changed, it is done through that service alone, thus enforcing a single point of access for that particular functionality and data.

SOA promotes that, data and logic that do not belong together are **decoupled** (or *loosely-coupled*) through the appliance of services. This loose coupling occurs on the level of ownership, business logic, data, and deployment.

Solutions

Now that you have a basic understanding of SOA and services. Let's take another look at the problems discussed in the previous chapter and see how SOA can offer a solution.

Example – utility company

Let's review the stated problem for the utility company and see how SOA can help:

 Problem: Organizations can't be changed fast enough because there is one big IT system with a lot of relationships between different entities.

The Solution

The company had problems splitting up their business, because of the monolithic system that was used to support their business activities. The following figure shows the difference between the two architectures schematically:

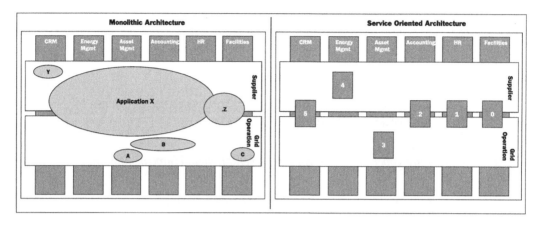

The left-hand side shows the monolithic architecture from the previous chapter. The left-hand side shows the services as they are offered by the different domains. The services are connected together in the user interface, other services, and process applications. Some Services (Service 5 in the CRM domain, service 2 in the Accounting domain, Service 1 in the HR domain, and Service 0 in the Facilities domain) support both the supplier role and the role of grid operator. Other services (Service 3 in the Asset management domain and Service 4 in the Energy management domain support either the supplier or the grid operator role. As you recall from the previous chapter, the company has to split in two, to separate the supplier from the grid operator role legally and physically. The company that has a service-oriented architecture can decide per shared service, who (new supplier company or new grid operator company) is going to keep the service and who is going to buy or make a new service. Because the services have a well-defined interface, the change can be made gradually, hiding the impact from the consumers. Note that having more and smaller building blocks does have a disadvantage: you need to integrate these building blocks.

Now compare this to the monolithic IT system of the utility company that has all the business logic and data intertwined and tightly coupled together. The impact analysis of changes, implementation of changes, testing of changes, as well as deployment of the split is far more complex.

When applying SOA, structural changes such as splitting an organization and its IT or outsourcing parts of the company with its IT can thus be dealt with as a set of smaller changes on several services; each change with less impact. Instead of suboptimal solutions such as duplicating entire IT systems or buying or rebuilding an entire new system from scratch, you can divide (ownership of) services based on the capabilities they offer.

>
> Improvement: SOA decomposes complex systems into smaller building blocks or services. Services are more easily changed than complex systems since they are simpler, well-defined through contract and interface, loosely-coupled, can be changed without impacting other services, and better address responsibilities and ownership of information and business logic. You don't have to change everything at the same time, as is often the case for monolithic systems.

International software company – changing existing processes

Let's review the stated problem and see how SOA can help.

>
> Problem: IT can't keep up with process changes because of the way the applications are structured.

A service is responsible for the capabilities it offers nothing more and nothing less. SOA is divided into smaller building blocks that offer a specific capability. These capabilities are implemented using business logic and data.

Let's have a look again at the previously discussed order-to-cash business process that is based on services. In this scenario, the services do not contain any process logic only business logic. The business process can for example be executed in a separate BPM tool. The process logic is separated (or extracted) from the business logic. This means you can change the process without modifying the business logic in the services, and vice versa.

The Solution

Suppose you need to change the order-to-cash process to enable upfront payment instead of payment after the customer receives the order. You can change the process in the BPM tool that executes the process. The process still calls the same services, but only in another order. You do not need to change the business logic within the services since the new process does not require changes to the business logic. Put simply, the Billing Service still bills customers the same way; it is simply invoked earlier on in the process than before.

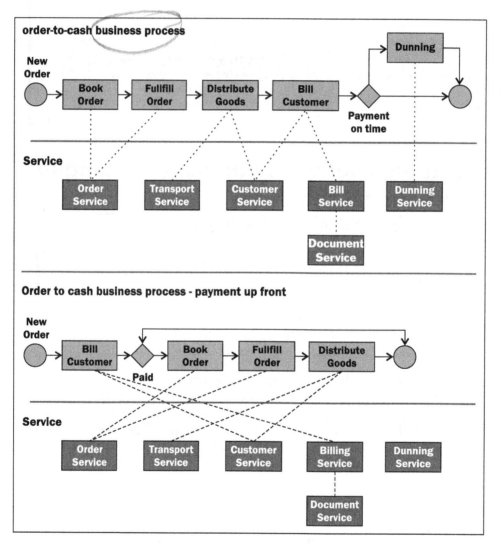

The top part is the process as it was run before. This was explained in the paragraph *From sunny-side-up eggs to IT* section in this chapter, for example the international software company. The bottom part shows the new process. The Bill Customer step has been moved to the front. It is now the first step that is executed. The Dunning step has been removed, since customers pay upfront, the company does not have to worry about that anymore. As you can see, nothing changes in the services; the only difference is the order in which they are called.

This change is easy, because the process logic is separated from the other business logic in this architecture. In the previous chapter, the process logic was intertwined with the other business logic inside the application. Changing the order of steps in the process impacted the other components such as data structures, and was therefore not that easy. Also, if you would need to support both upfront payment as well as payment after receiving the order you could face an even greater challenge when this needed to be supported through one application. In a Service Oriented Architecture (SOA), you can still use the exact same services and have two processes in the BPM tool. In this case, you don't need to change the user interface either, you just show the billing screen that is part of the service at the beginning of the process.

> Improvement: SOA enables faster change in processes since SOA separates business logic from process logic. Services encapsulate and divide business logic based on the capabilities they offer. Process logic is implemented outside of automated services in, for example, BPM tools. Changing process logic therefore has minimum impact on business logic and vice versa.

Functional duplication – rationalizing application landscapes

In the previous chapter, you saw if the insurance company wants to add a new product, this product needs to be registered in both the IAS system owned by the Claims department and the CMS system owned by the Marketing department.

> Problem: Companies lose against the competition because IT can't deliver solutions fast enough.

The Solution

By appointing a source for products and other data, the other applications can reuse the services to retrieve and update product data in one place. The following diagram shows the difference:

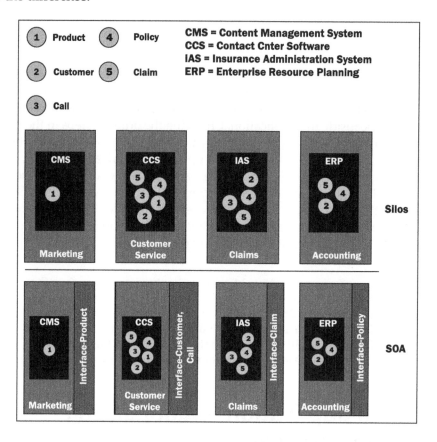

The diagram consists of three parts. The top part shows the legend for the middle and the bottom part. The middle part shows the architecture as it was discussed in *Chapter 1, Understanding the Problem*. This architecture leads to data and functional duplication. The bottom part shows a similar solution, but based on services. The systems retrieve and change data using services of other systems, not by duplicating it. Note that not all vendors create their system completely service oriented. Most will still require some local storage of data. This leads to physical duplication of data. But because of the services that are offered, this data can be retrieved automatically rather than by being entered twice. For example, if the CCS needs the product information to be physically available, it can be retrieved using `ProductService` of the CMS. This leads to better data quality in the organization, making it easier to add a new product every year. This only has to be done in one location: the CMS.

> Improvement: SOA enables reuse through services. Reuse speeds up solution delivery.

Standardization – enabling change

A lot of organizations face change, especially those organizations that are merged, split, outsourced, are part of a chain or network, and so on. Change often causes integration issues due to all the various frameworks, protocols, and technologies used. The more proprietary these are, the more difficult the change is.

Gradually changing a set of small building blocks is easier than changing one big thing at once. By the same analogy, splitting an IT system that is composed of a set of services is easier than splitting a monolithic IT system. For this to work however, you need services that are **interoperable**. The services need to work together and together provide the same functionality as the monolithic IT system.

SOA consists of a set of services that interact with each other to realize functionality in an organization. Services therefore need to be interoperable in order to be useable by other systems and services, especially in heterogeneous environments. Using open standards improves interoperability as it provides a "common vocabulary". Open standards are agreed upon by most major stakeholders, are publicly available, and maintained by non-profit entities such as W3C and OASIS in which major stakeholders are represented. Almost all major software vendors adhere to standards in their product stacks and frameworks.

> Improvement: There are open standards that you can base your services on to promote interoperability. Open standards improve operability compared to the use of proprietary and closed technologies and protocols since almost all major software vendors and their product stacks and frameworks support open standards.

Summary

This chapter revisited the problems stated in the previous chapter. Organizations need to be agile since they are confronted with changing external and internal drivers. The better an organization deals with these changes, the more successful it is.

You have seen how SOA can help address issues such as duplication of data and functionality, increase flexibility, and speed up time-to-market of new solutions. To do so you have first explored the concepts of SOA; the cornerstone of SOA is services. In the broadest sense of the word, a service is something useful a provider offers to consumers. This can be something tangible like a carton of milk, or something intangible such as an insurance product. A service in terms of SOA is regarded as a set of capabilities that belong together and whose capabilities are accessible to consumers. Services are building blocks that are well-defined, possibly reusable, and provide business value. Every service has a contract, interface, and implementation. For service consumers, contract and interface are visible and important. They describe under what conditions a service can be used and is accessible to consumers. The implementation is a "black box" and mostly important for the provider of the service.

SOA is a reference architecture that is based on services, and offers a number of improvements for the problems you learned about in *Chapter 1, Understanding the Problem*.

Now that you know what services are, the questions you probably are asking are: "What makes a service a useful service?" and "How do I find these services?" Without usable services you won't be able to achieve the promised benefits of SOA. The next chapter will dive into service design and discuss what aspects make services *successful*.

3
Service Identification and Design

We have seen that services are a key aspect of any SOA, and by now we know exactly what a service is! The next step is for you to find out what services you actually need based on the requirements of clients. This process is called **service identification**. Once you have identified what services your clients require, you can start designing these services by designing their operations, and the input and output of these operations.

It's important to start with service identification before going into the actual details of **service design**. Don't start with the design until you have a business case and a real project with real consumers, otherwise you might end up investing a lot of time and money in the design and implementation of services and operations that are useless. If you are not sure whether particular operations are needed, leave them out and only design and implement the ones you need. Later on you can always expand services and add operations, should the need for them arise.

> There are several methodologies and frameworks that focus on service identification and service design. For example, *Service Oriented Modeling and Architecture* (SOMA), *Arsanjani, 2004* makes a distinction between the service identification phase, the service definition phase, and the service realization phase. Another methodology, *Service Oriented Design and Development Methodology, Papazoglou* and *Van Den Heuvel, 2007* uses the term *analysis and design* instead of *identification and design*.

Service Identification and Design

This chapter begins by discussing service identification based on the different approaches you can take to find the services you need. The second part of the chapter then delves into service design to help you learn what sets good services apart from poorly-designed services. The chapter concludes by investigating an example of a poorly designed service. After reading this chapter, there'll be no secrets surrounding either service identification or service design!

Service identification

Service identification is not only about finding services that are already there, but also about identifying services that your organization needs but do not yet exist. These services can then be bought or developed. Identification can also result in the need to modify existing services, for example adding additional operations, or *promoting* existing IT assets into services. The latter is the case when the implementation is already there, but not yet exposed as a service, the service interface and possibly the contract are missing.

Service identification is an iterative process, meaning that you can't identify all the services in one large project all at once. Start small and realize the initially identified services before gradually expanding your service landscape in subsequent iterations.

There are generally two approaches to identifying services—**top-down** and **bottom-up**. Let's go into some more detail now.

Top-down

Top-down service identification typically happens when executing enterprise architecture or solution architecture activities. As you have learned in *Chapter 1, Understanding the Problem*, architectures typically consist of the following layers:

- Business architecture
- Information architecture
- Technical architecture

Using architecture to translate strategy into concrete activities and projects helps the organization to move into the desired direction in a controllable fashion. When the as-is and to-be architectures are compared you will discover discrepancies.

The next figure shows the order in which services are identified when applying top-down service identification based on the strategy of your company:

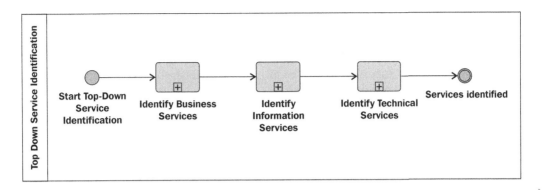

The following steps are executed:

1. **Identify Business Services**: You start by analyzing the business plans in your organization and determine what business services you need.
2. **Identify Information Services**: Once you know what business services you need, you can determine what information services are needed to support these business services.
3. **Identify Technical Services**: The technical services you need to support the information services are identified.

Examples of services you need are:

- On the **business level**, an organization might add new products to its portfolio creating the need for new business units to manufacture, market, and support these products
- On the **information level** this could mean we need information and applications to support selling and promoting these new products, while we might get rid of other less useful, older, or costly applications
- On the **technical level** we might have new standards we want to adhere to, or want to implement a new network to better enable working on premise, and so on

Service Identification and Design

>
> **Gap analysis**
> Analyzing the differences between two scenarios or plans, such as the as-is and to-be architecture is called a gap-analysis. In other words, you analyze what the differences or *gaps* between the two scenarios are. When the differences between the as-is and to-be architecture are clear, you can identify the concrete activities that need to be executed to *bridge the gap* between the as-is and to-be architecture. These activities are then planned in a roadmap based on priority, costs, benefits, and so on, and are executed.

The gap analysis in an SOA environment will identify what services need to be introduced, what services need to be changed, and what services need to be phased out. This is done on all the layers of the architecture, that is business, information, and technical, and often involves **make**, **buy**, or **reuse** decisions.

The next figure shows how make, buy, and reuse fits in the service identification process:

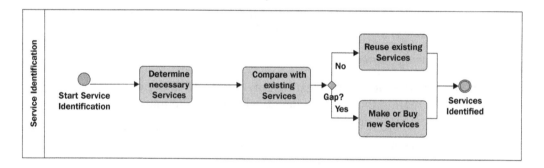

The following steps are executed:

1. **Determine necessary Services**
2. **Compare with existing services**: The services you need are compared with the existing services in your organization
3. **Make or Buy new Services**: If there is a gap, you decide whether the project will buy or make the missing services
4. **Reuse existing Services**: If there is a fit, you can use the existing services

Example of top-down service identification

A simplified example of the previous figure is a consumer electronics corporation whose strategy for the upcoming years is to become a quality brand (using product leadership as the strategy), as well as to diversify into other markets to increase revenue. To realize this diversification, the *to-be* business architecture identifies tablets and smart phones as new consumer products besides the current offering of televisions and computers.

Business service identification

On the business layer, you determine what services you need to be able to sell tablets and smart phones. The to-be architecture identifies the `TabletManufacteringService` for this purpose. Next the company decides how to realize this service:

- Reuse an existing service, for example one of their existing factories that produces laptops is modified to also produce tablets
- Buy a service, for example take over an existing tablet manufacturer
- Create a new service, for example set up a new plant and train new personnel

Information service identification

On the information level, services are identified that support the business service. The corporation identifies the need for an information service to support online sales of tablets and smart phones, and the need for an information service to implement an App Store to provide content for tablets and smart phones. Based on the company policy, it is decided to reuse the existing information services to support sales of tablets and smart phones, and to create a new service for the App Store.

Technical service identification

On the technical level there is the need to support new protocols for distribution of apps from the App Store to the tablets and smart phones and a way to push updates to these devices. A new `DistributionService` is identified, with two operations—`DistributionService.installApp` and `DistributionService.updateApp`.

This example shows us that top-down service identification provides a structured and systematic way to identify the services your organization needs. Top-down service identification is often based on gap analysis. To enable gap analysis you need to know both the current and desired state of your organization. The example shows that dividing the as-is and to-be situations in smaller parts such as a business, information, and technical architecture helps to make gap-analysis more manageable. Applying gap-analysis to the different layers of the as-is and to-be architecture in an SOA environment will result in a concrete set of services that need be created, changed, or phased out to realize the to-be situation.

Top-down service identification is an iterative process that needs to be executed periodically. The as-is and to-be situations keep changing due to economic, political, and internal drivers. As we execute the roadmap the as-is situation changes and looks more like the to-be situation.

Bottom-up

Bottom-up service identification occurs when you investigate your existing IT assets, and derive services from there.

An example of bottom-up identification is the implementation of an HRM system for the Human Resource department. The system offers several services out of the box, such as `EmployeeServices`, `SalaryService`, `AddressService`, and so on. A year after the system goes live the company wants to create a new intranet portal. One of the functionalities of the portal is to provide access to employee contact information such as e-mail, phone, picture, and work location. For this they can use the `EmployeeService` of the HRM service.

Bottom-up identification can be seen as harvesting services from your existing systems in which functionality is promoted as service; it is a more technical approach to service identification than top-down service identification.

Meet in the middle

Services that are identified in a bottom-up fashion are not less valuable than top-down identified services. Top-down services have the risk of being too abstract so nobody wants them or knows how to use them. Bottom-up services are there because there is a concrete need for them, but might need to be modified before they are usable for other departments or IT systems in the organization.

So, do we need to follow a top-down or bottom-up approach? As with so many things, the truth is in the middle—we need to do both. *Chapter 7, Creating a Roadmap, How to Spend Your Money and When?* will cover this subject further by explaining how to set up a roadmap for the realization of your SOA that includes service identification.

I have identified my services, now what?

It could be that your first iteration of service identification has resulted into the identification of three services for which there is an immediate need. Next, we are faced with the question of how to design these services if you choose to develop them or have them developed by someone else. If we buy these services we need to be able to analyze if we get our money's worth for them or not, we don't want to buy a pig in a poke!

The next part of this chapter will discuss service design principles that will help us in the design of new services and analysis of existing services.

Service design

Designing a service consists of several actions, such as:

- Define the functionality it offers
- Design the interface
    i. Design the operations and the functionality the operations offer.
    ii. Design the parameters of the operations.
    iii. Design the return value or the effect of the operation.
    iv. Design test cases for the operations.
- Design the contract
    v. Define who is allowed to use the service and who can use what operation.
    vi. Decide how often the service is available.
    vii. Define the load the service should be able to handle.
    viii. Define other relevant **quality of service** attributes.
- Design the implementation
    ix. Decide what tool or language you are going to use for the implementation.
    x. Design the components you need for the implementation.
    xi. Decide what tools to use to test the implementation.

Service Identification and Design

> **Quality of Service**, or **QoS**, is often used to describe the non-functional properties of (Web) Services such as performance, reliability, security, availability, and so on.

Service design principles indicate what qualities a service needs to have in order to be a usable building block in the architecture we are trying to achieve. When services are poorly designed or poorly implemented, our solution architecture will probably have little value for the business. What we need are sound design principles that help us as a **service provider** to create (re)useable services, and help us as a **service consumer** to judge if the services that we use (or want to use) are well designed.

The following list includes several service design principles in random order and **quality-of-service** aspects that can be used as checklist when creating, buying, or reviewing services. Note that the list is not in a particular order; the importance of each principle depends on the needs of your organization.

> These principles are both technical and non-technical in nature. It is important that you understand all principles and know why they are important. It depends on your role whether you need to apply the principles yourself and what principles have your primary concern. A software architect that designs and implements services may focus on implementation hiding and interoperability, while a security architect may focus mostly on trust; a business architect is concerned with the value that is provided by services.

Provide value

For every service, consider if and why you need it. If a service doesn't provide value to someone or something (organization's clients, internal departments, other IT systems, and so on) then it is probably not a good service, or only part of a service and not a service in itself.

Meaningful

It should be easy for (future) consumers to use a service. Therefore the service interface needs to be meaningful to the *consumer and not too abstract or complex*. If a service is not meaningful, the required effort to consume a service will increase. Consumers will not be able or are reluctant to use such services since they don't understand them or it is too expensive to use and integrate them into their landscape. Consider the breakfast example in *Chapter 2, The Solution*. We as consumers are not required to go through a week's training to learn how to order breakfast!

Implementation hiding

When it comes to services, consumers don't care about the actual implementation behind the service; this is a black box for them. Consumers focus on the contract and interface of a service to decide whether to use it and to be able to actually consume it. In short, a service and especially its interface and contract, should be self-describing and understandable.

Hiding implementation details is a common approach in several programming paradigms, even more so for SOA in which we specifically differentiate between contract, interface, and implementation. The service interface should abstract away (or hide) the specifics of the underlying systems and organizations that do the actual work. This makes it easier to change, upgrade, or swap the implementation without breaking interoperability since the interface can stay the same. It also doesn't burden consumers who don't need to know about the specifics of the implementation.

Trust

Consumers need to have faith in the service they consume. Consumers want services to be accurate; think about the weather channel, you want it to be accurate so you can trust the forecast. Services should do what they are supposed to do, especially in an SOA where services can be outside your own span-of-control in case of external services. Think about aspects such as security, fault handling, and auditing to increase trust in your services.

Idempotent *PREDICTABLE*

A service should be predictable; invoking a service operation with the same input more than once should result in the same outcome. Every time you order a soda in a bar, you expect a soda. You don't want sparkling water if somebody else ordered a soda before you, or a beer in case it rains outside.

Isolated *loosely coupled*

Services only provide flexibility and can only be easily changed if their operations are independent of other operations within the same or another service; this is called **isolation**. If a change to an operation results in changes to several other operations that are tightly coupled to the originally changed operation, we lose flexibility. Operations need to be separate building blocks that provide capabilities themselves.

Interoperable

Services should be easy to integrate into our IT landscape. Interoperability is a measure for the amount of effort it takes to use and invoke services. Interoperability is achieved by using standards for *describing, providing,* and *accessing* services such as XML, WS-*, WADL, and WSDL. The use of standards increases the ease of consuming services since most platforms and vendors adhere to standards. Note that only the service interface needs to be interoperable; the implementation itself can be proprietary. Think about the breakfast example again, as long as you can order breakfast in the language you as a consumer speak, you don't care what language the cooks speak, as long as the breakfast is good! Using standards to provide and access services helps to mix and match different technologies such as PL/SQL, .NET, Java, and PHP.

Interoperability is not equally important in all SOA environments. How important interoperabilty is for your organization, depends on several factors. Interoperability is especially important in the following cases:

- You need to integrate services in a heterogeneous environment in which different technologies and platforms are used
- Your services are used outside your own organization and you have no control or knowledge over the platforms used by the consumers
- You want to integrate services with packaged software or offer services as part of packaged software

Interoperability is less of a concern when you apply SOA within your own organization consisting of a homogeneous environment in which you have standardized on one or a few (possibly proprietary) platforms and technologies.

The principles of **isolation**, **trust**, and **idempotency** can be tricky and difficult to apply and will be explained in more detail next. We conclude service design by looking at **granularity** and **reusability** since these aspects build upon the service design principles that are introduced here.

Isolation

It is very important from a consumer perspective that operations of services are self-sufficient. This principle is called **isolation** or **autonomy**. This principle is also known as **loose-coupling** or **decoupling**, as opposed to operations that are tightly coupled to other operations, either in the same service or another service. Isolation means that an operation that is invoked by a consumer does not rely on the same consumer to have invoked other operations prior or after its own invocation to deliver the promised functionality. Consumers want to invoke only one operation to achieve what is agreed upon in the service contract for that operation, they don't want to be burdened with the task of invoking other operations to make the actual operation function properly.

Example: print service

Let's have a look at an example to demonstrate what happens if operations are not isolated. Suppose your organization buys a commercial off-the-shelf `PrintService` that can be used to create and send printing requests to the Repro department. The service provides a user interface from which employees can define and execute print jobs. This user interface is integrated into the existing customer care portal and intranet applications. The `PrintService` provides profiles for various departments that define who is allowed to use what type of printer and how many print jobs they are allowed to make. For example, senior employees of the marketing department are allowed to execute high-volume, color print batches, while junior finance staff are supposed to use the cheaper, standard black-and-white printers.

The following diagram shows the customer care portal and the intranet that integrates the user interface to print. The service has an interface and a contract that holds the profiles and other quality of service details. The correct printer gets called based on the profile of the user that calls the service.

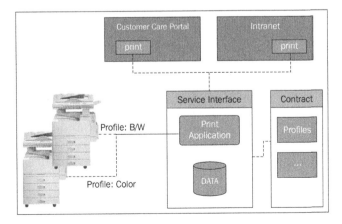

The `PrintService` offers two operations: `PrintService.setPrintProfile` and `PrintService.print`. The service requires us to invoke the `setPrintProfile` operation prior to invoking the print operation. Whenever we forget to invoke the `setPrintProfile` operation, invocation of the `print` operation will fail. It would be better to pass the print date as a parameter to the input of the `print` operation and forget about the `setPrintProfile` operation altogether. In other words, operations should be autonomous of one another. An operation alone should be sufficient to provide some functionality.

Changes to operations that are not isolated often results in cascading and undesired changes to other operations and their services that are tightly coupled to the initially changed operation. Tight-coupling also increases the chance that downtime and errors in an operation impact all coupled operations instead of one operation alone.

Trust

Important factors in trust are applying sufficient security, and fault-prevention and handling capabilities to your services. These are not the only factors in trust, but they are among the more important ones.

Security

Although security is just as important for services as for 'traditional' IT systems, the nature of services has an impact on how to address security. When we break down functionality into services as compared to monoliths we need to apply security on the level of services as well. Services are not only a unit for functionality but also a unit for security:

- An SOA environment typically has more automated interactions and straight-through processing than a 'traditional' IT landscape. We also need automated security mechanisms such as WS-Security and XACML.

- Service-orientation often involves message exchanges from consumer to provider and vice versa through one or more intermediate components such as an Enterprise Service Bus and message-oriented middleware. Security on the transport level alone (for example SSL/TLS) isn't always adequate if data needs to be protected *in rest* or within intermediaries. An example is that of messages that contain credit card information and can be viewed by operation teams that administer middleware platforms. Apply message-level security like signing and encryption of messages to provide end-to-end security from consumer to provider in such cases.

- Service-orientation often means that you use services provided by others or vice versa. When services are outside your own span of control you need to have faith in the quality of service and especially their security since your data flows through these external services. Explicitly state security in your service contracts so providers and consumers know and agree on the level of security that is provided.
- Security is part of the way that services are accessed and provided; it is part of the service interface. For example, if a web service is accessed over SSL/TLS, it needs to be defined if the service input and service output require signing. It is important that the security of a service is based on standards as well when interoperability is a concern. Examples of security standards are WS-Security (message-level security for authentication, authorization, encryption, and signing), SSL/TLS (transport-level authentication and encryption), SAML (message-based authentication and authorization), and HTTP basic access authentication (transport-level authentication).

Fault-prevention and handling

Another important aspect of trust is fault-prevention and fault handling of services. Faults can be seen as situations in which the outcome or effect of a service invocation is different than the 'happy flow'. Fault handling and prevention should be implemented on the level of services and operations, as is the case for security.

There are different types of faults. Services need to deal with these types of faults differently. The types of faults are:

- **Business faults**. Expected faults that have meaning to consumers: a failure to meet a particular business requirement.
- **Faulty user input**. Faults in the input of service operations so operations are unable to execute correctly or have an undesired outcome.
- **Technical and software faults**. Unexpected and undesired failures that cannot be easily recovered from by consumers such as a network failures, software programming errors, and corrupt disks.

Service Identification and Design

Business faults

Business faults have an impact on consumers and consumers need to act upon them. Consumers can recover from these faulty situations by taking appropriate action. For example, a bad credit check as output of a `PaymentService`, an `OrderService` that indicates that the client that wants to make a purchase is not yet registered in the system. In case the `OrderService` indicates the client is not yet registered, the application might redirect the client to a page where he or she can register. In case the ordered product is not in stock, the application can ask the client if they want to wait for it. Business faults should be identified during the design process and made an integral part of the service interface besides the *normal* input and output of a service and its operations. Every business fault should be listed individually in the interface so service consumers can act accordingly per fault.

The WSDL standard for describing web service interfaces, for example, makes it possible to explicitly define faults and their message definition per operation. The following code listing shows the part of the `OrderService` WSDL describing the `orderProduct` operation. As you can see, the operation defines two fault situations: the product is not in stock, and the customer that orders the product cannot be found.

```
<wsdl:operation name="orderProduct">
  <wsdl:input message="order:OrderProductRequestMessage"/>
  <wsdl:output message="order:OrderProductResponseMessage"/>
  <wsdl:fault message="order:OrderProductNotInStockFaultMessage"
    name="OrderProductNotInStockFault"/>
  <wsdl:fault message="order:CustomerNotFoundFaultMessage"
    name="CustomerNotFoundFault"/>
</wsdl:operation>
```

Faulty user input

An example of a faulty user input is a flight booking website where a customer enters a return date prior to the departure date which is then passed as input to a `BookingService`, or an online store where a user enters a wrong credit card number.

Faulty user input should be discovered as early as possible to prevent service operations from executing unwanted activities due to this faulty data. Consider a `CarRentalService` that books and bills a client for a rental period of 100 years and one week. Probably the client wanted to rent the car for one week and filled out the form incorrectly. Applying user experience techniques so that the service interface makes sense to the consumer and provides the required information that is needed to invoke the operation in a clear and structured fashion can prevent faulty user input. This way the overall quality of data entered by users increases. Services should always verify input before executing the actual operation that is invoked.

Technical and software faults

Services should be made robust to prevent technical errors. There are numerous patterns and techniques that can be applied such as:

- Retrying in case of network errors to prevent faults due to network glitches
- Throttling of service request to prevent overloading of services
- Pair-programming and code review to prevent programming errors
- Adequate monitoring of underlying infrastructure to prevent full tablespaces

Since consumers cannot recover from technical faults in services and these errors are unexpected, the different technical faults that can occur should not be specified as separate faults in the interface. Also make sure that exception messages and stack traces are not passed to the consumer directly since they can contain sensitive information that can be misused, for example specific versions of middleware components, usernames, operating system version, SQL statements, and so on.

> Hiding such information and wrapping specific technical faults as more generic technical faults is called **exception shielding**.

There is also a need for handling faults that span multiple services. An example is the order-to-cash process that invokes several operations from start to end of the process. If at some point a client cancels the order, we might need to deregister the order in our back office system, update the inventory, undo the credit card booking, and so on. Service operations define transaction boundaries meaning that once an operation is successfully completed, all activities as part of the operation are committed. These activities cannot be rolled back. In such cases compensation can be applied in which operations are undone by executing opposite actions. This can be achieved by invoking the same operation with the opposite input, or to have an accompanying undo operation for an operation, for example `createOrder` and `cancelOrder`.

Idempotency

Messages get lost or are duplicated by technical and human error. Invoking a service more than once should yield the same result. This is called **idempotency** and improves the robustness of services by making them predictable, thus increasing the trust that consumers have in the service.

Consider an HRM system that provides a `SalaryService` to modify salaries of employees. Suppose our HR manager is very pleased with our performance; after all, we wrote this book! She decides to give each of us a raise of $100 a month and uses a self-service portal to set the new salary. The portal connects to the HRM system using services such as the `SalaryService`. A poorly designed service would expose an `increaseSalary` operation. Since I get a $100 increase, the `SalaryService.increaseSalary` is invoked with $100 as input. Now suppose that the request message is delivered to the service, which increases my salary in the backend system, but the response message is lost due to a network error or other technical glitch. Maybe the underlying IT infrastructure is resilient, detects the failure and resends the entire input message, or maybe my manager sees an error in the HRM system and retries to increase my salary. In both cases, my salary will be increased yet again and the raise will be $200 in total. While I wouldn't mind this, the company loses money because the service is invoked twice, accidently. In other words invoking this service multiple times does not yield the same result (a given monthly salary).

It is better to have a `SalaryService.setSalary` operation instead. If our current salary is $3,000 and we want to increase it by $100, then setting the salary to $3,100 will always yield the same result independently of the number of times we invoke the service. Increasing the salary by $100 more than once does not.

Idempotency and statefulness

Automated services can run in a clustered configuration, that is there are multiple physical instances of the same service at runtime. You can compare this to a bank, library, and so on where you have multiple counters (or instances) that can serve you. A clustered configuration increases the throughput of a service, or the number of invocations that can be processed by a service and its operations, and increases availability. If one instance of a service fails, other instances can take over the load of the failed instance. Often consumers are unaware of the particular instance that they interact with, and with good reason too, since this is an implementation detail of the service and needing to know this as a consumer decreases the ease of use to consume a service.

Idempotency can be broken when service consumers are dependent on a particular *instance* of a service with or without knowing this dependency. This is mostly the case for services that are **stateful**, meaning a service instance maintains state (data) that is specific to a particular consumer.

Chapter 3

For example, consider a DocumentService that runs in a cluster with three instances. Instances of this service maintain their own local state (or cache) to improve performance. Every interval, this cache might be synchronized with a centralized datastore, but until that time the state per instance can differ. Suppose a client invokes the DocumentService to store a document. This invocation is routed by the underlying service infrastructure to instance 1. This instance stores the document in its local cache. The client invokes the service yet again to retrieve the document. If this invocation is routed to instance 1 of the DocumentService, the document is returned. However, if the invocation is routed to instance 2 of 3, a fault is returned since these instances do not have the document in their cache (yet) and are unable to find the requested document.

[Invoking the same operation more than once can yield a different result.]

The following figure shows the DocumentService that we discussed. As you can see the service consists of three instances at runtime and that all maintain their own state locally, thereby causing the DocumentService to lose its idempotency.

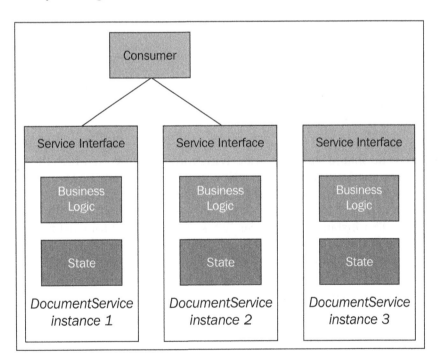

[71]

Service Identification and Design

Services should either be stateless or the state should be accessed and persist in a shared datastore, so it is accessible and the same for all instances of a service to guarantee idempotency. Such a datastore can be implemented using a relational database, in-memory grid, filestore, and so on.

The following figure shows the `DocumentService` again. Only this time all instances share the same state thereby preserving idempotency.

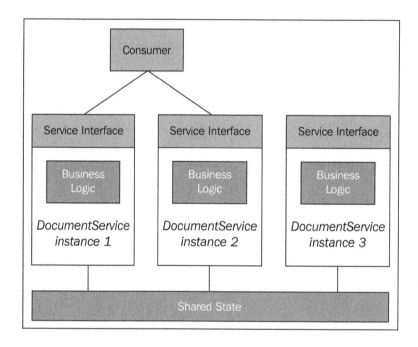

In case there is no shared state, the underlying infrastructure on which the service runs is sometimes configured to tie consumers to a specific service instance. This makes sure invocations from the same consumer always end up at a particular instance thereby improving idempotency. However, such configurations are less scalable since other instances cannot easily take over the load for existing consumers. The availability of the service is also more brittle since a failure in a particular service instance will most likely impact the consumers that are tied to this instance. Their invocations cannot be handled by other service instances without some (complex) synchronization mechanism of local state.

Granularity

So far we have considered all services to be of equal *weight* or relevance. However this is not the case in a real-life SOA. A service for converting AM/PM time notations into a 24 hour time notation isn't comparable to a service that is used to book a holiday including hotel reservations, car rentals, and flight bookings in terms of added value.

> Services are of different importance based on the degree of value or functionality they add. This is called **granularity**.

To illustrate granularity we will compare a traditional three-tiered architecture with an architecture based on services.

Three-tiered architectures consisting of web clients, a middleware component containing most of the business logic, and a datastore that stores the information has been advertised in the past as a solution to monolithic systems. Although three-tiered architectures offer decoupling between its **horizontal technical** layers, a large system can still be designed and developed as one monolith of different layers in which the layers themselves become monoliths, that is one very big lasagna, so to speak. Three-tiered architecture isn't flawed, but it shouldn't be applied on your IT landscape or large part of it as a whole as depicted in the following figure:

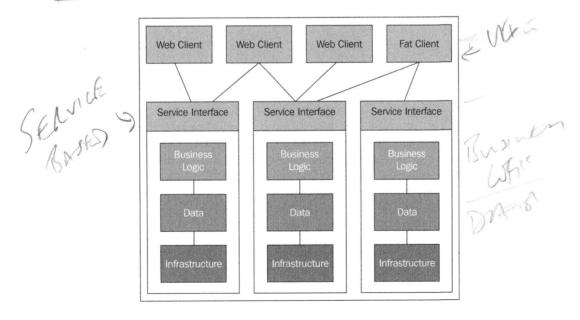

Instead we want to differentiate *vertically*, based on *functionality*, providing a limited and independent set of capabilities exposed by operations that belong together.

Services and three-tiered architectures can go hand-in-hand by applying three-tiered architecture to the implementation of services resulting in several smaller lasagnas. Now each lasagna can be changed without impacting other lasagnas. Using this approach, changing business logic and data becomes easier since it is separated (decoupled) from the other business logic and data layers in other services.

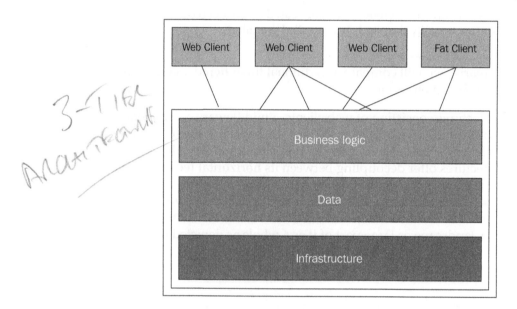

Solution architectures based on SOA are about dividing functionality in externally visible portions vertically before thinking how services are internally implemented in horizontal layers. This should also be reflected in the release management process that is responsible for promoting IT assets through development, test, acceptance, and production environments. The granularity of releases in an SOA is based on services we release vertically, per services, instead of big horizontal releases that impact several services at once. Releasing per service makes release management easier since the impact of a release is small (has little impact on other systems and services), and makes sure we focus on releasing functional building blocks that are useful to consumers instead of releasing based on technology (for example a complete horizontal layer) with less value and meaning to consumers.

How big should my lasagna be?

When thinking about granularity, the million dollar question we need to answer is: *How granular should a service and its operations be?* or speaking in terms of the lasagna example, *How large should my lasagna be?*.

In any case a service should be:

- Big enough to provide value on its own; a `setProfile` operation is too small since it provides no value in itself.
- Small enough to be able to change it, without changing the whole IT landscape in your department or organization. Putting all ERP-related functionality in one big monolithic service with thousands of operations that are used by almost everyone is too big. Every change in ERP-related functionality requires a change in this one service.
- Granularity should be derived from functionality, don't mix functionalities that are unrelated into a single service and don't split functionality that belongs together into different services.
- Granularity should go hand-in-hand with transaction boundaries; an operation defines a transactional unit; all activities as part of an operation are either successfully executed and committed together or in case an operation fails, all activities as part of the operation are rolled back.

It is important to realize that there is not just one correct granularity for all the services in your organization you need to settle on. Not all services are either fine-grained web services or coarse-grained process services alone. An SOA consists of various types of services with varying granularity. Different principles and guidelines apply to different types of services, and different types of services are designed and implemented differently.

Service Identification and Design

Classification

We need a pragmatic scheme to categorize our services into a set of different types of granularity. One way to do this is by means of a service classification. An example of a classification is one in different layers such as process services, composed services (combining smaller services into larger ones), and elementary services (smallest unit of services).

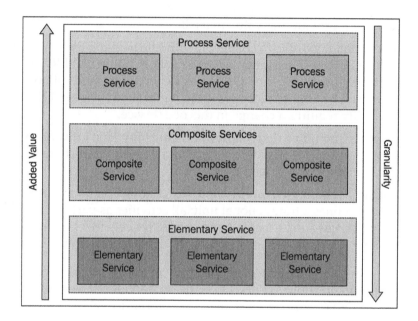

You can use another classification; every organization needs to pick their own classification that fits their needs. The next chapter will dive into the classification of services and provides a more detailed example of a classification scheme.

Reusability

Reusability means a service is used by more than one consumer or is meant to be used by more than one consumer in the future. In the latter case the service is designed with reuse in mind, but has not yet been used by more than one consumer at the time being.

 Reusability should not be confused with ease of use or usability of services.

[76]

The consumer of a service is the actual application, process, organizational unit, customer, or organization that uses a service:

- If a `StockQuote` web service is invoked from an Intranet application and a Financial packaged application, it is reused.
- If a `DocumentService` is used from the order-to-cash process and the HR onboarding process, it is reused. If the `DocumentService` is used from two different locations in the same process, it is also reused.
- If an organization's Shared Service Center IT provides services to the Marketing department as well as the Finance department, it is reused.
- If an invoicing company provides services to various clients, their services are reused.

> The terms consumer and client are often used interchangeably; actually they don't mean the same thing.
>
> The **consumer** of a service is the application, service, organization, department, or person that really uses, or invokes, a service.
>
> The **client** is the organization, department, or person that decides that a service should be consumed (by the consumer) and pays for it.
>
> For example, consider an HR application that invokes a `DocumentService`. The consumer of the service is the HR application; the client is the HR department that owns the HR application. Consider a Shared Service Center Finance that handles invoices for the Marketing department. In this case the Marketing department is both the consumer and client of the services offered by the Shared Service Center Finance.
>
> For automated services, clients and consumers are often not the same entity, for business services they often are. Making a clear distinction between different roles is important when considering SOA because every role has its own motives when (thinking about) using your services.

Reuse can save money. Instead of buying or building a new service, we can use existing ones, hopefully without too many modifications to the service we want to reuse. Measure the benefits of reuse not only by the current number of consumers but also by the possible future consumers that don't use the service yet but are viable candidates for using it. Reuse can also speed up the creation of new artifacts (processes, products, and so on) since we assemble already existing services instead of building them from scratch.

However, there is a price to pay; the more a service is reused the less flexible it often becomes. An increase in the number of consumers results in more wishes and requirements that need to be agreed upon by all stakeholders. We need to analyze whether changes impact other consumers. Consider for example a Shared Service Center IT in an organization, they cannot replace the existing e-mail application organization-wide based on wishes and requirements from the Marketing department without consulting the other service clients to see what their requirements are. This is not something you can solve by implementation hiding, because the e-mail program has a user interface (e-mail client) that is used by every employee in the organization.

Example – reusability

Let's have a look at an example. Imagine a sports article web shop that sells their goods online through a consumer-facing web application. This application is also used by their front office team that processes orders made via phone and e-mail. The web shop has built their own order management system that they integrate with the web application. Someone in the Marketing department reads in an article that sports fans that fit a certain profile (sports likes, gender, age, and so on) also have a keen interest in whisky. The chief marketing officer is also a keen whisky drinker and they decide to create a new web application to sell single malt whiskies that are advertised for customers that fit a certain profile.

The web shop now has two important decisions to make:

- **Technical level**: Buy or make a new ordering system specific for the whisky web application or reuse the existing ordering system?
- **Organizational level**: Form an additional front office team to process whisky orders or have a single front office team that handles all orders?

Chapter 3

Let's start on the technical level, we can either choose to reuse the existing order system or introduce a second order system. The following diagram shows the two possibilities:

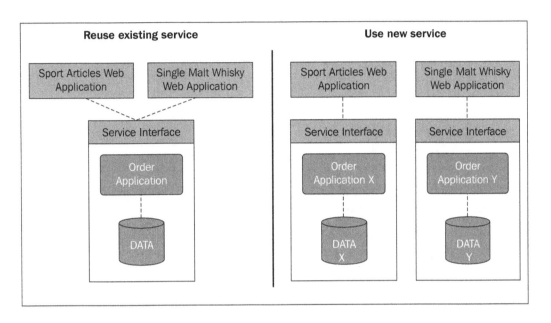

The diagram shows the two choices. On the left-hand side, the situation shown is if the organization decides to reuse the existing **Order Application**. The new **Single Malt Whisky Web Application** uses the existing service and has to comply with its interface and contract. On the right-hand side, you can see what happens if the organization decides to make or buy a new application. There is duplication of functionality, but the web application can use a service that is specific for its needs.

Service Identification and Design

A similar choice needs to be made on the organizational level as well; do we reuse the services offered by the existing front office team or introduce another front office team specifically for processing whisky orders? This is shown in the next diagram:

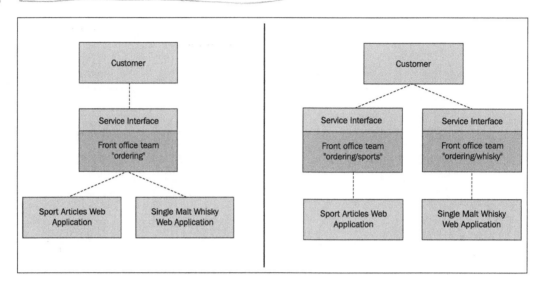

In the preceding diagram you can see what happens if a customer calls the front office team and if the company decides to reuse the existing front office team. The customer has one phone number, and the front office team figures out what application they need to use to order the goods: the **Sport Articles Web Application** or the **Single Malt Whisky Web Application**. In the case of a new business service, distinction is made between the order service for sport articles and whiskey. The customers call a specific front office to order whisky and another team to order sporting goods.

Reusability isn't a goal on its own and not every service is meant to be reusable. For example, a `ZipCodeService` is very reusable since we can use it from the Intranet, customer care service portal, and several front office systems. Now consider a municipality that used a `BuildingPermitService` that is capable of handling building permits, but offers no functionality for granting parking permits, felling permits, and so on. This service is not reusable, we only use it for a specific type of permit. Still both services are valid examples of services nonetheless.

Often the more added value a service delivers, the more specific it is and the less reusable it becomes, and vice versa. The `ZipCodeService` is reusable but has little business value, while the `BuildingPermitService` has more business value but is not very reusable. The `BuildingPermitService` is an example of a business service. The `ZipCodeService` is an example of an elementary service. Business services tend to add a lot of value, and are not very reusable, elementary services are very reusable but are not as valuable. Composite services offer something in between. This is also shown in the following diagram:

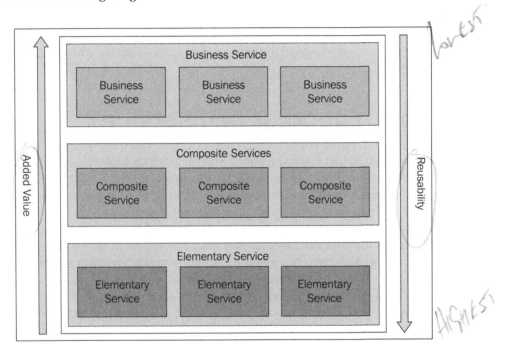

It is a pitfall to make services more generic per se to increase their reusability. It makes a service harder to use if it is too generic. First investigate if (future) reusability is necessary, before you end up with over-generic and non-understandable services and operations. Think for example of a service to change employee data. You can create a service `EmployeeService` with an operation `updateEmployee` with a parameter `newEmployeeData`. Now if a consumer wants to update the salary, the parameters that are needed are unclear. Do you need to provide the employee number, and the name, and the manager, and the new salary, or just the number and the new salary? An operation `setSalary` with parameters `employeeId` and `newSalary` is easier to understand.

>
> **Avoid over-generic services**
>
> Avoid the use of non-specific service. Service consumers don't know how to handle a service like `SuperService.doIt`, even though it is very reusable. It requires too much knowledge of the implementation of the service in order to be able to use it correctly.

This concludes the overview of service design principles. By now you should be able to differentiate between good and poorly designed services. The following section provides an example of a poorly designed service and an explanation as to why this is the case. With your newfound knowledge, the explanation shouldn't come as a surprise to you!

Example – good or bad service?

The customer care department owns a customer care service portal that stores phone calls and e-mails with the questions and orders that took place. The portal does not offer functionality to store related information with the customer contact events, nor does it store information that occurs through the self-service web application. The department has a requirement to store, edit, and retrieve this information for improving quality-of-service and to analyze customer satisfaction. If a customer calls the customer care department, the employee needs to see the entire history of the customer, not just the call and e-mails. Specific content items, for example letters that have been sent and that are related to the call should be accessible to the customer care agent. A project is started to integrate the customer care service portal with the organization's content management system through the `ContentManagementService`. This way all interactions between customers and employees through whatever channel (e-mail, voice, electronic forms) can be stored, retrieved, and inspected from the portal using the service. The following diagram shows the desired end result of the portal:

Chapter 3

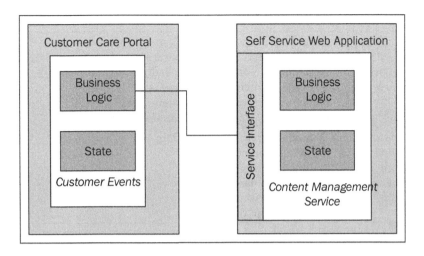

The application to the left-hand side is the **Customer Care Portal**. It calls the service interface that is part of the content management service of the **Self Service Web Application** to retrieve data about customer contact events and to store data that are collected in the customer care portal.

The following table describes the existing service interface of the organization's ContentManagementService that will be used to access the capabilities of the underlying proprietary **Content Management System (CMS)**. The service consists of two operations—storeData and retrieveData. At first glance the ContentManagementService may seem like a pretty useful service for the project.

The ContentManagementService is an automated service that can be used to store most types of electronic content such as XML payloads, digital documents such as MP3, DOC, DOCX, PDF, and ODF documents, and e-mail messages with attachments. The ContentManagementService can be invoked through the web service it exposes.

Service Identification and Design

Operation	Input	Output	Business fault
`storeData`: Stores data in the CMS according to the given parameters.	**Data**: Zero or more parameters and metadata elements formatted as name/value pairs to configure the storage of data.	Zero or more parameters and metadata elements formatted as name/value pairs that describe the stored data.	Storage not successful
`retrieveData`: Retrieves stored data according to the given parameters.	**Data identifier**: Zero or more parameters and metadata elements formatted as name/value pairs to configure the retrieval of data.	Data	Data not found

However, it turns out to be rather difficult to correctly invoke the `ContentManagementService` and integrate it with the customer care service portal. Let's have a closer look at an arbitrary invocation of the `ContentManagementService.storeData` operation.

The request message is listed as follows and contains the actual data to be stored, which is a snippet of binary data that contains the recording of a phone conversation between a customer care employee and a customer. Besides this voice recording that needs to be stored, the request message also contains relevant metadata that is important for the Customer Care department and parameters that are required by the underlying CMS to store this piece of data. As you can see from the request message, quite a few parameters need to be provided on top of the actual data to invoke the `storeData` operation. Examples of such parameters are the data markup (for example MP3) and compression algorithm to be applied (for example LZ77). These parameters are nested in some cases, meaning the parameter value itself is another set of parameters; for example the `Compression` parameters that are nested in the `StorageOptions` parameter.

```
<storeDataRequestMessage>
  <dataToBeStored>
    6tZuIKp$3wAzpL?jsUhgDSAq#a34pOP
  </dataToBeStored>
  <parameters>
    <parameter>
      <name>CMS_StorageType</name>
      <value>BASIC</value>
    </parameter>
    <parameter>
      <name>DataType</name>
```

```xml
      <value>
        <parameters>
          <parameter>
            <name>MarkUp</name>
            <value>MP3</value>
          </parameter>
          <parameter>
            <name>Standard</name>
            <value>MPEG-2 Audio Layer III</value>
          </parameter>
          <parameter>
            <name>Bitrate</name>
            <value>128</value>
          </parameter>
        </parameters>
      </value>
    </parameter>
    <parameter>
      <name>StorageOptions</name>
      <value>
        <parameters>
          <parameter>
            <name>Encryption</name>
            <value>false</value>
          </parameter>
          <parameter>
            <name>Compression</name>
            <value>
              <parameters>
                <parameter>
                  <name>Lossy</name>
                  <value>true</value>
                </parameter>
                <parameter>
                  <name>Algorithm</name>
                  <value>LZ77</value>
                </parameter>
              </parameters>
            </value>
          </parameter>
        </parameters>
      </value>
    </parameter>
    <parameter>
```

```xml
        <name>Metadata</name>
        <value>
          <parameters>
            <parameter>
              <name>Channel</name>
              <value>Telephone</value>
            </parameter>
            <parameter>
              <name>Date</name>
              <value>2011-10-25</value>
            </parameter>
            <parameter>
              <name>CustomerId</name>
              <value>389902</value>
            </parameter>
          </parameters>
        </value>
      </parameter>
    </parameters>
</storeDataRequestMessage>
```

The developers that are tasked with the integration between the customer care service portal and the content management service are asked why the integration proves to be more difficult than initially thought. The main reason is that the service is hard to use from the consumer's perspective. The developers encounter the following issues:

- **The parameters are too generic**: The interface specifies that request and response messages need to include parameters and metadata elements to store and retrieve data, although it is unclear what specific parameters and metadata elements are required and in what order. All parameters and metadata elements have the same element name (parameters, parameter, and value) and it is unknown if we need to add a set of nested parameters or just a value.

- **Exceptions are too generic**: The specified exceptions in the interface are so generic that it is unclear why an invocation failed; is it because of a technical error, is the passed data too large, did we provide a wrong set of parameters, are we missing parameters, and so on.

- **The implementation is not hidden**: The developers need to know about the internal implementation of the underlying CMS; for example, how to populate the CMS_StorageType and Compression parameters. These properties are specific to the underlying CMS but still exposed through the ContentManagementService.
- **The structure of the parameters is too complex**: Due to nesting and repeating elements in the request and response messages, the messages become complex so human programming errors are easily made. This complexity also makes bug fixing and monitoring by operations teams more difficult.

Because of the abstraction, developers don't know how to invoke this service without having in-depth knowledge about the inner details of the content management system and this had to be discovered by trial-and-error, which is time-consuming and error-prone. The service turns out to be tightly coupled to the underlying implementation—the Content Management System. It will be hard to switch the implementation of the service to another CMS or upgrade the CMS in the future without changing the service interface, thus breaking interoperability with the consumers of the service.

Service definition revisited

The previous chapter provided a basic definition of what a service is. With the design principles provided in this chapter in mind, let's have a look at a formal definition of services according to The Open Group:

The Open Group is a global consortium that enables the achievement of business objectives through IT standards. See: http://www3.opengroup.org/aboutus

A service:

- is a logical representation of a repeatable business activity that has a specified outcome (for example, check customer credit; provide weather data, consolidate drilling reports)
- is self-contained
- may be composed of other services
- is a *black box* to consumers of the service

Source: http://www.opengroup.org/soa/source-book/soa/soa.htm

This definition fits well with the service principles you have seen in this chapter. The following table maps the definition on our service principles:

Open Group Definition	Applicable Service Principles
A logical representation of a repeatable business activity that has a specified outcome	Provide value
	Meaningful
	Idempotent
Self contained	Isolated
May be composed of other services	Granularity
Is a black box to consumers of the service	Implementation hiding

Summary

In this chapter, you learned to identify what services you need before you dive into their design. Services are identified in a top-down fashion when they are derived from an overall strategy or plan, which is usually formalized in a to-be architecture and roadmap. Such a roadmap dictates what services to create, when, and in what order. Bottom-up service identification occurs when you investigate your existing IT assets, and derive services from there. This chapter explains why meet in the middle is the best approach.

This chapter also discussed what makes a good or a poor service based on design principles such as isolation and idempotency. Most important is that services need to be easy to use, must provide value, and that they can be trusted by (future) consumers.

As we have seen, not all services have the same *relevance* and we need to categorize services since different principles and guidelines apply to different types of services. The next chapter continues to explore such classification schemes.

4
Classification of Services

In the previous chapter you learned how to identify and design services. This chapter starts by revisiting the classification of services that was explained in the previous chapter, the aspects on which it is based and how the classification can be applied. The chapter briefly discusses why it is important to classify services based on your needs and what aspects can be used to create a classification of services.

You will then learn how services can be combined into larger services, which is called **service composition**. Composition is one of the building blocks for the classification scheme.

Next, the different elements of the classification scheme will be discussed in detail. Finally, the chapter revisits the design principle of isolation and explains why composition and isolation is a good match.

Service classification revisited

You have learned in the previous chapter that services can be divided into **elementary services**, **composite services**, and **process services**:

- **Elementary services**: The smallest possible components that qualify as services. For example, a service that can be used for zip code lookups.
- **Composite services**: Services that result from combining two or more other services into one service that provides more value. Composite services are executed in a single transaction and their execution time is relatively short. An example is a service to book a hotel and flight together.
- **Process services**: Longer running services that can take a couple of hours, days, or even more to complete and span multiple transactions. An example is a service for ordering a book online. The entire process (order, pay, ship, deliver) involves multiple transactions and takes a couple of hours at least.

The following figure shows this classification of different services:

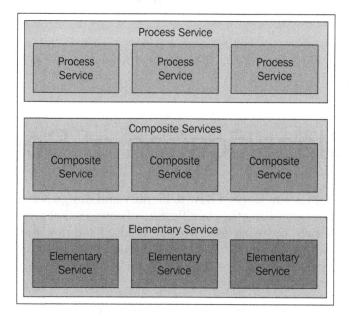

Example – insurance company

Let's take a look at an insurance company. The company offers a `ClaimToPaymentService`. We saw in *Chapter 1, Understanding the Problem* that this is a process service that consists of the following steps:

1. Receive claim.
2. Review the claim.
3. If the claim is valid, pay the claim.
4. Otherwise refuse the claim.

The steps are realized using the following composite services:

- `ClaimService`, operation `receive` and operation `review`
- `PaymentService`, with operation `pay`
- `CustomerService`, with operation `informCustomer`

The composite services are composed of the elementary services:

- `ClaimDataService`
- `DocumentService`
- `PolicyService`
- `AccountsPayableService`
- `CustomerDataService`

The following diagram shows the relationship between these services:

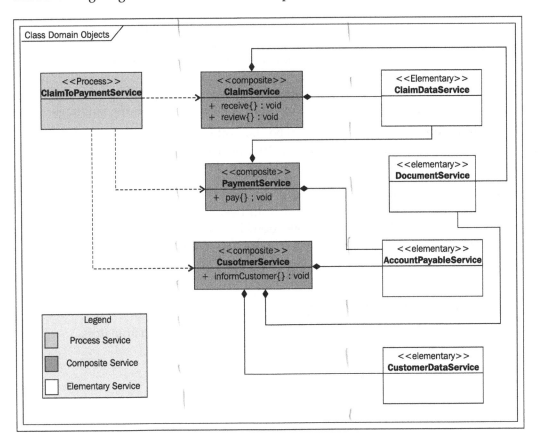

This diagram shows that **ClaimToPaymentService** depends on the composite services to execute. The composite services are composed of several elementary services. As you can see, an elementary service can be part of more than one composite service.

Classification of Services

The classification is based on the *granularity of the service* and the ability of *services to combine* into larger ones. Composite services can be created from elementary services and process services can be created from elementary and composite services.

Reasons for choosing this classification scheme are:

- Combining components into larger objects is a natural way of thinking. Consider the assembly of car parts such as tires and engines from small components, and the assembly of entire cars from these car parts. This is a natural way of differentiating between screws and bolts, a cylinder, and a Volkswagen Golf.
- Guidelines and implementation choices differ between these service types. For example, different error-handling mechanisms are required for long-running process services than for short-running composite services. Another example is the programming language used to implement services. It is not a good idea to program an elementary service in BPEL or XPDL; a more fit choice is Java, .NET, .PHP, or any other generic programming language.
- Its simplicity. Classifications can be elaborated into more dimensions, more layers, and more details that altogether provide more information, but more clutter as well. This is needs-based service classification.

There is no one true classification scheme to structure services. You can choose other aspects to classify services based on your needs – what do you want or what do you need to highlight using a classification? Perhaps you are the organization's security officer and security is the main concern you need highlighted in the classification model.

Other classifications

The following list names aspects that are frequently used as discriminators in classifications:

- **Granularity**: We discussed this already
- **Actor type**: Human, IT System, or both
- **Channel**: Telephone, web, and so on
- **Security level**: Public or confidential
- **Organizational boundaries**: Departmental, enterprise, and external
- **Architectural layer**: Business, information, and technical architecture

Actor type

If you base your classification on actor type, you divide services into two categories based on the question, *Who executes the service?*. The answer can be humans, IT systems, or both. Although you might think of services as automated building blocks without a user interface (for example, a web service), services can just as well provide their capabilities through a graphical interface next to (or beside) an automated interface. A `ZipCodeService` and `DocumentService` are examples of automated services executed by IT systems alone. An example of a service that is implemented by humans alone is bank employees who advise clients on the benefits and risks associated with buying a mortgage product. A service for invoice handling in which invoices are automatically stored and processed, but approved for payment by controllers is an example of a service in which the execution is mixed. Both IT systems and humans implement the service.

Channel

An organization has different channels to offer services to their customers or business partners. Examples are: mail, e-mail, telephone, internet, intranet, mobile applications, face-to-face conversations, third party resellers, and so on. An example is `BookService` which can be accessed from two channels, the telephone and via the Internet.

Organizational boundaries

The classification based on organizational boundaries is useful to get insight into who owns the service and who uses the service, external services are services that are owned by another organization; an example is a `StockQuoteService` offered by a stock exchange to banks. Internal services are owned by your own organization. These services can either be used by external consumers or by stakeholders from your organization alone.

The following figure depicts this. An organization creates client-facing business services by using its internal services. These business services are either offered to other businesses which is called **Business-to-Business (B2B)**, or offered to individual consumers which is called **Business-to-Consumer (B2C)**. An organization deploys people, IT, and processes, which are exposed as services to realize the required functionality.

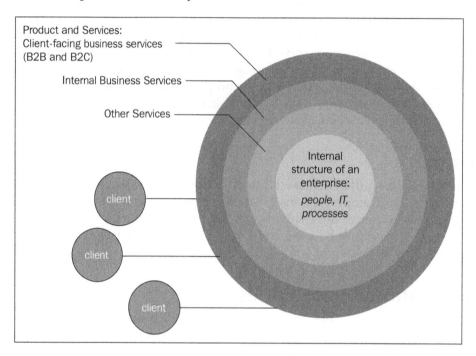

Security level

Another common classification is based on the sensitivity of the functionality and data that services operate on. This is expressed in terms of confidentiality, integrity, and availability requirements.

Architectural layer

This classification is based on the architectural layer to which services belong, that is business, information, or technology layer:

- **Business architecture layer**: The services you have identified in this layer are called **business services**.
- **Information architecture layer**: The services that are identified in this layer are called **information services** or **application services**.
- **Technical layer**: The services that are identified in this layer are called **technical services** or **infrastructural services**.

Combining classifications

The classification of services based on granularity can be combined with the classification of services based on architectural layer. The following diagram shows this:

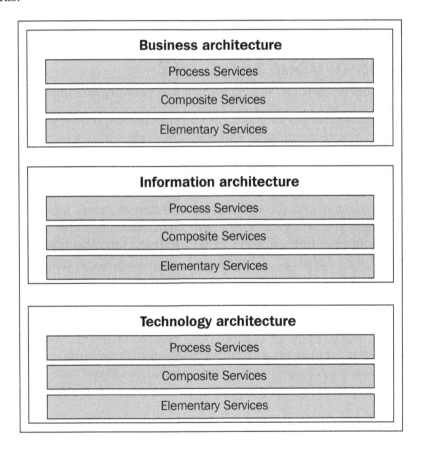

Classification of Services

The diagram shows that services in the business layer can be of type – process service, composite service, or elementary service. An example of a process service in the business layer is the `BreakfastService`. This service takes some time to complete, there are different transactions involved and it uses several other composite and elementary services like the `OrderService`, `PaymentService`, `CookingService`, `RefillService`, and `BuffetService`.

The `BreakfastService` is supported on the information layer by several services as well, such as `SupplierService`, `CheckService`, `HRService`, `RosterService`, `PrintService`, and so on. These can be classified as process services, composite services, or elementary services.

Finally on the technical layer there are services that support the information services. These can also be classified as process services, composite services, or elementary services. Examples are the `CashRegisterService`, `NetworkService`, `AlarmService`.

Why classify your services?

Classifying services has several benefits for you and your organization:

- Classification schemes help to focus on important aspects of services and filter out irrelevant details for stakeholders. A classification scheme divides services based on certain criteria. By choosing criteria that focus on important aspects, you can filter out details of services that are irrelevant to you.

- The importance of criteria differs per stakeholder. If the amount of value that services deliver is most important, you can categorize the services accordingly. This will yield a different classification than choosing ownership or the runtime platform of services as criteria in your classification.

- Classification of services also helps organizations to know what (type of) services they own and can be used to support decision-making processes, the architecture process, and new projects that want to reuse existing services.

- Classifying services into categories helps to decide what guidelines, best practices, and technology to apply per type of service. This helps an organization to create better services. Some guidelines apply to all services in general such as isolation and idempotency. However, there are guidelines and best practices that only apply to a certain type of service.

It is feasible to work with services without classifying them if you're only dealing with a dozen services or so in your organization. But as your SOA effort grows, you will find that classifications are helpful to inspect, analyze, and evolve your service's landscape in a controllable way. When you design solution architecture, the classification based on granularity is most suitable. It is based on service composition. Let's investigate that before we delve into the specifics of elementary, composite, and process services.

Composability

Service composition means the creation of new services from combining existing services. Following the design principles from the previous chapter improves the ability of services to be composed into larger blocks, thereby enabling rapid (re) use of functionality. Services need to be composable so that smaller services can be combined into larger services that provide a specific value. Think of it as building blocks that can be assembled into larger structures. A bank's MortgageService that provides loans to its customers for buying real estate is not comparable to the bank's ZipCodeService that validates zip codes in respect to the type of value they offer. Note however, that the ZipCodeService can contribute to the realization of the MortgageService.

Aggregation versus orchestration

Sometimes the terms **service composition**, **service aggregation**, and **service orchestration** are used interchangeably. While service composition denotes the fact that services are combined, it does not elaborate on the way in which services are combined. Aggregation and orchestration are specific ways to combine services:

- **Aggregation**: Combining two or more services into larger ones is fairly straightforward (for example invoke the service operation A, then service operation B, then service operation C). The CaseDocumentService that was discussed earlier on in this chapter is an example of service aggregation. Service aggregation involves short-running services.

- **Orchestration**: Combining several services into a flow or process that is more complex in nature and contains decision logic and different execution paths. Orchestration involves a central component such as a BPM platform that manages the orchestration of services. Service orchestration involves long(er)-running services. An example of orchestration is the order-to-cash process from *Chapter 2, The Solution*.

Example – DocumentService as a composite service

Another example of service composition is the combination of a `PDFService`, `SigningService`, `EmailService`, and `CRMService` into a `DocumentService` that is capable of creating documents in an automated fashion, storing these in the Document Management System, and e-mailing them to the customers. This new service can for example be used in an order-to-cash business process to automatically create invoices and send them to customers. Through composition, rather than development, you have created a larger service that makes it possible to completely handle a business function for consumers. This is a faster way of creating new services than developing similar functionality over and over. It is also less error prone since you reuse already tested and used software.

It is now time to investigate the different layers of the classification in detail, starting with the elementary services and then work our way up to the process services.

Elementary services

Elementary services are the smallest possible components that qualify as services. Splitting elementary services in smaller components yields components that violate the design principles you learned about in *Chapter 3, Service Design*. For example, splitting a `DocumentService` that is capable of storing and retrieving documents into a separate service that only stores the document, and another service that only stores the metadata violates the principle that services should be isolated or autonomous.

Realization

Elementary services in the information layer can be implemented in several ways:

- Existing applications such as packaged applications, custom developed systems, and legacy systems that are exposed as services using connectors, adapters, and so on. This can be coined as service-enablement of existing systems. An elementary service is implemented by one system, although a system can implement more than one elementary service.

- New functionality is created as a service right away. In other words, software is developed in an isolated manner and deployed as a separate service instead of a monolith that offers several services. Popular implementations for automated elementary services are .NET, Java, PHP, Groovy, among others. These platforms offer web service frameworks that can be used to easily expose software components as web services.

Composite services

Composite services are services that result from combining two or more services into a new service in a straightforward manner, and provide more value. Composite services avoid the need to implement reoccurring composition logic in clients.

Where to put the composition logic?

There are two options for the location of composition logic:

- **Service consumer**: The client invokes several service operations to accomplish a certain result.
- **Service**: A new service is created that invokes the different service operations and exposes this functionality as a new, single operation.

The following figure shows the difference between these variants using the example of the DocumentService. On the left-hand side, a DocumentService is created in which the generateDocument operation contains the logic to combine several underlying services. Service consumers invoke this new operation of the composite service. In the right-hand side service consumers implement the composition logic.

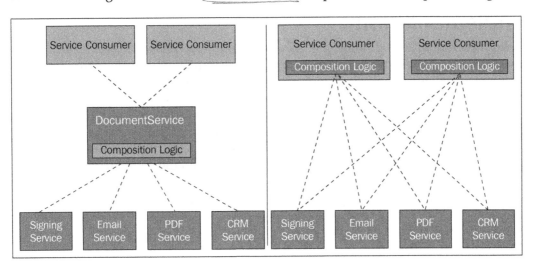

It pays off to create a new service that contains the composition logic in case multiple consumers require the same composition logic:

- Changes to the composition logic can be applied more easily since it is implemented in a single location instead of in different service consumers. Similar business logic is reused in the service that implements the composition.
- When you compose services into larger ones, the knowledge and complexity of how to combine these services and how they interact is hidden in a new service itself (**implementation hiding**). This makes it easier for service consumers to use the functionality.

When services are composed it is important that the entire service fails or succeeds. You do not want to end up in a situation where the document is generated and sent to a customer but not stored in the Document Management System due to some error. This means that a number of aspects need to be addressed in the composite service that relate to the behavior of the combination of the elementary services, not the elementary services in isolation. Such aspects are fault-prevention and handling, security, and transactionality.

Implementation

Composition of different building blocks can be implemented in several ways. Let's look at two examples. In both examples we use an insurance company that uses a case management system and a document management system. When claims are received, both systems are used to register the claim. For every new claim, a case is created using the `CaseService`, the accompanying documents are stored using the `DocumentService`, while the relation between case and documents is stored in the `CaseService`. Retrieving the documents belonging to a specific case requires two invocations: retrieving the document references from the `CaseService` and retrieving the physical documents from the `DocumentService`, using these references as input to the `getDocuments` operation. When such interactions occur frequently, you can compose this reoccurring logic into a new `CaseDocumentService` that offers a single operation for this functionality.

Example 1 – database link

The following figure shows `CaseService` that stores case information in its database. The case-related documents are retrieved using a database link that provides access to the `DocumentService` database. For the case data the data is retrieved using a database link to the datastore of the `CaseService`. For the business logic of the `CaseDocumentService`, it looks like the document data is in its own datastore.

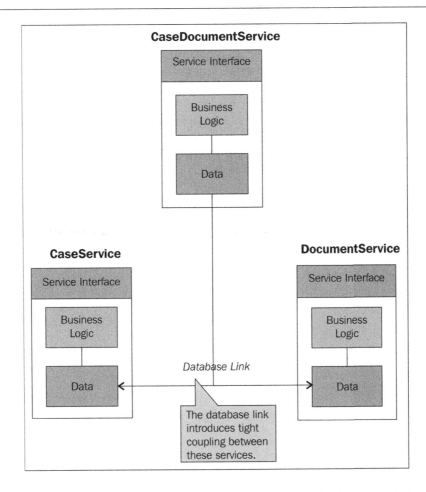

The figure shows CaseDocumentService that consists of a Business Logic layer and a Data layer. The CaseService and the DocumentService are composed of the same layers. The Business Logic of CaseDocumentService needs access to the data in DocumentService and CaseService. The database link offers this access, by creating a route directly to the database tables via the database layer of the CaseDocumentService.

When using a database link to directly access the DocumentService you need to have specific knowledge of the internal data structure and technical details. Whenever the internal implementation of the DocumentService changes, it will most likely impact the CaseService. In other words, the database link introduces tight coupling between the services.

Example 2 – service invocation

Not every change to DocumentService has an impact on its clients. It could be that a bug fix to the service affects the internal data model, but not the functionality that its clients need. Consumers should be unaware of such changes. In the previous scenario this would not have been the case since the service implementation was accessed directly. A better scenario would be to invoke the DocumentService using its service interface. The interface only exposes what the clients need, it hides the complexity of the service and its internal implementation, and shields service consumers from changes in the service that don't affect them.

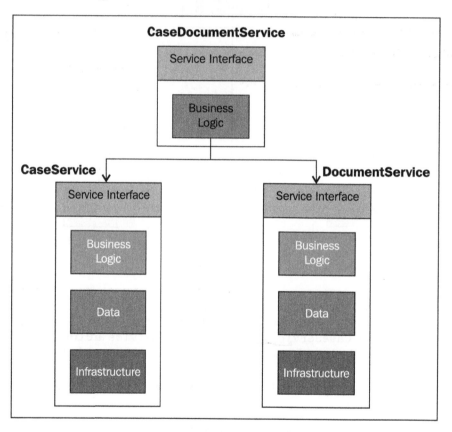

The figure shows the situation where the composite service CaseDocumentService combines the logic of the CaseService and the DocumentService. The CaseDocumentService contains business logic that was located in CaseService in the first example. The CaseService only contains business logic that is relevant for case management and DocumentService only contains business logic and data that is relevant for document management. You can see that there is no direct link anymore between DocumentService and CaseService.

Whenever one of the services is changed, this change is advertised through its interface in a technology-neutral way. This way it is easier to cope with changes to underlying services and their implementations. It could even be that changes in the implementation have no impact to service consumers at all. Composing services through their interfaces instead of implementation makes services work together instead of tightly-coupling them together.

Process services

Process services are services that use other services to execute their flow, like composite services. However, they take longer to complete and involve multiple activities and transactions. Process services invoke automated and human steps. The logic to combine these operations is more complex and contains more conditional logic than in composite services.

Examples of process services are invoice handling, the on boarding of new employees, a mortgage service, and so on.

The difference between process services and composite services is somewhat of a grey area. The main differentiators between the two types of services are:

- **Duration**: Process services are long-running processes that can take hours, days, weeks, or even longer, while composite services are short-lived services that take at most a couple of minutes to complete. A mortgage process that includes preparation, application, and underwriting, for example, can take weeks.

- **Transactions**: Process services can span multiple steps, or transactions; composite services are executed within a single transaction. A process service that spans multiple transactions needs other mechanisms to be undone. A common mechanism is compensation in which transactions are undone by executing an opposite action. An example is online booking of your holiday wherein you book a flight, a hotel, and a rental car. If you abort the holiday later in the process while the money has already been charged from your credit card using a service call, compensation means the money is deposited on your card by invoking the same operation with the opposite amount.

- **State**: Due to their complexity and duration, process services are required to maintain state between the different service operations that are invoked. For example, state can be used in a process service as part of a decision logic later on in the service. Composite services are stateless or volatile.

Implementation

Often, a business service is realized by orchestration of other services into a process. Every step in the process contributes to the end result of the business service that is offered to clients. A Business Process Management tool can be used to implement this orchestration. Most process services include both automated and human-centric services. A mortgage product for example is achieved by human steps (bank employee informing the client of the different mortgage products, a controller that validates the client's financial history and calculates risk) and automated steps (automated underwriting, automated debit for mortgage payments).

The term **Straight-Through Processing** is used to denote process services that are realized entirely in an automated fashion. An example is an `InvoiceService` that processes inbound invoices (scanning, extracting metadata, storing financial data, order matching, payment) without human intervention.

That finishes the explanation of the different layers in the classification scheme. The chapter continues by revisiting isolation and composition in light of the classification scheme that was introduced.

Isolation and composition – a contradiction?

The design principle **isolation** that was introduced in the previous chapter and **composability** that is introduced in this chapter might seem to contradict each other. How can you have autonomous services if you compose larger services out of smaller ones? Wouldn't that mean that the composed service is dependent on the smaller services?

The answer is that service composition promotes isolation of services. Isolation is viewed from the perspective of consumers, a consumer should be able to invoke a service independently without needing to know if other services need to be invoked before or afterwards. Service composition wraps such dependencies and knowledge of how to combine them into a separate service, thereby hiding this from the consumer and offering a new autonomous service.

Isolation is also known as **loose-coupling**, too many dependencies between services make them tightly coupled and therefore harder to change. As you know from the previous chapter, changes to services should have minimal impact, to maintain flexibility in SOA. Only create *direct* invocations from services to other services that are *in the same or higher level* of the classification when really needed. For example, it is better that the elementary `DocumentService` should not directly invoke the composite `CaseDocumentService`. Introducing this dependency would mean that changes to the `CaseDocumentService` can impact the `DocumentService` and vice versa. When avoiding the invocation from the composite service to the elementary service, changes to `CaseDocumentService` do not directly impact `DocumentService` anymore.

Passing information from smaller to larger services

Information and data need to be passed from elementary services to composite services or process services. The following list names different mechanisms that can be applied for this:

- **Request/reply**: In this message exchange, a service consumer invokes a service by sending a request message; for example, a composite service that invokes an elementary service. The invoked service responds by sending a reply message that can contain information for the service consumer to act upon. In this case, the data can be used by the composite service. This type of invocation is synchronous, meaning the consumer is blocked between the time the request was made and the time the reply was received. The following figure shows a request/reply message exchange:

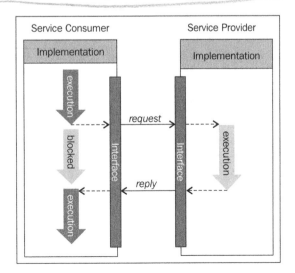

- **Callbacks**: Next to synchronous request/reply messages, services can also define callback operations in their interface. When using callbacks, the consumer sends the request and can continue with other activities. At some later point in time, the service that was invoked can send the response as a callback message to the consumer. Callbacks are used when consumers invoke long-running processes. Callbacks still introduce coupling between services, although this is made explicit by denoting operations as callbacks. The following figure shows a callback message exchange.

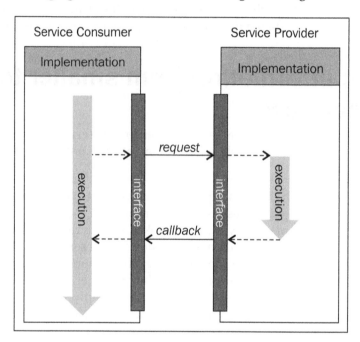

- **Events**: An event is the occurrence of something that is likely to be relevant to one or more consumers; for example the creation of a case, the approval of a loan, a new employee, and so on. In eventing, the originator of the event doesn't know which consumers are interested in what events and what actions these consumers will perform based on the events. The originator just publishes the event to some eventing platform. The platform knows which consumers are interested in what events and makes sure that events are sent to these interested consumers. This increases the decoupling between services. The following figure shows a message exchange based on events:

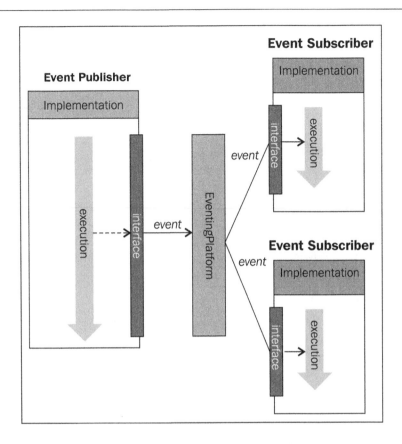

There are some important differences between these mechanisms in the light of passing information from smaller services to larger services:

- **Trigger**: While request/reply and callback mechanisms can be used to pass information from smaller services to bigger services, the bigger service that invokes the smaller service still triggers the information exchange. In eventing, the trigger of the message exchange is the originator of the event—the service that generates or captures a relevant occurrence. This publisher can be any service, and consumers of these events can be any service.
- **Decoupling**: Message exchanges using request/reply and callbacks require service consumers to know service providers, and the specific operation (that is action) to invoke. In eventing, publishers of events have no knowledge of the consumers and the operations that are triggered by the events they publish.

Classification of Services

The following figure shows the communication between the different types of services. The solid arrows indicate service invocations from one service to another. The communication of information between services through events is shown as dashed arrows in the figure:

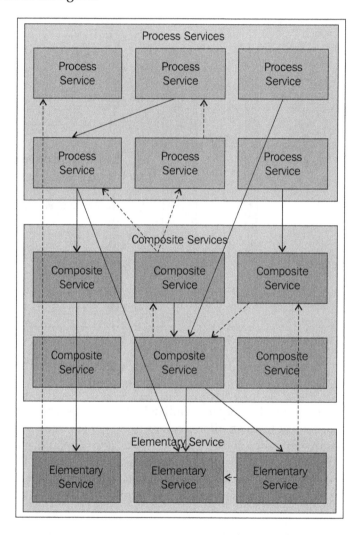

The figure shows the process services that call other process services, composite services, and elementary services. Composite services can call other composite services and elementary services. Elementary services don't call other services but use events to communicate. To minimize the complexity you can create design guidelines. For example you can limit the number of calls to elementary services that a composite service can make. If you exceed that number, it becomes a process service. Other guidelines are that elementary services are not allowed to call other services.

> Events can be classified as well as services. Examples of such classifications are those into **internal events** and **external events**, or a classification into **elementary events** and **complex events**.
>
> **Elementary events** are those events that in themselves are noteworthy, but when divided into even smaller occurrences are not meaningful anymore. Think of the events that signal the start and end of a telephone conversation. These are meaningful to the network operator to determine the duration and possibly cost of the phone call. The occurrence of the fact that one of the persons having the phone conversation presses the red cancel button to stop the call in itself isn't interesting to the network operator.
>
> **Complex events** are those events that are combined from smaller events to create a new and more meaningful event. An example is the occurrence of an ATM withdrawal by a particular client in New York at 13:00 GMT and an event indicating an ATM withdrawal by the same client in Amsterdam at 14:00 GMT that same day. These events can be combined into a complex event for the bank that issued the ATM card indicating the possibility of fraudulent activity. Complex events often involve a time aspect. If certain events occur within a specified timeframe, a complex event is generated that correlates these smaller events.

Summary

In this chapter you have learned how services can be categorized into a classification. This chapter introduced a classification into elementary services, composite services, and process services by looking at their granularity and the way services can be combined into other services; this is called composition.

In the next chapter, you will learn about the concrete building blocks that are used in SOA landscapes. These among others include business rules, user interfaces, BPM tooling, and Enterprise Service Buses.

5
The SOA Platform

So far, you have learned what SOA is, what benefits it brings you, and how you should design an SOA and its services. In this chapter, you will learn how to create an SOA by looking at the concrete building blocks, such as **Enterprise Service Bus (ESB)** and **service registry**, which are typically used as part of an SOA platform.

The chapter starts by providing an overview of a typical SOA landscape. The subsequent paragraphs each discuss what components can be used for:

- Services
- Events
- Service composition
- Business rules
- User interfaces
- Security
- Service registry and service repository
- Design tooling
- Development tooling

The chapter ends with an example that uses all components. Of course, there are other building blocks you need to run your SOA; think of networking components, storage, mail servers, web servers, system management tooling, and so on. However, this chapter focuses on those building blocks that are key, or unique, to SOA environments, not generic IT components

The SOA Platform

Overview

The following figure shows an overview of the various building blocks that are typically used to realize a service-oriented platform. It can be seen as a blueprint or **reference architecture** for SOA endeavors. You can create your own reference architecture that best suits your organization's needs and your customer needs and best fits the already available platforms. You won't learn how to create your own reference architecture; that is outside of the scope of this book.

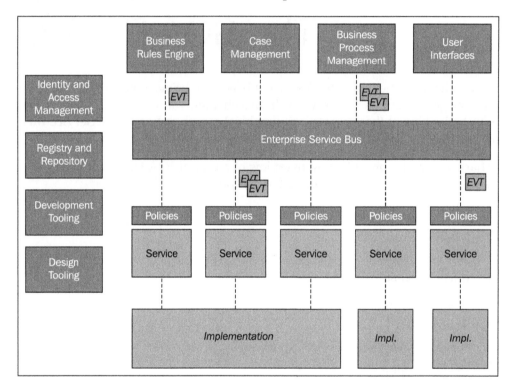

The following table gives a short description of the various parts of the platform:

Platform component	Description
Implementation	The realization of the business logic of the service.
Interface	Interface of the service.
Policies (contract)	Components that realize the contract of the service.
Events	Provider that publishes events, delivers them to consumers, and stores them in queues.
Enterprise Service Bus	Component that exposes the services to consumers and can also contain the implementation of composite services.

Platform component	Description
Case management	Component that hosts case management solutions. This can be the same as the Business Process Management component.
Business Process Management	Component to design, monitor, change, host and execute business processes.
Business rules	Component to host, create, and monitor business rules.
User interface	The functionality and data that is exposed through services is combined in **user interfaces** such as portals or web pages and mobile applications to provide good user experience to end users.
Registry and repository	The **registry** and **repository** are used to describe services and events and important metadata and artifacts for consumers to improve use of services.
Identity and Access Management	Services and processes need to be secured by managing identities, groups, and roles using **Identity Access Management** and by providing authentication and authorization capabilities.
Design tooling	Tooling to design applications, services, processes, and so on.
Development tooling	Tooling to develop applications, services, processes and so on.

Let's look at the different components of the SOA platform in more detail.

Services

Services are the key building blocks in an SOA. You know from the previous chapters that services provide access to well described functionality in an easy-to-use and transparent fashion for service consumers. They are composed of three parts:

- Interface
- Contract
- Implementation

There are three approaches to building services and linking interfaces to the implementation: **top-down**, **bottom-up**, and **meet in the middle** development.

In top-down or **contract-first** development, the service interface is the starting point for developing services. A framework is used to generate a code skeleton based on the service WSDLs and XSDs. The generated implementation can then be completed. This can be a good approach when there is no service implementation yet in place.

The SOA Platform

Bottom-up development works the other way around; the interface is generated based on an existing implementation thereby exposing its functionality. Bottom-up development can be a fast way of creating interfaces but gives you less control over the exact definition of the interface.

In meet in the middle approaches, both service interface and implementation are in place and the "glue" between them is created. This approach is ideal when the implementation already exists and you want to have full control over the service interface definition.

Let's take a closer look at the implementation and what components you can use in your IT landscape to create an SOA platform that takes into account existing and new software and services.

Implementation

The implementation of a service is the actual realization of the business logic of the service. There are three ways to realize services:

- Use existing software
- Build the logic or implementation for the service you need
- Combine existing services into a new service

Combining services into a new service is discussed in the paragraph *Composite Services*.

Using existing software

Your organization already uses software. If you have identified a service `PaymentService` you can decide to use your current financial software package as implementation for this service. The same is true for a service `EmployeeService`; you can decide to use your HR system for that. In these cases, the implementation of the services can be in any technology or programming language.

Build the implementation

If the functionality of the service is not available yet in your organization, or if you don't want to use the functionality that exists as a service, you can build a new implementation. You can realize that in the same platform component you use for your interface, or you can use any other platform or toolset in your organization.

> There are many platforms and toolsets to create implementation of services. You can use new languages such as Scala or Groovy. You can use object-oriented languages such as Java or C#, and you can use more functional oriented language such as PL/SQL. It is not important what you use for the implementation of your services as long as they adhere to the principles we discussed in *Chapter 3, Service Identification and Design*.

Interfaces

The interface is what is available to the service consumers. There are two types of interface:

- Proprietary interfaces, specific to a programming language or system
- Standard interfaces, based on **web services**

Proprietary interfaces

Proprietary interfaces are interfaces that use a specific protocol or language to communicate. Some examples are the interface tables and the PL/SQL APIs of Oracle E-Business Suite or ABAP for SAP. Both ERP vendors created their systems using specific technology and use the same technology to create interfaces for extensions, customizations, and integration with their systems.

Web services

Web services are standardized interfaces for services. They use web technology to communicate: HTTP and XML. Your SOA platform needs to have a component to host these web services, called a web container. Web services and web service clients are usually built in programming or scripting languages such as .NET, Java, PL/SQL, or JavaScript. Almost all vendors support web services, and there are a lot of web service frameworks available both commercial and open-source. Such frameworks help you in the development of services by generating boilerplate code, converters between objects and XML data structures, and so on, thereby speeding up development.

Vendors of ERP systems and other off-the-shelf software often offer web service interfaces for their systems. For example, Oracle E-Business Suite offers web service interfaces next to their proprietary interface we mentioned in the paragraph about proprietary interfaces. If the software you use does not support web service interfaces, you can use an ESB to expose the service as a web service.

The SOA Platform

There are two types of web service:

- SOAP-based services
- RESTful services

SOAP-based services

SOAP-based web services are services that are formally described, created, and consumed based on several web service standards and protocols. Together, these standards are denoted as **WS-*** and are maintained by standardization committees such as the **World Wide Web Consortium (W3C)** and OASIS. Examples of web service standards are WS-Security, **Web Service Description Language (WSDL)**, WS-RM (Reliable Messaging), and **Simple Object Access Protocol (SOAP)**.

SOAP-based services have interfaces that describe the available operations, the inputs and outputs of these operations, and the technology binding through which the operations are made available. These interfaces are documented using WSDL and XSD documents. A WSDL defines the operations of a service and can define input and output messages internally or refer to external XSD documents for this. It is a good design principle to define the operations in a WSDL, refer to an external XSD that defines the request and/or response messages, and refer from there to other XSDs that define the business entities such as customer and order entities that are part of the request and response messages.

The following code snippet shows how an SOAP-based web service request that retrieves the customer details for customer ID `56080086` might look:

```xml
<?xml version="1.0"?>
<soapenv:Envelope
xmlns:soapenv="http://schemas.xmlsoap.org/soap/envelope/"
xmlns:cust="http://www.foo.org/customer">
    <soapenv:Header/>
    <soapenv:Body>
        <cust:GetCustomerById>
            <cust:CustomerId>56080086</cust:CustomerId>
        </cust:GetCustomerById>
    </soapenv:Body>
</soapenv:Envelope>
```

A call to an SOAP based web service is packaged in an **envelope**. This is shown in the code snippet as `<soapenv:Envelope`. The envelope starts with the **namespace** declarations `xmlns:soapenv=` and `xmlns:cust=`. A **namespace** is used to avoid name clashes in your elements. The content of the message itself is in the **body,** denoted with `<soapenv:Body>`.

RESTful services

Representational State Transfer (REST) based services are based on a very different model than SOAP-based services. REST is a formal model based on resources. The idea is that you send a request for a resource. The resource that is returned shows you the options for the next step. For example, you can retrieve a resource customer list. The resulting list will show you the location of the individual customer data, for example in an URL. This model is very flexible and does not require that the client know in advance what services and service calls are available. The World Wide Web is an example of a REST architecture implementation. RESTful services rely on the HTTP protocol in which HTTP methods such as `GET`, `PUT`, `POST`, and `DELETE` are used to represent CRUD type operations (Create, Read, Update, Delete). The messages are exchanged using XML.

The following line shows how the same customer details that were retrieved using SOAP can be retrieved using REST. Basically, a RESTful service is invoked using a URL:

```
http://www.foo.org/resource/customer/56080086
```

In both customer examples, the server hosting `CustomerService` will receive the request, process the request, and return a response containing the customer details. While SOAP-based web services always exchange XML, RESTful services do not impose constraints on the data format exchanged. Data can be formatted as HTML, XML or **JavaScript Object Notation (JSON)**, and so on.

Contracts and Policies

Contracts specify the conditions under which services can be consumed and what consumers can expect from service providers. This can include guarantees on response times and availability, applied security measures, cost, and so on. You need to be able to monitor, manage, and enforce such contractual obligations and associated metrics, especially if you consume external services or offer your services to external consumers.

It is bad practice to implement such logic in services themselves; the business logic becomes entangled with management and security logic. Furthermore, the monitoring and security capabilities will vary per service in such cases. It is best to use a dedicated building block that is external to the services themselves.

A common approach in an SOA environment is the use of **policies**. Policies enforce a specific measure or enable a specific capability, such as applying a security mechanism, adding addressing information to messages, enabling logging of inbound and outbound messages, and so on. Multiple policies can be chained together to enforce and provide a set of capabilities for a service. Policies are applied to services and their operations so that isolation of services is preserved.

Policies can be applied on the consumer side as well as the provider side of the service. For example, a service contract specifies that a service should be secured using the WS-Security Username Token profile. A provider-side policy enforces that request messages contain a valid token, otherwise the message is denied. A consumer-side policy adds such a token to the outbound request, thereby relieving the service client of implementing such logic.

Policy platforms generally offer one or both of the following mechanisms to add policies to your services:

- **Gateway:** All service requests are tunneled through a centralized gateway by the underlying infrastructure. The gateway then applies the policies that are configured for the invoked service and monitors request and response metrics. Often, a gateway configures a set of policies that needs to be applied to a collection service. For example, enforcing SSL/TLS for all services.

- **Agents:** Agents define, apply, and enforce policies on a per service basis providing a more decentralized solution. Every service can have a different set of policies that needs to be enforced.

It is a good approach to have a mix of gateways and agents in which you use gateways to apply common or shared policies and agents to apply consumer- or provider-specific policies.

Events

The previous chapter introduced events as a mechanism to signal that something noteworthy happened. Events are important in an SOA platform, thus:

- From a business point of view, events are a natural way to represent information. Businesses and their surrounding ecosystem of suppliers, partners, and clients cause and react with events continuously: a customer moving to a different address, a new purchase order, receiving an invoice from a supplier, sending a bill to a partner, and so on.

- From a technical point of view, events improve the decoupling between software components. Software components are not required to know of each other's existence any more.

An event contains a payload that provides information on the occurrence. The following code snippet shows the event payload that describes a new order that has just been received. This event is published by the Customer Web Portal and received by the service `OrderService` for further processing.

```xml
<?xml version="1.0"?>
<order:NewOrderEvent xmlns:order="http://www.foo.org/order">
   <order:OrderId>789093609</cust:OrderId>
</order:NewOrderEvent>
```

You need components in your SOA platform that offer functionality to publish and consume events in your organization. Apart from that, you need a provider that will receive the events and deliver them to the registered consumers of the event. Publishers of events can be services, rules, business processes and user interfaces. Event providers can be dedicated **Message Oriented Middleware (MOM)**, or they can be part of application servers or ESBs. Such providers implement various event patterns, the most prominent being:

- **Queuing**: The originator of the event places a message (enqueue) in an intermediate channel (queue) and continues processing. Either the queuing infrastructure delivers the message to a consumer, or the consumer actively retrieves the message (dequeue) from the queue. You can have one event consumer for the queue, or a multi-consumer queue.

- **Publish/subscribe**: This pattern is very similar to queuing; in publish/subscribe the consumers register or subscribe to specific events that they are interested in. The event provider needs to maintain the event subscriptions.

Interfaces for events

Like services, events need an interface or API as well. Otherwise, the consumer of the event does not know how to read the content of the event. There are several standards and possibilities; depending on the other components of your platform, you can select one or more to use:

Java Message Service (JMS) is the official **Java Enterprise Edition (JEE)** standard API for communicating with MOM on the Java platform. JMS does not specify the implementation and protocol that should be used.

The **.NET Messaging (NMS)** API is an example of a standard API for messaging on the .NET platform; it hides the specifics of messaging implementations.

Advanced Message Queuing Protocol (AMQP) is an open standard that describes a messaging protocol, meaning it specifies the transport and message structure itself. AMQP is not bound to a certain platform, like JMS and NMS, but can be used in a heterogeneous environment as long as messaging client and provider both use the AMQP protocol.

The SOA Platform

Service composition

As you have seen in the previous chapter, services can be combined into larger services, which is called service composition. There are various building blocks that support composition. Services can be:

- Aggregated into composite services in a straightforward fashion using an **Enterprise Service Bus (ESB)**
- Strictly orchestrated into process services using **Business Process Management (BPM)** tooling
- Flexibly combined into process services using **Case Management** tooling

Enterprise Service Bus

Enterprise Service Bus (ESB) is an integration platform that connects the various service layers and provides consumers with access to services.

There are different definitions of what an ESB is and what it should do; there is no commonly accepted definition of the term ESB. Most modern providers of MOM have adopted the ESB concept as the de facto standard for SOA. Today's implementations of ESB use event-driven and standards-based MOM in combination with message queues as technology frameworks. Unfortunately, confusion is occasionally caused by software manufacturers who sell their existing middleware and communication solutions as ESB without adopting the crucial spirit of a bus concept. Common functionalities that an ESB should include are:

- **Validation**: The ESB can validate the incoming requests and/or the outgoing responses to the specified interface.
- **Composite services**: Elementary services can be aggregated into composite services using an ESB.
- **Routing**: Services are hidden behind the ESB and not directly visible to consumers. When a request from a service consumer is received, the ESB routes it to the correct service provider. This way, changes to services can be implemented without service consumers being aware. Sometimes, more than one service is available to fulfill the service request. The ESB can apply **content based routing** to determine which service the request needs to be routed to. The routing is based on the content of the message, hence the name. A special case of routing is to support multiple versions of a service, while the service provider only offers the latest version of the service.

- **Transformation**: An ESB exposes services in a data format and protocol that is suited for service consumers. It provides transformation of **protocols** and **data** between service consumers and service providers, for example, to integrate with legacy systems, message-oriented middleware, and (commercial) off-the-shelf software using adapters thereby exposing these proprietary interfaces as standardized interfaces.

The following figure shows a typical ESB flow that connects service consumers to a service provider. The ESB flow first validates the inbound request message sent by consumers, transforms the message into a format that is understood by the service provider (e.g. transformation from one XML structure to another), and then routes the message to the appropriate service provider. From the perspective of the consumers, the service is offered by the ESB.

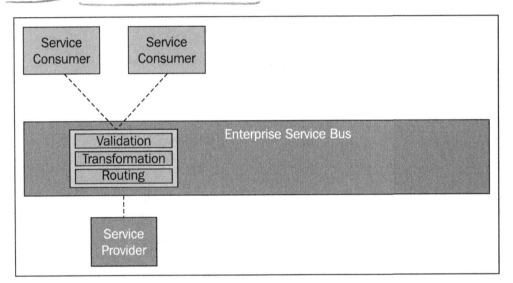

 A typical integration pattern supported by ESBs is **VETRO** — Validate-Enrich-Transform-Route-Operate. In such a flow, an inbound message is validated, possibly enriched with additional information, then transformed into a protocol and format intended for the receiver of the message, routed to a receiving service, and finally operated onto by the service receiver. See *Enterprise Service Bus*, D. Chappell, O'Reilly, 2004.

The main advantage of ESB is that it offers decoupling between services. ESB adds flexibility to your SOA environment. By using the capabilities we mentioned, an ESB can hide changes for current consumers, such as modification of the message format, change in the endpoint location, and change in protocol to services from service consumers. For service providers, it offers a single point to connect to service consumers rather than connecting to multiple consumers.

The main difference between ESBs on the one hand, and BPM and Case Management platforms on the other is that ESBs are geared towards integration scenarios and simple service composition, while the latter two platforms are aimed towards complex composition of services into process services. ESB is optimized for handling large volumes of small messages within short transactions and has little overhead. BPM and Case Management tooling deal with fewer but longer running processes.

Business Process Management

BPM deals with the management and improvement of your business processes. BPM is often expressed in terms of its life cycle that contains the following activities:

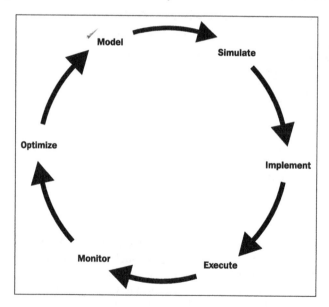

- **Model**: Design and model the business process that needs to be supported by the BPM platform. **Business Process Modeling Notation (BPMN)** is a popular standard for this.
- **Simulate**: Simulate the designed processes to see if requirements are met, given the predicted load and resources (people and IT).

- **Implement**: Build the business process in the tooling that the BPM platform offers. Popular execution models for processes are based on BPMN, **Business Process Execution Language (BPEL)**, or **XML Process Definition Language (XPDL)**.
- **Execute**: Deploy the process to the BPM platform and run it.
- **Monitor**: Monitor the processes and instances at runtime by collecting metrics and other information. This is often dubbed as **Business Activity Monitoring (BAM)**.
- **Optimize**: Based on runtime metrics, you can improve the design of your process thereby starting another iteration of the BPM life cycle.

BPM suites can contain more than one product or tool that each implements some aspect(s) of the life cycle; an example is a separate BAM product.

Case Management

A **Case Management** platform shares much of the capabilities of a BPM platform but is more geared towards executing dynamic processes that can vary per instance and require knowledge to make decisions about the next step.

Not all processes are straightforward, highly automatable, and predictable. Some processes are more knowledge intensive and the actions that need to be executed vary per instance of the process. The following figure shows an example of how a case management tool can show the flow:

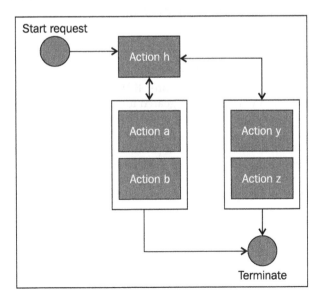

The SOA Platform

The diagram shows that after the request is received, action *h* is taken. Depending on the decision or outcome in action *h*, the next action or actions are executed. As you can see, an action can be executed multiple times and the next step after an action is not determined. After a while the case is done and it is terminated.

An example is the approval of complex permit requests. When it comes to approving the construction of a new factory, one needs to take into account the environment, nearby residential areas, economic benefits, and so on. Handling this request will differ significantly from handling a permit request for building a simple dormer in a residential area. Other examples of such dynamic process are:

- Immigration and naturalization cases
- Document-centric processes that involve decision making and approval

In dynamic case management, users work together in a collaborative fashion to complete the process. Users that handle the case can influence how specific process instances are executed and what steps are needed, which is a major difference with BPM. Case Management is **knowledge driven** while BPM is **task driven**.

In Case Management, you do not model an entire process but define the conditions that need to be met in order to complete the process, the conditions specifying when certain process steps need to be executed, and the services that can be used during process execution. The Case Management platform is responsible for coordinating the various process steps and to help finishing the case.

The separation between BPM and Case Management platforms is not always clear; some BPM tools are also capable of more dynamic case management of processes, and vice versa.

Mixing BPM and Case Management

A business process is rarely "pure" BPM or "pure" Case Management. A process as a whole is often geared towards one of these types, while parts of it can have more affiliation with another type. An example is invoice processing. The main flow of this process is predictable, can be automated, and is ideal to implement in a BPM platform. However, knowledge workers are required to handle exceptional behavior during invoice processing. Only employees of the financial department are able to investigate what went wrong and what actions to take. These actions probably vary per case. In other words, exception handling of the invoice process can be best implemented using Case Management instead.

Business rules

The term **business rules** is used to indicate relatively fast-changing decision logic in processes and services, as opposed to more static business logic. **Business Rules Engines** (BRE) or **Business Rules Management Systems** (BRMS) implement business rules in such a way that the logic can easily be changed at runtime by separating the "know" (Business Rule) from the "flow" (process), using a graphical user interface without the need of software development and redeployment of services.

Business rules contain decision logic that is important to business stakeholders. Let's look at some examples of such logic:

- The order-to-cash process in which customers with platinum status get a 15 percent discount, while silver status customers get a 5 percent discount and other customers no discount. Over time, you might want to introduce gold status customers or change the discount percentages.
- A service `InvoiceService` that contains a rule that invoices under $10,000 can be processed in an automated fashion, while senior financial staff should manually validate invoices over $10,000.

Business rules consist of the following components:

- **Input or facts**: The data that is needed by the rules engine to make a decision, for example, the customer status, total amount of the order, order date, and so on.
- **Decision logic**: The decision logic can range from a simple if-then-else construction or decision table to more complex logic that generates intermediary facts. The decision logic might include callouts to (other) services to retrieve data or execute functionality.
- **Output or decisions**: The outcome of the business rule. This can be a simple `true` or `false` value, an amount, or a more complex data type.

Business rules are frequently used as decision points in business processes. Such decision points can be implemented by invoking the rules engine from the process platform. Sometimes, BPM and Case Management tooling also incorporate (light-weight) rules engines.

Let's have a look at the order-to-cash process example using discounts. The following figure shows part of this business process including the decision point *Determine discount*. Here, the rules engine is invoked passing relevant process data as facts. The rules engine returns the applicable discount. In case of no discount, the process continues with the sub process *Ship order*, otherwise the automated action *Calculate discounted price* is executed in which the order amount is lowered with the discount percentage. A business analyst can use the rules engine's user interface to alter the discount percentages (outcomes) and decision logic determining the discount type.

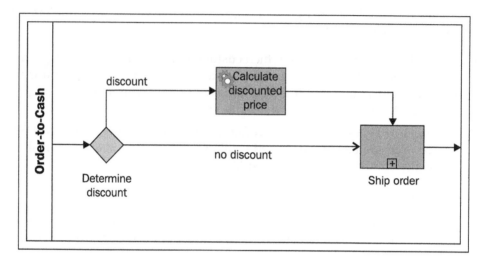

There are two types of business rules: rules that are only applicable in the context of a specific process and rules that are reusable. An example of the first is the discount percentage as part of the order-to-cash process. If the business logic is reusable, the business rules can be exposed as a service. An example is a rule determining the solvency of companies. This logic can be reused for processing loan requests, mortgages, insurances, and so on. In such cases, it is important that a rules engine be capable of exposing a business rule as a service. In other words, the business rules engine becomes the implementation of a service.

User interface

The **user interface** layer is a consumer of services, just like your BPM component, but it can also be a service in itself.

> Services are often regarded as automated components without a graphical user interface such as web services. However, services can have any interface, also a user interface. An example is a service `PrintService` that provides a portlet interface for creating print tasks. Another example is any app from any app store.

In silos, users have to switch between using different user interfaces during the execution of a single task. For example, an employee in your HR department might need to switch between her email client, HRM application, financial application, and network file system containing documents to finalize salary changes. The main reason is that these applications were designed as separate (or "**stovepiped**") systems without looking at other systems or looking at the end user's needs. This situation is shown in the following figure:

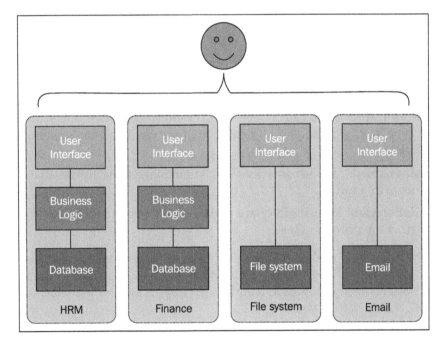

In an SOA, landscape information and functionality is better accessible through services giving you the possibility to create:

- User interfaces to expose the functionality of a single service
- User interfaces that combine multiple services and their user interfaces into a single interface to offer a more integrated user experience to your end users

An SOA landscape can consist of a mix of these.

The following list contains important capabilities of user interfaces in an SOA environment:

- **Location and device transparency**: The user interface is accessible through the web or apps so that users have the freedom to use it from different devices and locations.
- **Mash-up**: The user interfaces combine, or **mash up**, different sources of information and functionality that are offered by services. The mash-ups can include multimedia and social media components such as blogs, twitter feeds, and apps.
- **Contextual**: The information displayed in user interfaces is linked to other relevant information that the user might need for his or her tasks.
- **Event-driven:** The user interface is able to consume events and thereby notifying the user of relevant changes without the need for users to periodically check for new events. Conversely, the interface should be able to publish events.
- **Customizable**: Users can change the user interface to their needs by selecting the type of information and functionality they need and customizing how it looks.
- **Task-enabled**: The user interface helps to manage the activities that the user needs to execute.
- **Collaboration**: The user interface makes it easy for different people to work together on a common task.

HTML is the dominant presentation language for user interfaces of (web and mobile) applications. A lot of vendors supply tools and frameworks that render HTML user interfaces, possibly using plugins and embedded objects such as videos, music, and apps. HTML 5 is the latest standard.

Integrated user interfaces

Integrated user interfaces offer the following benefits in your processes:

- Operational processes boost productivity for end-users
- Products and services improve customer satisfaction
- Management processes help management of decision-making

The following figure shows an integrated employee user interface that combines data from several services that better serves the needs of end users. The user interface in the figure contains four sections that hold certain information, for example, a section presenting the task overview for a user and a section showing the relevant documents for the selected task.

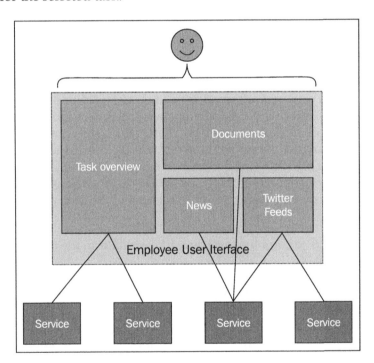

A **portal** is a common implementation for integrated user interfaces. Portals can be used to combine several user interface building blocks into a single interface using a catalogue of available building blocks called **portlets**.

The SOA Platform

A portal product provides several out-of-the-box portlets that provide a specific feature, such as a news portlet, blog portlet, task portlet, email portlet, and document portlet. Portals also offer the capability of creating your own portlets that can consume services, present information, and be integrated into the portal. The downside of portals is that it is an extra middleware component, it can be complex to install and configure, and will give you features and portlets that you don't need.

Other examples of implementations of integrated user interfaces besides portals are dashboards, online web portals and (HTML) user interfaces that divide a user interface into different regions and sections thereby creating a similar user experience.

Information mismatch

Services are bounded building blocks that are centered on a particular type of information or functionality. This is especially true of elementary services. Think about services such as `InvoicingService`, `EmployeeService`, `DocumentService`, and `ZipCodeService`. While such boundaries help you to create manageable services, users have a different information need. Users need information in context to make decisions and execute tasks. Different services need to be combined in such a way that the users are most productive and have all the information they need. An employee of the finance department not only needs information as provided by `InvoiceService`, but also relevant documents, supplier details, and order details. Several services all provide part of this information need. There is a mismatch between the information offered by a single service and the information need from users.

There are several ways to combine services and their data so the information need from end users can be satisfied:

- The user interface is capable of invoking several services and combines the data and functionality itself.
- Create composite services that combine data and functionality to fulfill the needs of user interfaces. This approach is especially useful if the composition is needed in more places or if the user interface is not capable of such combinations.

Creating logic in the user interface can lead to discussion with architects who believe that the user interface should not contain any logic at all. It is important to realize that user interface logic (think of a wizard, the position, and the fields you want to show) is very important. A machine might have enough to work with a technical identifier of an order. A user needs the context to be able to help the customer make a decision or change data. So, you either create a specific composite service for the user interface layer or put this logic in the user interface itself. Either way, you create something for a specific purpose or task. This does not violate the design principles of services and keeps the logic in the layer it belongs in: process logic in the business process and user interface logic in the user interface layer.

>
> **Apply user experience techniques**
> Architects often design services based on criteria that do not take into account the information needs of end users. Employ user experience techniques and methods to identify the needs of end users and validate your user interface. The wizards, page flows, and so on that result from these techniques are specific to the user interface and don't belong in the business process.

Security

Security is important in your architecture, independent of the reference architecture or style you apply. For this reason, you need Identity and Access Management (IAM) tooling. It provides the following functionality:

- **Identity management**: The storage and retrieval of identities that require access to your services and processes, and relevant attributes of these identities, such as username and email address. Identities can represent (external) employees, customers, organizations, and systems. Identity management is also responsible for provisioning identities and their attributes between different identity stores. A common protocol used by identity stores is **Lightweight Directory Access Protocol (LDAP)**.

- **Authentication**: Verifying that the identity is in fact who she/he/it claims to be. Authentication mechanisms can include username/password validation or stronger forms of authentication such as voice recognition and the use of tokens in addition to a username/password combination.

- **Authorization**: Granting authenticated identities access to resources. Authorization is often granted to identities based on membership to groups and roles. Groups can for example reflect the hierarchy and structure of an organization, while roles are frequently based on function. Often, groups and roles are also stored in identity stores, in addition to the identities. Authorization and application roles are stored with the service or application. These authorizations are more fine-grained and specific to the application or the service implementation. Think for example of the authorizations that are stored in SAP: approving a timesheet or entering a creditor in the system.

> Single Sign-On (SSO) is a type of authentication in which successful authentication provides access to more systems without the need for re-authentication. An example is a corporate marketing employee successfully logging into Windows. The user does not need to log in again when accessing his email and CRM application since these systems are connected to the SSO infrastructure. Common implementations of SSO are based on the **Security Assertion Markup Language (SAML)** protocol. Sometimes, SSO is referred to as **identity management as a service**, because other services and systems can use the authorization services of SSO as a service.

Identity and Access Management is a required building block in SOA and non-SOA environments alike. The main aspects in an SOA that impact Identity and Access Management are:

- **Higher degree of automation**: There are more automated message exchanges between various automated services and processes. This means that the identity store will contain identities and attributes for services and systems, besides human identities. Automated message exchanges also require automated authentication and authorization mechanisms in addition to manual authentication.
- **Use of intermediary components**: Messages pass through several components between the moment they are sent by clients and the arrival at the service provider where consumers are authenticated and authorized. Such intermediaries can, for example, include ESB and BPM platforms. Identity information needs to be propagated as part of the message from the original sender (service consumer) to the ultimate receiver (service provider). This is called identity propagation.

Applying security in your SOA

There are several locations in your architecture where you can apply security. The following figure illustrates this:

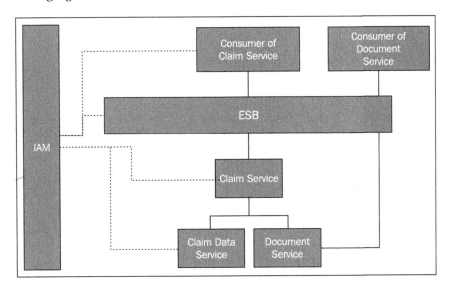

The dotted arrows in the figure represent locations where you can apply authentication and authorization. The solid arrows represent request/response message between the different components.

The locations are:

- Service consumer, in the figure `ClaimService` consumer.
- ESB
- Composite service, in the figure the `ClaimService`
- Elementary service, for example `DocumentService` and `ClaimDataService`
- A combination of the previous locations

You need to consider the location carefully. Applying security on a high level (for example, a service consumer) has the disadvantage that other consumers are not authenticated or authorized automatically. This might be a risk if the services are easily accessible and well known. Applying it on a low level (for example, an elementary service) has the disadvantage that it is a lot of work and is very complicated. A good start is to apply it on the ESB and make sure that only requests from the ESB are permitted to the services, not directly from service consumers.

Apart from applying authorization and authentication, you can also encrypt and sign your messages or the transport layer. Signing your messages can be achieved with policies, as was discussed in the paragraph contracts. When you only encrypt on the transport layer, the message itself is not encrypted, for example, when it is logged. The message is, of course, encrypted while it is transported from the provider to the consumer and vice versa.

The following table shows several standards that can be applied:

Standard	Use	Remark
WS-Security	Security, authentication	Encrypt, sign messages, authentication token
OAuth	Authentication	SSO
SAML	Authentication	SSO
Basic HTTP authentication	Authentication	Username/password
SSL/TSL	Authentication	Certificates

Service registry and service repository

A **service registry** is used to describe processes, services, events, and important metadata. Consumers search a registry to find services they can use and retrieve information, such as the status of a service, the owner of a service, its endpoint location, and dependencies on other services. Registries can be compared to the yellow pages. Registries can be used at design-time for service discovery, but also at runtime for endpoint virtualization.

A **service repository** also stores artifacts of processes, services, and events such as WSDLs, XSDs, and other relevant documents.

The more mature and scaled-out an SOA gets and the more services you create and use, the more need there is to manage them using a registry or repository. You can read more about registries and repositories in *Chapter 8, Life Cycle Management*.

Canonical Data Model

Registries and repositories can also publish data definitions of processes, services, and events. The **Canonical Data Model** (or CDM) is the **common** definition of operations and data structures that is used by your services and their consumers. A common technical implementation of CDM uses WSDLs and XSDs.

Different operations can operate on similar data. An example is the `CustomerService.getCustomer` operation and the `OrderService.getOrderDetails` operation; the responses of both operations contain customer data. Data definitions are defined by the service providers and often differ from each other. The disadvantages of having different data definitions for the same type of data within your enterprise are:

- The burden of handling different data formats for the same type of data is passed to the consumers of the system, resulting in more complex integration for consumers.
- The same type of transformation logic to cope with differences in data definition is duplicated in several places. In the worst-case scenario, you need data transformation logic for every combination of different data definitions.
- Differences in data format result in inconsistencies and decreased data quality in other systems.

These issues can be addressed by using a CDM to define important data elements, also referred to as business entities, and the service operations. Canonical Data Models can have a departmental scope, be valid enterprise-wide, or can be used globally or industry-wide. An example of the latter is **Health Level 7 (HL7)** for exchanging medical data, and **eXtensible Business Reporting Language** (XBRL) for exchanging financial data.

The following figure shows a CRM system and two order systems that each have their own specific definition for customer data that is passed on and out of the respective systems. The CRM system defines a customer name that encompasses first name, middle name, and last name, while one of the order systems might specify separate fields for these attributes, and the second order system has a separate attribute for last name and a combined field for first and middle name. The following table shows this situation:

System	Attribute	Value
CRM	Name	John Patrick Jones
Order System 1	First name	John
	Middle name	Patrick
	Last name	Jones
Order System 2	First names	John Patrick
	Last name	Jones

The services that are exposed by the ESB translate the proprietary data models for customer data to the unified customer data format as defined in the enterprise Canonical Data Model. The service consumers are unaware of the underlying differences in data formats. An ESB can also be used to enrich data, in case the underlying system does not provide all elements as specified by the CDM.

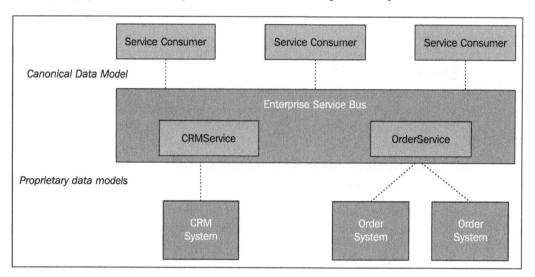

Design tooling

Architects and designers need tools to create solution architectures, functional designs, technical designs, and so on, and more importantly, to communicate these designs to other stakeholders, such as developers, end users, testers, and project leaders.

In the process of creating architectures and designs, **whiteboards** are essential. The creation of architectures and designs is a process that involves several persons and is iterative by nature. You hardly ever get the (solution) architecture or design right the first time. In the early stages, it helps to discuss, brainstorm, and explore different variants of a design using a whiteboard or some other easy-to-use medium.

When formally describing and documenting architecture and design, and communicating it to other stakeholders, software tooling can be used. This can range from documenting architectures and designs in a free-format way using graphics suites, word processors, and presentation tools to using specialized software tools that capture architecture and design in formal notations. Examples of the latter are the use of:

- BPM modelers to design your business processes
- UML (Unified Modeling Language) modeler to design software architectures and technical designs of services
- Tools to model enterprise architectures in languages such as ArchiMate
- Design tools for user interfaces and web pages

The creation of architecture and design shouldn't be a goal in itself. These artifacts are merely the means to an end: working services. That implies that up-to-date and useful architectures and designs are preferred over hundreds of pages of out-of-date designs and architecture documents.

Development tooling

Developers need tools to create code and other artifacts, test them, and assemble them into services, processes, rules, user interfaces, and so on. Good tools help developers to produce better code more efficiently. Development tools can range from simple text editors in which you just type your code to extensive **Integrated Development Environments (IDEs)** that provide features such as:

- Compilers, validators, code inspectors, optimizers, and so on that verify the correctness of your code and point out possible improvements.
- Debuggers and code analyzers to track and solve bugs.
- Documenting code and publishing this documentation.
- Graphical editors and wizards to generate code. Examples of these are XSLT mappers to graphically map a particular XML format into another one, and editors to create HTML pages.
- Support for frameworks that provide out of the box functionality for frequently occurring constructions and boilerplate code. Frameworks speed up development and provide best practices for solving particular problems.

    Examples of frameworks are Object-Relational Mappers (ORM) that help in the transformation of relational data into objects and vice versa, Model View Control (MVC) frameworks that help you bind data to user interfaces, web service frameworks to generate web services on top of code, clients to web services, or code skeletons based on web service contracts.

- Creating and running unit tests for your software and generating test reports.
- Building, assembling, and packaging code into runtime components.
- Generic tooling such as code completion, code formatting, indentation, highlighting, and so on.

The SOA Platform

In addition to tools for creating code, you also need supporting tools such as source control or versioning systems, issue trackers, and continuous integration tools to help the development team. IDEs provide functionality to integrate with such tooling, for example, extensions to integrate with Subversion (SVN) or GIT for version control of your software.

Some IDEs provide a runtime environment so you can run your software and services inside the IDE. This can be helpful for testing and debugging your services. In such cases, IDEs include functionality for deployment of software to a server: either the internal runtime of the IDE or a separate server (development, test, acceptance, or production).

It is a best practice to deploy your code using scripts instead of the IDE. The main reasons are that you don't burden administrators that deploy software with the need to learn an IDE and that scripts generally provide a more predictable, controllable, and stable way of deploying software to a runtime environment.

You will probably need to use more than one development tool in your SOA environment. Over time, you will employ more building blocks, such as a rules engine, portals, and ESB, and will have different service implementations such as .NET, Java, Python, and HTML. Different building blocks often have their own development environment that is tuned for effective development in that particular environment. This is especially true in a best-of-breed situation. Some vendors also offer extensions or plug-ins for popular IDEs to support development in your IDE of choice. Only when you have a very homogeneous environment and a single suite that provides the building blocks you need, will you have a single IDE. In real life, the need to employ multiple development tools is very real, though.

This could mean you need to make a trade-off between using more specialized IDEs that are more productive but have a higher learning curve (you need to work with more tools), or have fewer generic, all-purpose IDEs that are less productive.

There can be overlap between architecture, design, and development tooling. Some IDEs also offer design and architecture tooling such as UML modelers and BPMN modelers. The other way around, some design tools can generate code based on designs. You need to decide where the handoff is between the design and development tools that you use, so that there is minimum overlap in how you use these tools.

Chapter 5

Example – Order-to-cash revisited

The international software company you read about in the first two chapters wants to create a more flexible solution for their order-to-cash process. They decide to rebuild the solution using their SOA platform.

Designing the solution

First the solution architect designs the overall architecture, which is designed using design tooling. The design shows that the business process will be created using BPM tooling and the services will be exposed using the ESB. The implementation of the following services will remain in the CRM system: `OrderService`, `CustomerService`. The implementation of `BillingService` and `TransportService` will be done in the ERP system. The `DocumentSerivce` will be implemented using the Document Management System (DMS). There are two events that are relevant: an order is received and a payment is received. The customer care portal can access the state of the process; it is the interface to the order-to-cash process. Authentication and authorization is done with the IAM component. There will be a system account for the BPM component.

The following diagram shows the solution architecture that is the result of design.

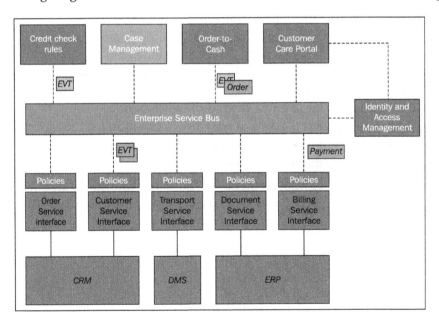

Next, the business process is designed using the BPM component. The services are designed and registered in the registry and repository.

[139]

Developing the solution

The realization of the different components is carried out with development tools. The following components need to be developed:

- **Business Process Management component**: The business process that is designed needs to be developed; the service calls and manual tasks need to be built and tested.
- **User interface**: The user interface for the customer care portal needs a portlet to expose the state of the order to the employee. This portlet calls `OrderService` and `CustomerService` to access the relevant data.
- **Business rules**: For certain amounts, a credit check is conducted. This logic is built in the business rules engine.
- **Events**: Two events are defined in JMS: `OrderReceived` and `PaymentReceived`. The business process subscribes to the events to start the process and to continue the process.
- **ESB**: The services need to be exposed on the ESB. A composite service for billing the customer is developed in the ESB. The ERP system does not expose standardized interfaces, so their interface is transformed in the ESB.
- **Policies**: The policies on the services are configured based on the requirements from the organization.
- **Interfaces**: The CRM system comes with out of the box web services, so nothing has to be developed. However, the interface `DocumentService` needs to be developed. A web service is built with JEE, based on the WSDL that was defined and the API that the DMS offers; the development tool offers support for this meet in the middle approach.
- **Implementation**: The implementation of the service is already available, so no development effort is needed, except for the implementation of the composite service that was already discussed.
- **Identity and Access Management**: The authentication and authorization is configured in the portlet, and on the ESB, the system accounts are checked.

Running the solution

Once the solution is in production, orders are queued in a JMS queue. The Business Process Management component reads from this queue and starts an order-to-cash process instance. The first step in the process is to determine whether the customer needs a credit check by calling the business rules engine. If this is not necessary or the customer passes the check, the next step is to bill the customer. The process calls this composite service on the ESB. The ESB authorizes the BPM component and calls the service `BillingService` of the ERP system and the service `DocumentService` of the DMS. The process will wait until the customer pays the bill. If the customer calls, the customer care employee who is logged in will look up the state of the order in the customer care portal. This portal calls the service `OrderService` and the service `CustomerService` to look up the data for this customer. The IAM component determines whether the employee is logged in and whether he or she is authorized to use these services. Once the payment is received, the process continues by calling the appropriate services. The CRM user interface that the CRM system offers to the sales people is still used to support their core business processes that are specific to CRM.

Summary

In this chapter, you learned about the most common building blocks of an SOA environment, such as an ESB, a registry and repository, and a BPM platform. These building blocks can be combined into a reference architecture that acts as a blueprint for your SOA environment. In the next chapter, you will read about the different offerings from vendors for these building blocks.

6
Solution Architectures

Now that you know what Service Oriented Architecture means, what building blocks are used in Service Oriented Architecture, and what type of services can be distinguished, it's time to investigate how we can technically implement this. In this chapter, you will learn the main features and architecture of the product suites that are offered by three large software vendors: Oracle, IBM, and Microsoft. There are a lot more vendors on the market, but it would take up too much space to describe the entire market. After reading this chapter and this book, you should be able to assess other suites yourself.

Comprehensive suite or best of breed

In the previous chapter, you learned about the building blocks of SOA. These building blocks can be realized in a number of ways, such as by creating homegrown frameworks, using a comprehensive suite, or using a mixture of different tools from different vendors, thus creating a best of breed solution.

The advantages of comprehensive suites are:

- Integration of the different building blocks is tested and supported by the vendor.
- Performance of a suite is often better, because the vendor optimized the communication between the different building blocks, for example by using native calls.
- Documentation of the integration of the different building blocks is more widely available.
- The purchase department of your organization only has to deal with one vendor. Discounts and other perks are easier to get when buying more than one component.

Solution Architectures

- Resources are easier to find as there are more people experienced with one whole suite than people that are an expert in multiple products from multiple vendors.
- Environments (Development, Integration/Test, Acceptance, and Production) are easier to create because there is one homogeneous suite involved.

Obviously, there are some disadvantages as well:

- There is no suite that consists of the best solution for every building block. So purchasing a comprehensive suite, means compromising in terms of some requirements. It is important to know the weak points of a suite as well as the strong points so that you can have optimal return on your investment.
- The building blocks are packaged in suites. You pay for the suite, not for the individual building blocks you use. Especially in a first project, you might not need all these building blocks at once.

If you chose a best of breed solution, you will need to integrate the building blocks from one vendor with the building blocks of another vendor. Two factors determine the ease of this integration:

- The way the interface of the building blocks is defined. For example if you want to integrate a rules engine from one vendor in the suite of another vendor it is important that the rule engine has a standardized API (SOAP or REST services for example).
- How the building blocks are realized. Often you need some type of development environment (IDE) for the different building blocks. If you need a different IDE for every building block, this becomes very cumbersome for your developers.

The following table summarizes the advantages and disadvantages of using a comprehensive breed versus a best of breed solution:

Factor	Comprehensive suite	Best of breed
Ease of integration	High	Average
Cost	Low	High
Supplier management	High	Low
Support	High	Average
IDE	High	Average
Quality	Average	High
Resources	High	Average
Performance	High	Average

If performance and other quality requirements are more important than price and ease of integration, then a best of breed solution is more suitable for you. If price is important you can choose a cheaper suite and extend it with homegrown frameworks. Your organizational goals, the experience of your IT department, and the size of your organization all determine what the best solution is: using a suite, build some building blocks yourself, or use a best of breed solution.

It is important to think carefully about this before you start, because there exist a lot of standards for runtime integration. So you can communicate between a Java web service that is hosted on an Oracle WebLogic server and a Microsoft WCF service that is hosted on IIS. However, there are not a lot of standards that allow for the seamless import and export of components. For example, if you define a composite service using the ESB toolkit for BizTalk Server, you can't export this and then import it in Oracle Service Bus, or some other vendor's ESB. The following table shows the parts of the solution architecture from *Chapter 4*, *Classification of Services* with standards for implementation of these components and an estimate of how easy it is to switch to another implementation or vendor.

Component	Standard	Switch to another implementation or vendor
Services	JEE	Yes, all JEE compliant services. Note that Microsoft does not offer this implementation.
Events	JMS	Yes, all JMS compliant message providers. Note that Microsoft does not offer this implementation.
Service Composition	BPEL	BPEL: A lot of vendors created extensions specific for their environment
	BPMN	BPMN: No, Only the definition is standardized, the implementation is not. You can export and import the design. The implementation has to be redone in another environment.
Business Rules	RIF	Most vendors support only parts of the standard.

Comparison

Now let's take a look into the suites that the three big software vendors—Oracle, IBM, and Microsoft—have to offer. You will learn about these suites based on the reference architecture that was described in the previous chapter. There are a number of cross-cutting concerns and additional tools and frameworks that are also part of the suites that were not discussed in the previous chapter. To make a good comparison you will, apart from the building blocks, also learn about:

Solution Architectures

- **Test tools**: The services that are created need to be tested before you integrate them with the rest of the services.
- **Deployment tools**: The services need to be installed in the different environments (QA environment, acceptance environment, and production environment).
- **Monitoring tools**: Once the services are installed in the different building blocks, they need to be monitored. Performance, errors, and load are important aspects you need to keep an eye on.
- **Error-handling mechanisms**: Errors occur. Especially in an SOA environment, you have to have a mechanism to handle them. The communication between the different types of services can cause different types of errors. Asynchronous communication and long-running business processes need to be flexible and you should be able to find and fix errors.

The following table shows the different products and runtime environments that the three vendors (Oracle, IBM, and Microsoft) offer for the different building blocks and tools that are needed to realize the reference architecture. These products are discussed in more detail in the remainder of the chapter.

	Oracle	**IBM**	**Microsoft**
Services	Self hosting in Java application	Self hosting in Java application	Self hosting in .NET application
			Windows Service
	Oracle WebLogic Server (WLS)	IBM WebSphere Application Server (WAS)	IIS
Events	JMS (WLS)	JMS (WAS)	-
	Oracle Advanced Queuing (AQ)	IBM WebSphere MQ	MSMQ Server
	Oracle Event Processing (OEP)	WebSphere Operational Decision Management	Microsoft Stream Insight
	Oracle Business Activity Monitoring (BAM)	IBM Business Monitor	BizTalk Server Business Activity Monitoring (BAM)
Service composition	Oracle Service Bus (OSB)	IBM WebSphere Enterprise Service Bus	BizTalk Server ESB toolkit

	Oracle	IBM	Microsoft
	Oracle SOA Suite	IBM Process Server	BizTalk Server
			Windows Server AppFabric
	Oracle BPM Suite	IBM Business Process Manager	-
Business Rules	Oracle Business Rules	WebSphere ILOG BRMS	BizTalk Server Business Rule Framework
User interface	Oracle Application Development Framework (ADF)	-	Silverlight
	Oracle WebCenter	IBM Portal	MS SharePoint
Security	Oracle Web Services Manager	Tivoli Access Manager	-
Registry and repository	Oracle Service Registry	-	UDDI Services
Design tooling	Oracle Enterprise Repository (OER)	WebSphere Registry and Repository (WSRR)	-
	JDeveloper plugins	Rational Application Developer	Microsoft Visio
	Eclipse plugins	Integration Designer	
	Browser based (OS, BPM and business rules)	Process Designer	-
	Oracle BPA Suite	-	-
Development tooling	JDeveloper	Integration Designer	Visual Studio using Windows Communication Framework (WCF)

Solution Architectures

	Oracle	IBM	Microsoft
Test tooling	Eclipse plugins	Rational Application Developer (RAD)	-
	NetBeans	-	-
	SCA test framework	Rational Tester For SOA Quality	Visual Studio Test Professional
	Browser based test consoles	-	-
Deployment tools	IDE (JDeveloper, Eclipse, NetBeans)	IDE (Rational Application Developer, Integration Designer)	IDE (Visual studio)
	Consoles	Admin tools	BizTalk Server Task (BTSTask)
	Scripting (Ant, Maven, WLST)	Scripting (Python)	Microsoft Windows Management Instrumentation (WMI)
	-	Rational Build Forge	Team Foundation Server
Monitoring	WebLogic Console	WAS Console	Event viewer
	OSB Console	Process Server Console	BizTalk Server Administration Console
	Enterprise Manager with SOA Management Pack Enterprise Edition	Tivoli Composite Application Manager for SOA	-
Error handling	Retries	Retries	Retries
	Fault policies for SCA	Exception destination	-

Oracle

Oracle has a number of product families, such as hardware, databases (Oracle, MySQL, and so on), packaged applications (Fusion applications), and Oracle Fusion Middleware. The latter offers different suites, like Oracle SOA Suite, Oracle BPM Suite, Oracle WebLogic Server Suite, and so on.

Services

Elementary services, either SOAP-based or REST-based services are usually exposed using a web container. In Oracle Fusion Middleware, WebLogic Server is used to host these services. This application server supports **Java Enterprise Edition (JEE)**, including standards for web services.

> JEE is divided into a number of logical layers or tiers, such as the client tier, the web tier, the business tier, and the **Enterprise Information Systems (EIS)** tier. The standards for the web services can be found in the business tier. The following standards are relevant when creating web services: JAX-RS RESTful Web Services, JAX-WS Web Service endpoints, and some supporting standards such as JAXB for the transformation from Java objects to XML and vice versa. More information about these standards can be found on the Oracle website.

Events

Events need to be generated, transported, and published by a message provider, or message-oriented middleware. Furthermore, there needs to be a mechanism for clients who are interested in them to subscribe to these events. Oracle Fusion Middleware supports the following types of events:

- **Java Messaging Service (JMS)** and **Oracle Advance Queuing (AQ)** as message-oriented middleware solutions or messaging providers. These techniques were discussed in the previous chapter.

- **Event-delivery Network (EDN)** is a layer on top of JMS or AQ, that hides the implementation details from the programmer and offers a way to describe events in a way similar to describing services such as **Event Definition Language (EDL)**. This is an Oracle-specific solution that can only be used within a WebLogic Server domain.

- Data from sensors, for example physical events such as rise in temperature or pressure, reading a radio frequency identification (RFID) tag, and also software events, such as firing of process sensors, database triggers, and so on.

Oracle recognizes two main concepts for processing these different types of events: **Complex Event Processing (CEP)** and **Business Activity Monitoring (BAM)**. CEP is used to process a high throughput of events with extremely low latency and to evaluate patterns in event data. Oracle BAM is used for *larger* business events that occur in your organization.

Oracle Event Processing (OEP)

Oracle Event Processing (OEP) is the name for the product that Oracle delivers to handle complex event processing. It is a component of the Oracle SOA Suite. An OEP event-driven system is comprised of several **event sources** that come from data stores, sensors, and devices. These sources generate streams of **ordinary events** (as opposed to **notable events**). The Oracle CEP applications, listen to these event streams, process these events, and generate notable events. These events are subscribed to by so-called **event sinks**. Typical use cases for this product are security and fraud detection, algorithmic trading, and patient monitoring in health care.

Business Activity Monitoring (BAM)

Oracle **Business Activity Monitoring (BAM)** is the product in the Oracle Fusion Middleware product family that helps organizations to monitor the business process, correlate them to KPIs and to take corrective actions if some change warrants that. It is part of both the Oracle SOA Suite and the Oracle BPM Suite.

Service composition

Oracle offers several solutions to compose different services into a composite service or process service:

- Oracle Service Bus (OSB)
- Oracle SOA Suite
- Oracle BPM Suite

Oracle Service Bus

As you have read in the previous chapter, an Enterprise Service Bus is used to expose services and to create composite services that are short lived, and (usually) part of a single transaction. The Oracle Service Bus is an Enterprise Service Bus that consists of the following components and functionality:

- **Service management**: This component offers monitoring features using the OSB Console, SLA alerts and reporting facilities.
- **Service virtualization**: This component offers content-based routing, transformation of messages, and service chaining.
- **Security**: The security capabilities of the OSB include authentication, authorization, identity, and encryption and signing. Note that WebLogic Server handles securing services on the transport layer. WebLogic is the underlying server that OSB runs on.
- **Adaptive messaging**: This is realized by offering adapters for different protocols and enterprise integration, such as HTTP(S), JCA, JMS, WRM, REST, MQ, SMTP, FTP, File, Tuxedo, AQ, EBS, SAP, SBL, JDE and so on.
- **Configuration framework**: This component offers validation of changes, import and export capabilities, and a metadata store using the change center.

An example of a typical composite service for the OSB is an automated `OrderService` that is exposed on the Oracle Service Bus and is enriched with another service to fetch the customer data that is needed to store the order in the ERP application.

Oracle SOA Suite

Oracle SOA Suite is used to create composite services, or composite applications. Typically this is used for service composition that is more complex or spans multiple transactions. Think for example of an alternative, more complex `OrderService` that consists of an automated service to execute a credit check and a human task to approve the order before it is stored in the ERP application. The infrastructure of the Oracle SOA Suite is based on the **Service Component Architecture** (**SCA**) standard. This standard is maintained by OASIS. It is defined on their website (http://www.oasis-opencsa.org/sca) as follows:

> *Service Component Architecture (SCA) is a set of specifications which describe a model for building applications and systems using a Service Oriented Architecture (SOA). SCA extends and complements prior approaches to implementing services, and SCA builds on open standards such as Web Services.*
>
> *SCA is based on the idea that business function is provided as a series of services, which are assembled together to create solutions that serve a particular business need. These composite applications can contain both new services created specifically for the application and also business function from existing systems and applications, reused as part of the composition. SCA provides a model both for the composition of services and for the creation of service components, including the reuse of existing application function within SCA compositions.*

Solution Architectures

The Oracle SOA Suite offers different technologies to create (composite) services that are packaged as a composite: Spring contexts, BPEL processes to orchestrate services, business rules, Mediator components to transform and route within the composite application, and human workflow tasks to allow interaction with people in the composite application.

> A composite is the unit of deployment in SCA and is described using XML. A composite consists of **components**, **services**, **references**, **property declarations** and the **wiring**. A component is the implementation of the service. Services are the exposed interfaces of the composite. References are the services that are consumed by the composite and the wiring connects the different components within a composite. Property declarations offer the possibility to declaratively set properties like location, currency, and so on.

Oracle BPM Suite

Apart from Oracle SOA Suite, Oracle offers Oracle BPM Suite. It is used to automate and improve business processes. It is more oriented towards business analysts and business processes, whereas Oracle SOA Suite is more aimed at IT developers and the realization of composite services. BPM Suite packages some of the same components as the SOA Suite, and some additional components to support **Business Process Modeling Notation (BPMN)**. As you can see in the following list of components, Oracle BPM Suite supports two standards for executing business processes – BPEL and BPMN. These two types of business processes can be combined with the human workflow component. Apart from that, the tooling supports **Social BPM** and case management, by integrating portals and social media features with the BPM functionality.

The Oracle BPM Suite consists of:

- **Oracle Business Process Manager (OBPM)** to model and execute processes that are defined using BPMN
- BPEL Process Manager to execute processes that are defined using WS-BPEL
- Human Workflow to support human tasks and patterns in workflow in your business process
- Adapters to connect to databases, JMS queues and so on
- Business Rules to define business rules outside of your business process declaratively
- Business Activity Monitoring (BAM) to monitor your business process
- Process Portal to discuss cases and cooperate with other people on your business process (Social BPM)

Business rules

Oracle Business Rules is a rules engine that is part of both the BPM Suite and the SOA Suite. It can be used in conjunction with a process or composite service, but also as a standalone service. It supports both `if.... then...else` rules and decision tables. The business rule engine is based on the **RETE algorithm**.

> The RETE algorithm is a pattern-matching algorithm that was developed in 1974 by Dr Charles L. Forgy of Carnegie Mellon University. The performance of the algorithm is independent of the number of rules; the Rete algorithm is designed to sacrifice memory for increased speed. This algorithm is used in a large number of rule engines nowadays.

User interface

As you have learned in the previous chapter, the user interface in SOA can expose a single service, or a collection of several services that are combined into a portal.

To expose services in your user interface, Oracle offers Oracle **Application Development Framework(ADF)**. It is based on **Java Server Faces (JSF)**, a JEE standard for web applications. The framework offers widgets, renderers for different platforms and a number of technologies to map the Java objects to relational data or XML.

Next to ADF, Oracle offers a portal platform called Oracle WebCenter. This name is used for a family of products:

- **WebCenter Content**: For content life cycle management.
- **WebCenter Sites**: To build intranets, extranets, and other sites.
- **Application Adapters for Oracle WebCenter**: To access, view, and act on business transactions from ERP software such as Oracle E-Business Suite, PeopleSoft, Siebel, and Microsoft SharePoint.
- **WebCenter Portal**: To create portals and mash-ups.
- **WebCenter Social**: To help people work together.

Security

Oracle sells a whole range of products around identity management, access management, directory services, and identity governance. An important product when working with services is **Oracle Web Services Manager** (**OWSM**). This is a component of the Oracle SOA Suite and offers a solution for policy management and security of your service infrastructure. It offers support for several industry standards like WS-Security, WS-Policy, WS-Reliable Messaging, and several signing and encryption algorithms.

Registry and repository

Oracle offers the combination of **Oracle Enterprise Repository** (**OER**) and Oracle Service Registry for SOA governance. In *Chapter 8*, *Life Cycle Management* you will learn about the differences between repositories and registries and how they aid you in life cycle management.

Design tooling

Oracle offers a number of different tools for designing your solutions, depending on your role.

Design tooling for developers

Most of the design tooling that Oracle offers is integrated into their development tooling: Oracle JDeveloper and plugins for Eclipse.

Design tooling for business analysts

For business analysts, Oracle offers design tooling in a browser. There are tools available that can be used to model business processes and tools to define business rules. Apart from the design capabilities it offers versioning, support, and role-based security.

For the design of enterprise grade business process models, Oracle has a partnership with Software AG, parts of the ARIS Suite are packaged and rebranded as Oracle BPA Suite. The main difference between the Oracle BPM Studio and Oracle BPA Suite is that the Oracle BPA suite is used to model strategic goals and higher level (abstract) processes and the Oracle BPM Studio is more geared towards lower level (executable) business processes. This might change in the future; this part of the market is changing rapidly.

Development tooling

For development in an SOA-environment, Oracle offers different integrated development environments (IDE). This is due to the fact that Oracle purchased several companies, each with their own development environment.

The strategic development tool for Oracle is Oracle JDeveloper. It can be used to access the database, program Java and JEE, program SOA building blocks like BPMN and BPEL, create user interfaces and portals, and so on. Apart from this core functionality you can deploy your applications to a JAR, EAR, or directly to an application server, access the database, and run unit tests. The tool has an architecture based on plugins. Oracle creates the plugins that are needed for the Fusion Middleware stack such as Oracle SOA Suite; other companies or teams can create plugins of their own.

Apart from JDeveloper, Oracle offers a distribution of plugins for Eclipse, the open source Java development tool. This distribution is called **Oracle Enterprise Pack for Eclipse** (**OEPE**) and can be used to develop code specifically targeted to JEE applications and Oracle Fusion Middleware such as OSB and OEP.

Last but not least, NetBeans can be used to develop applications. NetBeans is a powerful development tool that offers support for Java and for several scripting languages and front-end technologies.

Test tooling

The Oracle Fusion Middleware product family offers several options to test your services, next to the available open source frameworks such as JUnit.

Testing transformations

Both OEPE and Oracle JDeveloper offer testing tools for transformations that you program. For example, in JDeveloper you can define an XSLT document that transforms an XML document to the canonical format that is used in your organization. You can then test this transformation by pointing to an example XML document, or generating one. The document is then transformed and you can compare the result to a predefined output XML, or inspect it visually. OEPE offers the same functionality for XQueries that you define for the Oracle Service Bus.

SCA testing framework

The SCA testing framework is part of the SOA Suite. This testing framework allows you to create and run automated tests on an SOA composite application. It offers the following features:

- Simulate references (web services your application calls)
- Validate process actions with test data, you can assert that a certain result is returned
- Create reports of the test results

With these capabilities you can test a BPEL process, a mediator, a business rule, and so on. To execute the tests, you need to deploy the composite with the test suites to the Oracle SOA Suite runtime environment. Unfortunately, it is not possible to test this from within the IDE.

Testing from the console

It is also possible to test services from the various consoles. Web services that are deployed to WebLogic Server can be tested from WebLogic Console. When you access the testing URL, a form is generated automatically, enabling you to enter data that will be used as input for the web service. The same is true for composites that are deployed in the SOA Suite. If they expose themselves as a service, the Enterprise Manager (the console for the SOA Suite) offers a screen to enter the input document for the service and execute it. Last but not least, the OSB Console offers a testing opportunity for services and transformations.

Deployment tooling

There are three ways to deploy services in the Oracle stack: from the IDE, using scripts, or from a console.

Deployment from the IDE

When you are done programming a web service, a composite, or an OSB project, you can deploy this directly from the IDE to the server. This is usually done in development environments, to test your code. Both JDeveloper and Eclipse support this. You point the IDE to a server that is reachable from your development machine and deploy the service, composite, or OSB project to it.

Deployment from the console

Another option is to package the web service, composite, or OSB project in the IDE to an archive (WAR, JAR, EAR file) and deploy it from the appropriate console. This can be done for web services in WebLogic Console, in the Enterprise Manager for composite applications (SOA Suite), and in the OSB Console for OSB projects and artifacts.

The WebLogic Console and the OSB Console have the notion of a change center. This gives you the opportunity to apply a number of changes and *commit* or *rollback* these in one transaction. You can even test the changes before you actually apply them.

Deployment using the console is most often used for demonstration purposes, in development environments, or to learn the tooling.

Deployment using scripting

The best way to deploy software in a professional environment is to use scripting. This is the least error prone method, and repeatable by anyone in your organization.

Depending on the technology you used, you can use one of the following scripting options:

- **Maven**: Maven manages dependencies and also has some built-in tasks for deployment to WebLogic Server and generation of web service projects. This method can be used for JAX-WS services, and also for RESTful Web Services.
- **Ant**: Oracle has created Ant tasks for packaging and deployment of SCA composites to Enterprise Manager. This technique can also be used for *regular* web services, both SOAP-based and RESTful-services. OSB projects can also be deployed using Ant, calling WLST scripts from within the ant scripts.
- **WebLogic Scripting Tool (WLST)**: It is based on Jython, and lets you manage, create, and monitor WebLogic Server domains. With these scripts you can deploy SCA composites, JAR files, WAR files, EAR files, and OSB projects. Apart from that it lets you create resources such as JDBC connection pools and start and stop the server.

Monitoring

Once your services are running, you need to monitor their health. You need to keep an eye out for errors, monitor performance and throughput, and watch for security breaches. Apart from the different consoles, Oracle offers Oracle SOA Management Pack Enterprise Edition to offer administrators a consolidated view of the SOA environment, enabling them to monitor and manage all their components from a central location.

Error handling

In every IT application, handling of errors is very important. This is even more important in an SOA environment. Part of the Oracle SOA Suite is the Fault Management framework. This framework uses policies that are defined in XML. These policies can catch both runtime and business faults. Once a fault is caught, the policy defines actions that can be used to mediate faults in the SOA instance. Possible actions include **retry**, **human intervention**, **replay scope**, **rethrow fault**, **abort**, and custom Java actions. When human intervention is the action that is defined for a particular fault, the console of the SOA Suite (Enterprise Manager) provides a GUI for managing the faulted instance.

IBM

IBM also offers a complete set of solutions for your SOA building blocks.

Services

IBM **WebSphere Application Server (WAS)** is the JEE application server that can run web services, both SOAP Web Services and RESTful Web Services.

Events

IBM has a number of products available to handle events: JMS in WebSphere Application Server, IBM WebSphere MQ, IBM WebSphere Message Broker, WebSphere Operational Decision Management, and IBM Business Monitor.

JMS and IBM WebSphere MQ are similar to JMS as offered by Oracle on WebLogic Server and to Oracle Advanced Queuing (Oracle AQ). IBM WebSphere Message Broker is built on top of IBM WebSphere MQ, giving MQ ESB like capabilities, for example data transformation.

WebSphere Operational Decision Management and WebSphere Business Monitor warrant a little more discussion, you will learn about them next.

WebSphere Operational Decision Management

WebSphere Operational Decision Management consists of two components: WebSphere Decision Center and WebSphere Decision Server. The Decision Center provides a repository and management components to define business logic based on rules and events. The Decision Server is the runtime environment. WebSphere Operational Decision Management is comparable to Oracle Event Processing. The biggest difference is the way patterns are recognized. Oracle Event processing uses Continuous Query Language (CQL), a query language to analyze the events that are generated. The IBM solution uses a rules engine to detect patterns.

IBM Business Monitor

IBM Business Monitor provides real-time visibility and insight into operational processes, transactions, and events. It has built-in support for IBM BPM and IBM SOA offerings. It consists of role-based dashboards and integrates with Cognos Business Intelligence Server for advanced analysis and reporting on historic data.

Service composition

IBM offers several ways to compose services from other services. Two major products are discussed in this paragraph: IBM WebSphere Enterprise Service Bus, and IBM WebSphere Process Server.

IBM WebSphere Enterprise Service Bus

The IBM WebSphere Enterprise Service Bus (ESB) is used to realize composite services that are short lived and are executed in a single transaction. An Enterprise Service Bus typically offers a service to consumers and routes the request to another service. Apart from the routing between these **endpoints** (the address of the service), transformation and other logic can be added. **MediationFlows** provide the essential functions for WebSphere ESB. Mediation is the dynamic intervention between services. This mediation can be used to transform data, to log data, filter data, route data, and so on. A **Mediation Flow** implements mediation. A mediation flow component has one or more flows; for example one for the request and one for the response. The mediation framework is based on the **Service Component Architecture (SCA)**. The product supports connectivity between endpoints through a variety of protocols and APIs like **Java Message Service (JMS)** and a variety of transports, including TCP/IP, SSL, HTTP, and HTTPS. WebSphere ESB supports the following web services standards:

- SOAP/HTTP, SOAP/JMS, WSDL 1.1
- UDDI 3.0 Service Registry
- WS-* Standards including WS-Security, WS-Atomic Transactions

The ESB capabilities are closely integrated with the IBM Process Server, part of the IBM Business Process Manager that is discussed next.

IBM Business Process Manager

The IBM Business Process manager can be used for composite or process services that contain multiple transactions, are longer running, or too complicated to realize with the IBM WebSphere Service Bus.

These process services or composite services are assembled into **Process Applications**. IBM Business Process Manager consists of two main parts: a Process Center and a Process Server. The Process Center consists of a BPM repository that stores the Process Applications, shared assets, and a server registry. The Process Server is the runtime environment for Process Applications. It is built on WebSphere Enterprise Service Bus, thus providing it with the mediation functionality of the ESB and the Quality of Services that WebSphere Application Server provides (for example clustering, failover, scalability, and security).

In the past, IBM offered two types of runtime environments: WebSphere Process Server and WebSphere Lombardi edition. The newest edition integrates both of them. It supports the following:

- **SCA**: To assemble composite applications, originally in WebSphere Process Server. This is part of the core that WebSphere Application Server offers and that is also used by WebSphere Application Server.
- **BPMN**: To model business processes, originally in WebSphere Lombardi Edition.
- **BPEL**: To develop executable business processes and composite services, originally in WebSphere Process Server.
- **Rules**: The engine to externalize business rules, originally in WebSphere Lombardi edition.
- **ESB**: To mediate between services, originally in WebSphere Process Server and inherited from WebSphere Enterprise Service Bus.
- **Monitoring**: To monitor your business processes and your services, both from WebSphere Process Server and WebSphere Lombardi edition.
- **Process Portal**: For management of human tasks, originally in WebSphere Lombardi edition.

- **Configurable Business Space**: For creating a customized user interface (originally in WebSphere Process Server).
- **Add-ons**: For MS SharePoint and MS Office integration.

Business rules

IBM offers the WebSphere ILOG **Business Rule Management Systems Suite (BRMS)** to externalize business rules from your application. As you learned in the previous chapter, the main purpose of a BRMS is to separate the life cycle of business rules from the life cycle of application development. This way you can change a business rule separately from changing something in the application. Externalizing business rules in your application accomplishes this. ILOG BRMS has two editions—one that runs in a Java runtime environment and one that runs in a .NET runtime environment. It consists of the following modules:

- **Rule Studio**: Eclipse-based development environment.
- **Rule Execution Server**: Runtime environment.
- **IBM WebSphere ILOG Rule Team Server**: Business user rule management environment.
- **IBM WebSphere ILOG Decision Validation Services**: Testing, simulation, and audit functions that are integrated with Rule Studio, Rule Execution Server, and Rule Team Server.
- **IBM WebSphere ILOG Rule Solutions for Office**: Guided authoring and editing of rules through Microsoft Office Word and Excel.

User interface

IBM WebSphere portal supports workflows, content management, social, mobile web delivery administration, open standards, security, and scalability. If you don't need a portal, you can develop your own user interface using Java development tools and the IBM WebSphere Server as a runtime environment.

Security

IBM offers a number of products for security and access management, including Tivoli Identity and Access Manager and IBM Security Access Manager for Enterprise Single Sign On. Security policies can be stored in WebSphere Registry and Repository and integrated with the Enterprise Service Bus where they are applied on services.

Solution Architectures

Registry and repository

WebSphere Registry and Repository (WSRR) is the registry and repository building block of the IBM stack. It can be integrated with the Enterprise Service Bus. This packaged offering of WebSphere Service Registry and Repository and WebSphere ESB is called WebSphere ESB Registry edition.

WSRR provides registry functions that support publication of metadata about services. This allows service consumers to find services and to analyze their relationships with other services. Apart from publication, WSSR provides repository functions to store, manage, and assign a version number. It also enables governance of service definitions by providing the following features:

- Control access to the metadata by using authentication and authorization
- Model the life cycle of service artifacts
- Manage promotion of services through phases of their life cycle in various deployment environments
- Perform impact analysis and communicate changes of the governed service metadata

To facilitate communication with service consumers and service providers, WSRR supports the following types of APIs:

- Java-based
- SOAP-based
- REST-based
- Atom-based APIs

Note that WSRR does not support UDDI, but IBM offers a WSRR-UDDI synchronization module. IBM offers IBM WebSphere Registry as a UDDI Registry solution. In *Chapter 8, Life Cycle Management* you will learn more about the difference between a registry and a repository.

Design tooling

In the IBM stack, the Rational product line offers support for design and development. These can be used to create services and user interfaces. Tools to create composite services, process services, and mediation are part of separate products.

Services

IBM **Rational Application Developer** (**RAD**) for WebSphere software cannot only be used to design web, service-oriented architecture, Java, JEE, and portal applications, but you can also use it to develop, analyze, test, and deploy these applications. RAD is built on Eclipse.

Composite services

Process Designer, which is part of IBM Business Process Manager, is the authoring tool to design and model business processes using BPMN 2.0. WebSphere Integration Designer is an Eclipse-based tool for integrating your business processes with your SOA assets. You use this tool to create solutions for WebSphere Process Server, WebSphere ESB, and WebSphere Adapters.

Development tooling

Development is done in the same tools as the design tooling: Integration Designer and Rational Application Development.

Test tooling

IBM offers Rational Tester for SOA Quality as part of the Rational Suite. It is a tool to automate the testing of web services and supports testing of BPEL, SOAP, JMS, WS-*, and RESTful services.

Deployment tooling

In the IBM stack there are several options to deploy an SOA artifact:

- Deployment from the IDE
- Deployment from the consoles
- Deployment using scripting

Deployment from the IDE

You can define the WebSphere server you want to deploy your application to in both Rational Application Developer and "vanilla" Eclipse. This is usually done during development. For your integration and SCA artifacts you can deploy your business process using WebSphere Integration Designer.

Solution Architectures

Deployment from the web interface of the server

WebSphere Application Server and WebSphere Process Server offer the option to deploy artifacts from the console. The consoles are browser-based, making it easily accessible for everyone in your organization.

Deployment scripts

You can create Ant scripts or Maven scripts and combine them with python to connect to the WebSphere Administration Tools to deploy artifacts.

IBM offers Rational Build Forge as a centralized build and releases management solution for your software projects. It integrates with different IDEs and different build-tools such as Ant and Maven. The product consists of the runtime engine, a management console, and workforce agents that are used to execute the automation jobs.

Monitoring

IBM offers IBM Tivoli Composite Application Manager for SOA to manage your SOA artifacts. It supports heterogeneous SOA platforms: IBM WebSphere, Microsoft .NET, and Oracle WebLogic Server. Application Manager offers three main functions:

- Service Management provides the monitoring and management of message flows.
- Application Management can help monitor application performance and availability at the resource level for web servers and application servers.
- Messaging management monitors the status of WebSphere MQ servers, queues, queue managers, channels, and critical performance data related to WebSphere Message Broker. It provides real-time status on the availability and performance of the messaging environment.

Error handling

A number of IBM products offer error destinations to handle errors. Usually this is a queue that is used to store failed processes or messages. The administrator is responsible for monitoring these queues and for fixing the errors. Apart from the error destination several of the products offer *retry* options to handle temporary errors like bandwidth or availability errors.

Microsoft

Like Oracle and IBM, Microsoft offers an SOA platform. To make the comparison with IBM and Oracle a little easier, the Microsoft products are mapped on the reference architecture that you learned about in the previous chapter.

Services

Services are created using **Windows Communication Framework (WCF)**. This development framework can be deployed or hosted as follows:

- Self-hosting in a managed .NET application
- Hosted as a Windows service
- IIS, the web server of the Microsoft platform

Events

Message-oriented middleware

As a queuing solution, Microsoft offers **Microsoft Message Queuing (MSMQ)**. It is part of the Windows operating system. Messages are stored and forwarded by MSMQ until they reach the destination queue. Later, when a recipient application runs, it can retrieve the messages from the queue. MSMQ provides built-in security and transaction support.

Complex Event Processing (CEP)

Microsoft StreamInsight is the platform that you can use to analyze large amounts of data that are streaming in from different sources. It consists of a CEP engine that contains queries, input adapters, and output adapters. The platform that it uses underneath is Microsoft SQL Server, the database solution by Microsoft.

Business Activity Monitoring

BizTalk Server offers business activity monitoring for business users. It offers capabilities to monitor and analyze data from business process information sources both in real time as well as historically.

Solution Architectures

Service composition

The Microsoft platform offers two solutions for service composition:

- Microsoft BizTalk Server (BTS)
- Windows Server AppFabric

BizTalk Server

The heart of the server is the BizTalk Server engine. This consists of two parts:

- Messaging component – to communicate with other systems. Using adapters, the engine supports a variety of data formats and protocols. Adapters exist for:
    - WCF components
    - Protocols like HTTP, SMTP, SOAP, and so on
    - MSMQ
    - Line of business applications (LOB), such as SAP, Oracle E-Business Suite, Oracle database, and so on
- Orchestration component – to support process services.

Apart from the adapters, BizTalk Server provides an ESB toolkit. This toolkit extends the basic BizTalk Server capabilities to provide for service composition using itinerary services, dynamic resolution of endpoints and maps, Web Service and WS-* integration, fault management, and reporting.

BizTalk orchestration provides a transactional programming model for process services. You can define three types of transactions when creating an orchestration: non-transactional scopes, atomic transactions, and long-running transactions. The orchestration consists of an Orchestration Designer and an Orchestration Engine. The orchestration is defined using a proprietary format, not WS-BPEL; however WS-BPEL can be imported into the engine.

Windows Server AppFabric

Windows Server AppFabric extends Windows Server to enhance hosting, management, and caching capabilities for web applications and services. This makes it easier to deploy, configure, and manage WCF-based and **Microsoft Workflow Foundation**-based services.

> **Windows Workflow Foundation (WF)** is a framework that enables developers to create system or human workflows in .NET applications. It provides an API, an in-process workflow engine, and a designer to implement long-running processes.

It is possible to combine the adapters that BizTalk Server offers with the WF and WCF features of AppFabric using AppFabric Connect. This offers the developer the possibility to use the LOB adapters and the XML mapper from BizTalk Server in combination with WF workflows that are exposed as WCF endpoints in Windows Server AppFabric.

Business rules

BizTalk Server includes the Business Rules framework as a standalone .NET-compliant class library. The primary modules include the Business Rule Composer for constructing policies, the Rule Engine Deployment wizard for deploying policies created in Business Rule Composer, and Run-Time Business Rule Engine that executes policies.

User interface

There are several solutions that are offered by Microsoft for the user interface. SharePoint is the portal solution that offers the following capabilities:

- **Sites**: This is used for business sites, or intranet. It offers the possibility to share documents, manage projects, and publish information.
- **Communities**: This contains collaboration tools and a platform to manage them.
- **Content**: This product is used for content management.
- **Search**: Helps you to find information.
- **Insights**: This product gives you access to information from databases, reports, and business application.
- **Composites**: Offers tools and components for creating do-it-yourself business applications.

If you don't want to use a portal, you can use Silverlight to build your own applications. Silverlight is a plugin for .NET that helps you build web and mobile applications. Apart from Silverlight, ASP.Net web applications can be used to expose a specific set of services.

Security

To secure web services, you can use the built-in security features of the Windows Communication Framework, or one of the security protocols that .NET offers.

Registry and repository

Microsoft offers UDDI Services to manage your SOA artifacts.

Design tooling

Microsoft Visio can be used to design applications, data, processes, and network infrastructure. It is part of the Microsoft Office Suite. The resulting diagrams can be exported as pictures and imported into other Office applications such as Microsoft Word. Visual Studio also supports the full UML design functionality. The resulting UML diagrams can be used to generate code. Note that the Oracle and IBM UML tools offer similar functionality.

Development tooling

Visual Studio is the integrated development tooling that Microsoft offers. To build web services you can use Windows Communication Framework (WCF) in which both SOAP and RESTful services are supported.

Test tooling

Microsoft offers Visual Studio Test Professional as a tool to manage test plans and tests cases for all project types including SOA applications. If a service has a user interface (for example, a web page), the tool can record the clicks from a manual test and automate them as Coded UI tests. You can develop unit tests for services without a user interface in Visual Studio and associate them with the test cases. They can then be run in Test Professional.

Deployment tooling

A deployment in .NET is called an assembly. In Visual Studio you can create a deployment project that will package all the code in your workspace, using Team Foundation Server.

BizTalk Server

There are three ways to deploy an assembly for Microsoft BizTalk Server:

- **Visual Studio**: The developer can create BizTalk assemblies in Visual Studio and use the *deploy* command to automatically deploy them into a BizTalk application.
- **BTSTask command-line tool**: BTSTask allows you to perform many application management tasks from the command line.
- **Scripting and APIs**: You can use Microsoft Windows Management Instrumentation (WMI) or Windows PowerShell to create and run scripts that automate many application management tasks.

Monitoring

Microsoft has several tools for managing and monitoring your IT infrastructure. You can find plenty of information about this on the Internet. An example is **System Center Operations Manager** (**SCOM**). Of specific interest is the monitoring of BizTalk Server, since this is an important component in the Microsoft SOA platform. It can be split into three categories:

- Availability monitoring
- Health monitoring
- Performance monitoring

All of these categories can be either monitored with Event Viewer of Windows, SCOM, or BizTalk Server Administration Console. For performance monitoring you can also use Microsoft Business Activity Monitoring (BAM).

Error handling

SCOM can automate error handling across the Microsoft stack. The ESB Exception Framework provides error-handling capabilities for BizTalk. It includes retry capabilities.

Summary

You have learned about two approaches to realize the solution architecture from *Chapter 4, Classification of Services*: best of breed or comprehensive suites. Both have advantages and disadvantages. Components from the solution architecture can interact with each other using standards. Using a component you built in the environment of one vendor is not so easy; this is not supported for most components. Therefore, it is important to think about the choice in advance. To show you what a suite can offer, the different products to realize and support SOA from three major software vendors—: Oracle, IBM, and Microsoft— were discussed. Oracle and IBM offer solutions for SOA and BPM that are composed of different acquired products and are integrating their products into comprehensive suites. Microsoft takes a more programmatic approach; they offer tooling that allows system integrators to build products for specific industries. Other vendors and open source solutions offer similar solutions as the vendors mentioned in this chapter. Remember, you don't have to buy a suite; you can also choose a best-of-breed solution or only use part of the building blocks, integrating them using standards such as Web Services.

In the next chapter, you will learn how you can plan and realize your SOA based on a roadmap and business case.

7
Creating a Roadmap, How to Spend Your Money and When?

Now that you know how to design and implement SOA, it is time to investigate how to organize this endeavor in your organization. In this chapter, you will learn how to analyze the benefits an SOA offers to different stakeholders in the context of a business case, approaches to realization, and how to set up a roadmap. The chapter ends with describing maturity and other organizational issues that you might run into during this process. After reading this chapter, you should be able to create a business case, pick a suitable approach, and draw a roadmap to realize an SOA in your organization.

Organize the SOA effort

In the following figure, the steps needed in your organization to create an SOA that realizes the goals of your organization are described. As you can see, this is a process that ends either because there is no (longer a) positive business, or because you have finished with all the features on the roadmap.

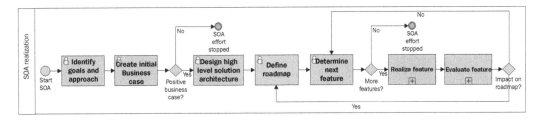

Let's look into the steps in more detail:

1. **Identify goals and approach**: There is a strategy or business goal associated with why a company wants to start with SOA. It is very important to make this explicit, so you can base your business case and solution design on the right facts. These goals are also important during the realization. They guard the whole process; to make sure that the SOA will actually satisfy the needs of the business.

2. **Create initial business case**: Create a business case for the SOA endeavor; we will discuss in the next paragraph how to create a business case for the strategy and the goals we want to accomplish. If the outcome of one of the (SOA) business case scenarios is positive, we create a roadmap or order in which we want to accomplish the realization of our SOA. If the outcome is negative for the SOA scenario, the SOA effort is stopped.

3. **Design the high-level solution architecture**: Based on the scenario that came out of the business case, the solution architecture is created on a high level. Choices such as a complete suite or a best of breed solution, the use of a portal or separate user interfaces, the use of workflow, and so on is described in this architecture. The solution architecture can contain some services, but no operations or interfaces yet.

4. **Define the roadmap**: The roadmap is defined, based on the high level solution architecture, the business case, and changes that are planned in the organization. The roadmap describes the necessary actions to get from the current situation to the desired situation as described in the solution architecture. The actions or work packages are put in order.

5. **Determine the next feature**: The roadmap contains the features and order in which we want to realize the architecture. This step is very simple; we just pick the first item on the roadmap and start a project for this.

Features are things you want to be able to offer or improve as an organization. This can be services, but can also be an attribute of a service. For example, an online store might want to implement a wish list feature, or an insurance company might want to offer a new channel to ask questions about policies.

6. **Realize the feature**: This sub process has several steps, as can be seen in the following figure:

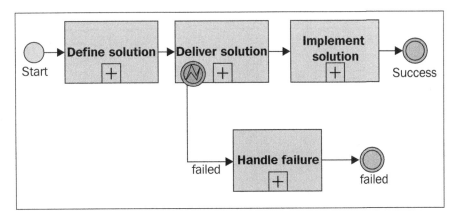

   i. **Define the solution in detail**: This means we need process design, service design, and user interface design, preferably written down in a project architecture. These all describe what part of the overall solution architecture will be realized.

   ii. **Deliver the solution**: Using the development process and development tools of your organization, the solution is delivered.

   iii. **Implement the solution**: After the software is successfully built, the solution needs to be implemented in the organization. People might need training, documentation needs to be updated, working processes might need to be adjusted, conversion needs to be executed, and so on.

   iv. **Handle failure**: The previous steps, were all 'regular steps' in a software development cycle. A possible outcome, like in all projects, is that a project fails. If it fails, it is important to handle the failure. It needs to be determined what the cause of the failure is and whether this has impact on the business case and architecture that has been described. Projects can fail for several reasons, especially if you are doing something new for your organization.

7. **Evaluate the feature**: After you realized the feature, it is important that it is evaluated. The following figure shows the steps you need to take to evaluate the feature:

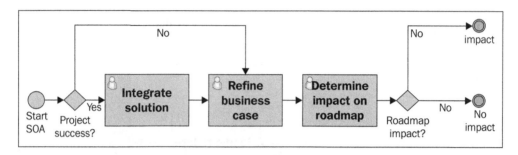

   i. **Integrate the solution**: If the project was successful, we integrate the solution into the overall architecture. The services that are delivered need to be registered in the service registry, the business process documentation in the tool that is used to describe processes and the user interface, and manuals need to be documented.

   ii. **Refine the business case**: You refine the business case based on the experience with the realization of the feature. Regardless of the outcome of the project, things change. You gain new insights in cost, time needed to complete services and features and the impact on the organization.

   iii. **Determine impact on the roadmap**: Refining the business case can have an impact on the roadmap. You need to determine if and what the impact is.

8. **Define the roadmap**: Update the roadmap, if this is necessary, based on the refinement of the business case. This may mean you need to remove features or processes, or that you need to change the order in which you want to accomplish things, the size of the features, and so on.

9. **More features**: You check that there are still items on the roadmap and pick the next item. Otherwise you stop the effort. You repeat steps 5, 6, 7, 8, and 9 until we have no more items on the roadmap.

To summarize this process: you start by identifying your goals and approach. Then you define the initial business case. If the business case is positive, you create a high-level solution architecture. Once that is finished, you define the roadmap and pick the first feature that you want to implement. You realize the feature and evaluate the result. If the business case is still positive and you have more features on the roadmap you repeat the steps until there is no longer a positive business case or until there are no more items on the roadmap.

Business case – benefits for different stakeholders

We have seen in the previous chapters how you can design and implement an SOA based on the solution architecture. A new company can design their architecture and organization from scratch, but most companies don't have that luxury. They need to redesign and implement the architecture, while running the operation. This means that it is not feasible to change the architecture in a big bang scenario, but that you have to grow the architecture gradually. The order in which you execute this depends mainly on the benefits the new architecture offers for different stakeholders.

Apart from benefits, an SOA can result in additional technical complexity and organizational challenges. The technical complexity is caused because SOA introduces new components and standards such as an Enterprise Service Bus or Business Rule Engine in the organization, as you learned in *Chapter 6, Solution Architectures*. The organizational challenges have to do with the changes the way IT is organized. Instead of the silos in the department, departments share services. If a change is needed by one client, the impact on other clients has to be taken into account.

Business case explained

A business case captures the reasoning for initiating a project or task. A business case can be created for the entire realization of your SOA or for parts of it. In general it is a good practice to create an overall business case for the entire program and refine this for every project that you start.

In your business case you describe the following items:

- The background for the transformation:
    - What type of problems do you face today, what is the history?
    - What business goals does the transformation contribute to?
    - What other projects are related to this transformation?
    - What trends and developments are relevant?
- Problem:
    - In this paragraph you describe what you want to accomplish, the mission of the program, or transformation.
    - Describe the business processes that are impacted by the transformation and the problems or ambition that apply to the processes.

- Goal:
    - What are the results of the transformation? Describe this for the business processes that are impacted.
    - Quantify the goal for the problem owner in terms of money, time, and other measurable, specific results.
- Future developments:
    - What are the future developments that you expect?
- Specific requirements of the solution: Apart from company-wide goals, there can also be specific requirements for this specific domain.
- Summary of the scenarios:
    - What are the different possible solutions to accomplish the goals?
- Analysis of the scenarios: List the scenarios, one of which usually is 'doing nothing'. List per scenario the costs and the benefits of each solution, the impact on the organization, the feasibility, the risks, the turnaround or completion date, and the net worth of the scenario. The benefits and costs should be related to the problem and the goals of the organization.
- Advise: Advise the organization to pick one of the scenarios based on the analysis.
- Next steps: Describe what needs to be done next if a positive decision on the business case is made.
    - Describe how many projects will be started
    - Describe who will be the project manager
    - Describe who the stakeholders are
    - Verify the business case during the course of the projects, as was described in the process in the previous paragraph

There are different ways of looking at the business case; from the perspective of the company as a whole, the perspective of a specific department, or from an IT perspective. In the next section, we discuss the possible benefits from these different perspectives and illustrate this with the examples we saw earlier in *Chapter 1, Understanding the Problem?*.

Company as a whole

If the SOA endeavor stems from a strategic decision, the business case is described from the perspective of the entire company. This can mean that for a specific department or business process cost, effort, or other measures deteriorate. But for the company as a whole the business case is positive. When a company makes a strategic choice for SOA, the business case typically is linked to the strategy of the business (operational excellence, customer intimacy, product leadership) and corporate benefits and costs.

Take, for example, the insurance companies that we discussed in *Chapter 1, Understanding the Problem?*. There are several insurance companies that compete with each other. In the following examples you will see two different types of (fictional) business cases for two different strategies of insurance companies.

Example 1 – insurance company WATB needs shorter time to market

Background: Insurance companies that sell health insurance the Netherlands are in a very competitive market. People are obliged to have health insurance, and by law they can switch insurance company in a set period of time: between January 1st and February 1st. The insurance market is consolidating, leaving a few big players who operate different brands. The same is true for an insurance company named **WATB (We Are The Best)**. It is a company that is the result of several mergers, and wants to compete by offering products for very specific target groups. WATB is a product leader and needs to decrease the time to market of the products, because the competition is catching up. Combining existing information in new products and reusing existing information and processes in new products is why SOA is an important step in the right direction.

Problem: Because of changing rules and regulations, mergers and the small time window for customers to switch, the company needs to be able to create new products and launch and market them in a short period of time. This means that information about the new products needs to be available to the entire company and that changes to them need to be available at the same time. Core processes that are impacted by this transformation are policy administration, underwriting and acquisition, and reinsuring. There are also supporting processes impacted: marketing and customer service processes need information about products too.

Goal: WATB wants to create an enterprise architecture in which data and functionality are not duplicated, and changes are available in all systems that use this data and functionality right away. For customer service it is also very important to have up-to-date information about customers in combination with information about products and available policies for the customer, based on their profile. At the end of the project, the information about products, policies and customers should be the same, no matter what the channel or timing of the question is.

Future developments: It is expected that the company will start operating in Europe, not just in the Netherlands. Therefore, the solution needs to take into account different rules and regulations. These regulations need to be flexible and need to be changed without a complete new release of IT systems.

Specific requirements: Communication about claims between healthcare providers and health insurance companies is organized using a central portal that is hosted by an organization named **Vecozo**. The new solution should support the processes and data that are exchanged using this portal.

Summary of scenarios

0-scenario means that the architecture of WATB stays the way it is right now. The current architecture will remain the same, changes in rules and regulations are executed in different systems and synchronized using batch programs.

- **Scenario 1**: Migration to an SOA, using BPM and business rules to support straight through processing and declarative programming. This means a major rewrite of most IT systems and a lot of changes in the current business processes in the organization.
- **Scenario 2**: Migration to an SOA with no specific workflow or BPM parts. Business rules will be applied in the services as needed.

In the table given as follows, the scenarios are summarized in terms of cost, benefit, risk, impact, change, and time it takes to complete the scenario:

- Cost is calculated as the cost to realize the scenario. This includes (IT) development, migration, implementation, training, and so on.
- Benefit is the amount that will be saved in the operation, either because of lower administration cost, savings on cost of labor, increase in customers, and so on.
- Risk is the chance that something goes wrong, combined with the impact if this goes wrong.
- Change is a measure of how much of a change the scenario is for the organization.
- Time is the amount of time it takes to realize the scenario.

Scenario	Cost	Benefit	Risk	Change	Time
0-scenario	500,000	-100,000	high	low	3 months plus
SOA plus BPM	3,000,000	1,500,000	Very high	extremely high	2 years
SOA	750,000	1,500,000	neutral	neutral	1year

[In a real business case, you would also quantify the risks and change that is associated with each scenario.]

In this example, all scenarios are compared with each other over a five year time period. The arguments and numbers here are examples; in your business different conclusions or cost and benefits can apply. You can specify the amount of change that is needed and the risk that is involved based on the knowledge that you have of your organization.

Analysis of the scenarios

In the 0-scenario, we don't change anything about the architecture and the current way of creating new products. Every year 500,000 Euro is needed to create changes to the systems, synchronize the data between the systems, and maintain the synchronization between the systems. The benefit is -100,000 Euro; the company can't keep up with the competition, and is losing customers every year. The systems and synchronization is becoming more complex every year, so the risk of doing nothing is high. The rate of change of this scenario is low; it is business as usual. The time to complete all the necessary work is about three months, but increases slightly every year.

In the SOA plus BPM scenario, the total cost to create the IT support with workflow is estimated to be 3,000, 000 Euro. The estimated benefits are approximately 1,500,000. The benefits are mainly caused by introducing SOA and consist of an increase in customers because the time to market is smaller and they are able to create more sophisticated products. The operation becomes a little more efficient because of the introduction of BPM; this saves some money too.

In the SOA scenario, the total cost is much lower because we only change to an SOA; the BPM part is left out. The benefit is still significant, because the number of customers that can be reached increases just as much as in the SOA-BPM scenario.

In this case, the company decides to go ahead and create a solution architecture based on the third scenario.

Now let's look at the next insurance company. The strategy of the company is based on operational excellence; it competes based on the price.

Example 2 – insurance company TPIR needs to decrease operational cost

Background: Company **TPIR (The Price Is Right)** operates in the same market as WATB, but their strategy is very different. They are owned by a big investment company and target the low end of the market with cheap insurance policies. TPIR was the cheapest, but their operational cost is increasing because they have been adding channels (Internet, for example). All these channels have their own operation and systems.

Problem: As keeping up with changing rules and regulations is expensive, the company needs to cut costs in order to stay ahead of the competition and be the cheapest. This means that they need to use more straight through processing and standardized processes. Straight through processing means that some processes are handled automatically by the systems, without human intervention. This cuts labor cost. Standardizing the process means that employees can work on different products, because they are all handled the same way. More efficient use of available labor will also cut cost; in the number of workers needed, but also in training cost, number of errors in the processes, and so on. Core processes that are impacted by this transformation are policy administration, underwriting and acquisition, and reinsuring. Supporting processes are also impacted: marketing and customer service processes will be changed too.

Goal: Company TPIR wants to create an enterprise architecture in which processes are standardized and data is shared. For customer service this means it does not matter what product the customer is calling, the procedure is always the same. The information on the website is the same as the information that customer service offers, and reinsuring an existing customer is handled by a completely automated system, unless some very specific circumstances apply (bad payment track record, for example).

Future developments: It is expected that the company will start offering other forms of insurance, not just health insurance. Therefore, the solution needs to take into account different rules and product groups. Addition of new product groups should be easy to configure and the processes for these product groups should be similar to the process of health insurance.

Specific requirements: TPIR uses the same portal and is part of the same organization (Vecozo) as WATB. Communication about claims between healthcare providers and health insurance companies is organized using the central portal. The new solution should support the processes and data that are exchanged using this portal.

Summary of scenarios

0-scenario means that the architecture of TPIR stays the way it is right now. The current architecture will remain the same, different departments have different processes and functionality and data are duplicated.

- **Scenario 1**: Migration to an SOA, using BPM and business rules to support straight through processing and declarative programming. This means a major rewrite of most IT systems and a lot of changes in the current business processes in the organization. Processes are standardized, and are as efficient as possible to cut cost in the operation.
- **Scenario 2**: Migration to an SOA with no specific workflow or BPM parts. Business rules will be applied in the services as needed.

Scenario	Cost	Benefit	Risk	Change	Time
0-scenario	500,000	-100,000	high	low	3 months plus
SOA plus BPM	3,000,000	4,500,000	Very high	Extremely high	2 years
SOA	750,000	1,000,000	neutral	neutral	1 year

> Note that the cost for TPIR is very similar to the cost for WATB. This is because we work with imaginary examples and imaginary companies. The cost of implementing SOA and or BPM varies wildly, depending on the current state of the IT, operations, size of the company, and so on.
>
> In this example, all scenarios are compared with each other over a five year time period.

Analysis of the scenarios

In the 0-scenario, we don't change anything about the architecture and the current way of creating new products. Every year 500,000 Euro is needed to create changes to the systems, synchronize the data between the systems, and maintain the synchronization between the systems. The benefit is -100,000 Euro; the company is no longer the cheapest, and is losing customers every year. The systems and synchronization is becoming more complex every year, so the risk of doing nothing is high. The impact of this scenario is low; it is business as usual. The time to complete all the necessary work is about three months, but increases slightly every year.

In the SOA plus BPM scenario, the total cost to create the IT support with workflow is estimated to be 3,000,000 Euro. The estimated benefits are approximately 4,500,000 Euro. The benefits consist of an increase in customers because the time to market is smaller, and TIPR is able to save considerable amounts in the operation because of the standardization and the straight through processing that is achieved by applying BPM techniques.

In the SOA scenario, the total cost is much lower, because we only change to an SOA; the BPM part is left out. The benefit is also lower, because the number of customers that can be reached is increased by less, as in the SOA-BPM scenario. This is because TIPR gets their customers mainly based on their competitive pricing. To be able to offer cheap products, their operation needs to be efficient.

In this case, the company decides to go ahead and create a solution architecture based on the second scenario.

Note that in the previous two examples, the companies decide to change things in their organization, based on their corporate strategy. The changes don't just impact the way IT is handled. In the example of TPIR, operations are standardized so that employees can work on more than one product or brand. The trigger and sponsoring of these projects is strategic and come from the board.

IT

Sometimes, the trigger for changing the architecture in a company stems from the IT department itself. As we saw in *Chapter 1, Understanding the Problem?*, not just strategic drivers exist for moving to SOA. A very common scenario is when IT wants to cut cost, by standardizing systems.

Example – insurance company TMS needs to consolidate systems

Imaginary insurance company **TMS (Too Many Systems)** the company has three systems that use a Document Management System. The Document Management System that is used by the **Insurance Administration System (IAS)** was bought at the time of the implementation of the IAS. The other Document System was purchased as part of the ERP-CRM implementation. Customer data and policy data is duplicated, causing some problems in the operations. This is especially true when they try to make a change to the fields or in the products (policies) they sell. The IT department of the company would like to reduce the number of duplicate systems; they want to consolidate their IT landscape. The benefit in these cases is two-fold: more efficient use of hardware and software (license cost, administration cost, and so on) and an increase in data quality.

The cost of this type of change usually lies in the complexity of the whole IT landscape. The following figure shows the data objects in each system, and the use of the document management systems.

The IAS contains functionality to enter and maintain customers, policies, and claims. It uses DMS-1 to store and retrieve documents (claims that are sent, letters, and so on). The ERP contains information about customers, policy conditions, and finance data. It connects to DMS-2 to store and retrieve documents. The CRM application stores information about policies, customers, and proposals that are sent to prospective customers.

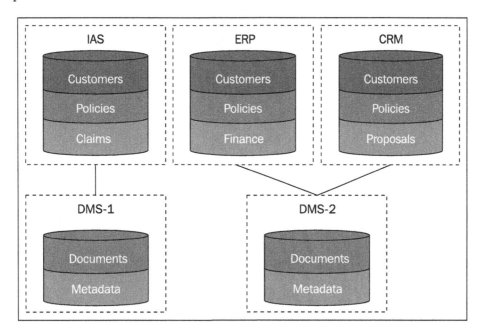

Cost can be cut, in this case, by consolidating the Document Management Systems into one system. This saves on maintenance and license cost. The organization can improve data quality by appointing one source SPOT for customer data and one SPOT for policies.

 A **Single Point of Truth** (**SPOT**) is the definite source you have appointed for a piece of information. The information can be a price, a name, a salary, an office number, and so on. For example, TMS can appoint the CRM system as SPOT for customers and the IAS as the SPOT for policies.

The following figure shows the result. As you can see, there is also an increase in complexity; if the Customer Relationship System is down, the other systems are impacted as well. This means that from an administration perspective, cost and complexity increases.

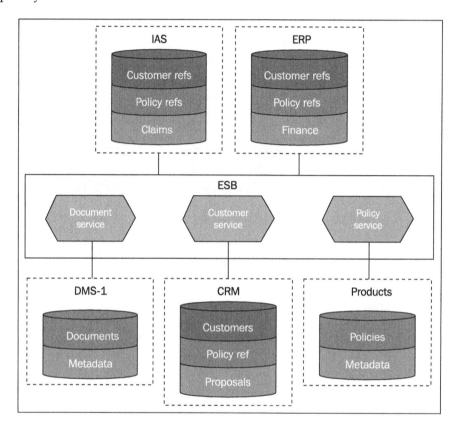

Another solution could be to only consolidate the Document Management Systems, and leave the situation with the customer and policy duplication as is.

To determine the best solution for the company, a business case comparing these three scenarios is created:

1. **0-scenario**: Do nothing, allow for multiple Document Management Systems in the organization.
2. **Consolidate all systems**: Create an SOA and consolidate all systems. This increases data quality and cuts license cost for the DMS systems.
3. **Consolidate just the DMS**: This has a positive effect on the license cost and the administration cost. The data duplication and possibly synchronizations that take place is left as is.

We won't repeat setting up a business case for this example; the steps are the same. First, the goal of the project is determined, second the cost, benefits, risks, impact, and change are described. Based on these aspects, and the qualitative and quantitative comparison of the three scenarios, the company decides which scenario to choose. In this case, the company decided to do a partial consolidation of systems (scenario 3). The cost of changing the big legacy systems at this time is too high compared to the benefit. However, the architecture they want in the future is described in the second scenario. As soon as the ERP, IAS, and/or CRM systems need to be replaced, the business case will be created again.

So far we have seen examples of business cases with strategic perspectives and an example of a business case with an IT trigger. The trigger or perspective has an impact on the choices you make. A strategic decision for operational excellence has lead to a choice for BPM in combination with SOA, an IT-driven need to cut cost has lead to consolidation of systems in the IT landscape. This is not a general rule; the outcome for your organization might be different. This depends on many factors: the current IT costs, the current flexibility, the size of the company, and so on. The third perspective we describe in this chapter is not from the IT department or the company as a whole, but from a specific department.

Departmental benefits

The business case is very similar to the strategic case. The biggest difference is usually the size of the project/program, and the scope of the changes.

Example – insurance company X wants to cut cost

The HR department of the imaginary insurance company X wants to cut costs by outsourcing the recruitment of temporary staff. Most of the changes in architecture will focus around enabling the outsourcing of this process by this department. There are several scenarios with which to approach this: exchanging information electronically periodically, exchanging information real time, or having no integration between the systems of the HR department and the company that is handling the recruitment. There is no 0-scenario in this case, because the company already decided to outsource the process. Doing nothing is not an option the company wants to explore further.

- **Scenario 1**: No information is exchanged electronically. In this scenario, the company outsources the process, including all the information that is needed to support this process. That means that the recruitment agency offers systems to the company for requesting labor, job descriptions, timesheets, and attendance. Information that is needed by the HR department or the finance department is delivered on paper and entered manually by the employees. The following figure illustrates this situation. Both organizations have their own IT systems and there is a connection between them.

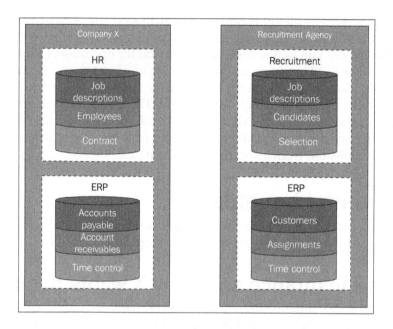

- **Scenario 2**: Information from the HR department is synchronized on a regular basis. Job descriptions, user profiles, and financial data are exchanged. This is done based on batch jobs; data is synchronized or duplicated. The following figure shows this situation:

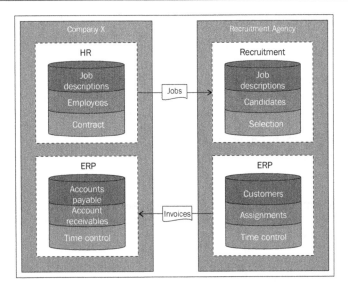

- **Scenario 3**: The recruitment agency uses the information they need from the HR department directly, by calling services. This is shown in the following figure. The Recruitment Agency software calls services to get information about job descriptions, contracts, or employees. The ERP system of the Recruitment Agency calls the financial service that the ERP system of company X offers to get data about accounts payable and time control.

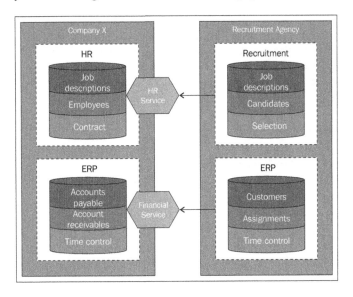

The advantage of this scenario is that company X can change their HR system, without having to change the interface with the recruitment agency.

Analysis of the scenarios

After some market research the company concludes that the HR-XML standard (see http://www.hr-xml.org/) is used by most recruitment agencies. This makes scenario-3 more feasible: they don't have to come up with service descriptions; they can simply use the standard that is already available in the market. A snippet showing one of the WSDLs from this standard is shown as follows:

```
<?xmlversion="1.0"encoding="utf-8"?>
<wsdl:definitions
……
<documentation>
Copyright HR-XMLConsortium. All Rights Reserved. http://www.
hrxmlconsortium.org and http://www.hr-xml.org.Terms of license can be
found in license.txt.

This "noun-specific" WSDL has been auto generated applying a sub-set
of the OAGIS verbs against the draft nouns within the HR-XML library.

Your paths maybe different and need adjusting. This was generated
relative to the entire HR-XML library. If included in a standalone
package, paths and edits will be necessary. However, the patterns and
practices are intact and recommended.

Developers may find this useful in designing their own WSDL in cut and
paste fashion.

Position Opening. Contains details about a position opening, including
requirements for the position as well as administrative information,
such as how to apply.
</documentation>
  <wsdl:types>
    ...
  </wsdl:types>
    ...
  <wsdl:messagename="GetPositionOpening">
    <wsdl:partname="Message"element="hrx:GetPositionOpening"/>
  </wsdl:message>
    ...
  <wsdl:portTypename="PositionOpening_PortType">
    ...
    <wsdl:operationname="GetPositionOpening">
      <wsdl:inputmessage="tns:GetPositionOpening"/>
      <wsdl:outputmessage="tns:ShowPositionOpening"/>
      <wsdl:faultname="GetPositionOpeningFault"message="tns:ConfirmB
OD"/>
```

```
        </wsdl:operation>
        ...
    </wsdl:portType>
    <wsdl:binding name="PositionOpening_Binding" type="tns:PositionOpening_PortType">
        <soap:binding style="document" transport="http://schemas.xmlsoap.org/soap/http"/>
        ...
<wsdl:operation name="GetPositionOpening">
        <soap:operation soapAction="GetPositionOpening" style="document"/>
        <wsdl:input>
          <soap:body use="literal"/>
        </wsdl:input>
        <wsdl:output>
          <soap:body use="literal"/>
        </wsdl:output>
        <wsdl:fault name="GetPositionOpeningFault">
          <soap:fault name="GetPositionOpeningFault" use="literal"/>
        </wsdl:fault>
    </wsdl:operation>
        ...
</wsdl:binding>
    <wsdl:service name="PositionOpening_Service">
      <wsdl:port name="PositionOpening_Port" binding="tns:PositionOpening_Binding">
        <soap:address location="http://www.hr-xml.org/3/ws/PositionOpening"/>
      </wsdl:port>
    </wsdl:service>
</wsdl:definitions>
```

Realization of the batch process is not much cheaper than realization of the services. The HR and ERP systems of company X have features to expose functionality as a web service. They decide to use a light weight open source service bus that can handle the translation of the ERP and HR format of the company to the HR-XML standard. If the company ever decides to implement SOA on a larger scale, they can replace the light weight service bus for an enterprise grade bus.

Approaches

As you learned in *Chapter 3, Service Identification and Design*, there are different approaches you can take to realize an SOA.

When you design a service top-down, you start by analyzing the need for certain operations from the perspective of the consumers of the service. There are two types of consumers relevant in this case: the processes and the user interface. Sometimes multiple processes and interfaces use the same service; other services are specific to one process or user interface component. These services then can be designed: we design the service interface, a contract and build it from scratch. This approach works well for green field situations, when a service or the type of data needed by the processes and the user interface do not exist yet.

Example – Document Management Service

Take for example a company that does not have a Document Management System yet. In that situation it makes sense to identify the document service operation and messages based on the requirements of the consumers and to start building them. Often, however, you already offer (part of) the service in the organization. Take the same example of the Document Management Service. If a company already has a Document Management System, this system often offers an API based on standards or the programming language the system is built with. In that case, designing the service top-down can lead to a mismatch between the API the system offers and what your detail design prescribes.

Top-down identification

The following figure illustrates the problem that arises if top-down identification is applied in this situation. After analyzing the claim process, two services are identified: `ClaimService` and `PaymentService`. The operations needed are `registerClaim`, `reviewClaim`, `payClaim`, and `registerPayment`. The systems in the company in this example don't offer these services, so now there is a mismatch between the services that were designed top-down and the IT that is already available in the organization.

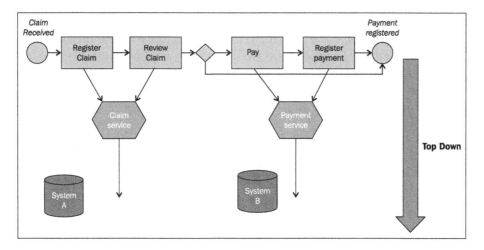

Bottom-up identification

Another approach is to identify services bottom-up as a solution to the problem with top-down service design. However, identifying services bottom up leads to another problem: If you start identifying services by analyzing all your existing systems in the enterprise and offer the functions of these systems to other consumers as services, you end up with a lot of services that don't match the need of the service consumers. This problem is illustrated in the following figure. The APIs that are available from the IAS system, the ERP system, CRM system, and the Document Management System are exposed as services. The APIs are fine grained. The operations or methods and the data structures are very specific; they don't match the need of the claim-to-payment process. For example, to register a claim, a call to the IAS service and a call to the document service is needed. Other services might not be needed, like the ERP system might expose a service for accounts receivable that no process or user interface needs.

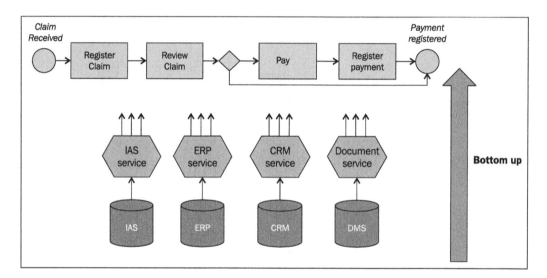

Meet in the middle

A meet in the middle approach solves these problems. You identify the services from the perspective of the consumers, and to make sure the services exist or can easily be realized in the organization you do the detailed design of the operations and the interface based on the existing systems. This is shown in the following figure:

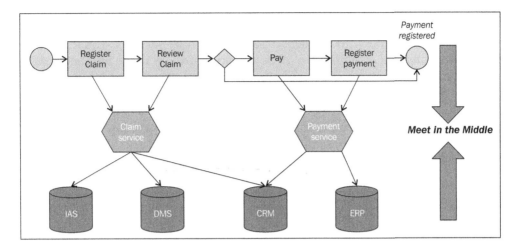

Two composite services are defined: the `ClaimService` and the `PaymentService`:

- The `ClaimService` uses the API of the DMS, the IAS, and the CRM system. The data that is needed by these systems is required by the operations of the service. For example, the DMS needs the author as a parameter to the API to register a document. So one of the parameters of the `ClaimService` is `Author`.
- The `PaymentService` uses the API of the ERP and CRM systems.

This way services are defined that can be realized using existing systems in the organization.

Roadmap

Now that we have seen how you can create a business case, and what the best approach is to identify and design your services, we can look at planning the features, services, and processes. The way to approach this is to create a roadmap. A roadmap is a plan that matches short-term and long-term goals with work packages. It consists of work packages in a specific order.

Work packages

There are several ways of attacking this. You can decide to build service by service, process by process, feature by feature, or a mixture of these three.

Service by service

This means you organize your project scope around entire services. You identify, design, and implement an entire service before you move on to the next service. In our recruitment outsourcing example, two services were identified: HR service and a financial service. If you decide to realize service by service, it means that you first finish the HR service, before you realize the financial service. Often the problem with this approach is that you can't implement it in the organization, because you only support part of the business process. This type of work package is most fit for IT-driven business cases, like the document management example.

Process by process

This means that in the roadmap, you realize and implement the assets you need based on the business process. In our recruitment example, we would identify several processes (from job opening to selection, from work to invoice, and so on). Each process calls different operations on different services. After the first project, the job opening to selection process is implemented in the organization. The HR service and the financial service are partially realized. Only the operations that are needed for the selected business process are implemented and in use. The rest is realized if and when the next process on the roadmap needs it: from work to invoice.

Feature by feature

This means an entire feature is implemented before we move on to the next feature. These features can be technical in nature, or functional. For example, a company that offers the recruitment software in our previous example might want to implement support for self billing as a feature, or single sign on for customers that want to use their company authentication with the recruitment software. The self billing feature is part of a service (invoicing) with particular attributes and requirements. It uses services from other organizations. After a feature is realized, this can be sold to customers who are interested, and the next feature is realized. The scope of a feature is somewhat arbitrary, as opposed to business process or service work packages.

System by system

This is a very special case. If you want to remove a system from your IT landscape, realization of the service and operations that are needed by the users of that system are implemented. Think, for example, of an ERP system that is replaced, or a Case Management System. The roadmap is then oriented towards replacing the system. At the end of the project the old system is obsolete and the organization has migrated to a new system using services. The use of services is introduced to make sure that in the future it is easier to replace the system, because the consumers can still use the same services.

Comparison

It very much depends on your business case, what the approach for your organization is. If you have a business case where you want to consolidate your IT landscape and get rid of duplicate functionality, realizing this by consolidation service by service can be a good approach. If you want to get rid of an entire system, working system by system is a better approach. But, if your business case is based on standardization of processes, breaking down the work packages in processes makes more sense. In the following table, the work packages that fit the trigger and the business case best are listed:

Trigger	Business case	Unit of work	Advantages	Disadvantages
Strategic	SOA and BPM	Process	Return on investment is assignable to a specific budget	Reuse has to be taken into account
Strategic	SOA	Service	Reuse is possible from the start, flexibility is built in from the start	Risk of building services nobody uses. Return on investment is hard to specify
IT	Consolidation	System (or Service, depending on what you are consolidating)	Return on investment is assignable to a specific budget	Replacement of systems means the service design is driven by an application, not by good service design

Trigger	Business case	Unit of work	Advantages	Disadvantages
Departmental	SOA and BPM	Process	Return on investment is assignable to a specific budget	Local process improvements
Departmental	SOA	Feature	Return on investment is assignable to a specific budget	Local calculation, the benefits and cost for the whole company can differ significantly

Of course you can decide to break down the work packages further. Services can be broken down into components, processes can be broken down into services, or sub processes. The point is that the business case and the company goals determine for a large part the way you scope your projects.

The biggest advantage of using processes and features as work packages is that it is easier to calculate the costs and benefits. A service is most of the time used by different consumers. Calculating the cost can become difficult, because investments are done by other departments, not in the department the savings are earned. It is important to use the same scope for calculating the cost and the benefit. If the trigger is strategic and thus covering the whole company, the business case should take into account the company as a whole. If the effort is IT driven, the cost and benefit should take into account all cost from an IT perspective.

We saw that the roadmap you create depends heavily on the type of initiative. A strategic choice for SOA will lead to a longer and more challenging roadmap. If the start of the realization is successful and enforced by management, the chance of success for the whole roadmap is fairly high. An initiative from IT has a much lower chance of success because the business problems are solved indirectly and choices are made based on IT problems. A departmental SOA project is very easy to start but is harder to maintain, because other departments don't have an incentive to cooperate or improve the results.

This does not mean that an SOA program or project based on a strategic trigger is better than a program or project based on an IT trigger or a departmental trigger. It just means that you have to make sure you take all these factors into account when creating the business case in order to be able to make the right choice at the right time.

Maturity and stages

Most maturity models look at SOA in a 'clinical' way and talk about how repeatable and planned the activities to realize the architecture are.

> A **maturity model** is a model that allows executives to review the progress of processes. By having a standard maturity model, it becomes possible to benchmark the SOA levels in your organization. The term maturity relates to the degree of formality and optimization of processes. From ad hoc practices to formally defined steps, to managed result metrics to active optimization of the processes.

While this can be a good way to measure the software maturity in an organization, it does not focus or describe the challenges that are encountered when trying to change something in an organization. As with all change, the organization will hit some hard times during the entire effort.

The most important part is picking the right business process, feature, or service to start with. After that, the follow up needs to be closely guided. A lot of organizations that implement SOA are going through some phases that are very similar to the phases you go through in a relationship: at first you are excited and in love, because you've only just started to get to know each other and everything is new. Then the first disappointments occur, you notice we are all only human. The same is true for SOA; the new approach is not the silver bullet you thought you had found, it is quite hard to keep the discipline and keep communicating about the new design principles. The next phase in the relationship starts, when children are born. This is similar in SOA; after some initial hurdles, you go live with the first project. After a while, you decide to realize the second business process (or feature or service). These children of your SOA, so to speak, are harder to handle than you anticipated, like raising children that hit puberty. They challenge your values and want to do things their own way.

In SOA the same happens with the service providers and consumers, and in new projects. "How is that possible?" you despair. You did everything you could to make everything flexible and reusable, and still it seems to be a lot of work. Finally, your kids grow up and are mature. They find a job and get children of their own. Again, in your SOA endeavor the same thing happens; you keep up with the best practices and your 'children' will grow up to become useful and responsible citizens or your architecture. The SOA will grow and people see the benefits in a realistic way. The next business process (or feature or service) is easier, but you still run into some issues. You are experienced now, so you can solve them quickly and after a while, your SOA is in a maintenance state.

This analogy results in six stages that an organization often goes through when executing the steps to realize an SOA. It is based on the expectations and perceived success of the SOA endeavor by the organization, not on the capability of the organization to execute steps in a controlled way or to measure the success formally.

Stage 0: Starting with SOA

When a company starts with SOA, it is a new exciting endeavor. The business case is promising and people are enthusiastic and expect SOA to solve all the problems. Usually the expectations are a little higher compared to what realistically can be achieved. The architecture is new, and a lot of people need to learn new ways of working. This is not apparent to everyone at this stage.

Stage 1: Newlyweds

During the first project, the first disappointments occur. Solutions that were bought are not performing exactly the way you hoped. Some problems are technically challenging and especially at the beginning the coordination of service consumers and service providers is difficult. Enthusiasm for the project declines and becomes more realistic.

Stage 2: Live

After the first project goes live, some people in the business will be disappointed. The effort that went into the project is not always apparent to them; it took a long time and not everything they needed has been realized. The fact that a foundation is being laid and a lot of new things (architecture, technology, change management) need to be learned is not visible to them. However, some of the benefits are achieved and the foundation for the next steps on the roadmap is laid.

Stage 3: Growing up

When the second project starts, things become more complicated. There are already users from the first project, so changing something requires more meetings and involves more people than in the past. Also, people expect everything to be reusable. Most of the time, this is not the case. The first project will have run into some time or budget issues, not everything is known in advance and it will be necessary to invest some money in improving the things from the first project.

Stage 4: Experience

After a while, things become easier. The change process is in place, administrators know the drill and most services are of good quality. Also, when new services are identified and designed they are of better quality because of the increase in experience in the organization. The organization now gets full benefits of the architecture and more people are satisfied with the status quo.

Stage 5: Maintenance

Now the architecture hits maintenance mode; every major item in the solution architecture has been realized. Now and then systems or services are replaced, outsourced, in-sourced, and so on. Identifying, designing, and maintaining services has become business as usual for your organization.

The stages of the organization are depicted in the following chart. It shows the enthusiasm for the realization of your SOA. The enthusiasm is a measure for the perceived success, or buy-in from stakeholders and sponsors. It is important to keep track of it, because it may result in cancelation of the realization of the SOA, not based on the results in relation with the business case, but based on this perception and expectations.

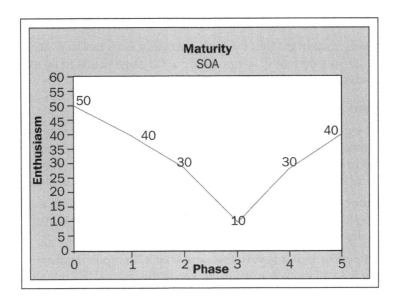

As you can see in the chart, the enthusiasm for the SOA endeavor is unrealistically high, 50 out of the maximum of 60 when you first start with SOA, defining the business case, creating the roadmap, and so on. Once the project starts, enthusiasm drops to a more realistic number. Once the project is live (stage 2), enthusiasm for SOA drops to a low. The project did not live up to the expectations from stage 0, and there are very few notable benefits for the organization. In stage 3, when you start to change and add things, enthusiasm drops to an unrealistic low. In stage 4, you are more experienced and learned from your mistakes. You still need to put effort in, but enthusiasm is back to normal numbers. Once you have a mature SOA, enthusiasm is at its optimum again: there is no silver bullet. The benefits are clear to the organization, as are the costs. Expectations are neither unrealistically high nor unfairly low.

The speed in which your organization travels through these stages depends heavily on the return of investment and the visibility of the successes. That's why it is important to pick small processes where the stakeholders embrace the need for change. The process, feature, or service that is picked as the first to be realized should be something technically challenging. But, not too challenging so everybody can learn and success is likely. It is important to keep the expectations realistic in the beginning, and to communicate clearly that creating reusable services is a learning process. A lot of companies never make it past stage 3, because the willingness to change has disappeared. Often this has no relationship with the actual cost, objective maturity (ability to plan or repeat projects), or actual return on investment.

Therefore, it is very important that your organization does not look at SOA as an architectural or IT-only endeavor. Organizational change needs to be guided. To help this process, a couple of measures are important:

- **Communicate the SOA drivers clearly**.
- **Train the people involved**. Key users, administrators, programmers, project managers; everybody is impacted by a new architecture. Make sure everybody knows what is going to happen. Don't start training too early, make sure the training precedes the actual implementation closely.
- **Communicate your successes**. Often all that is known about a project is its delays, extra money, or other frustrations. It is important that the successes are equally well known.
- **Reward people that adapt to the new way**. Often people don't take a stand and take a 'wait and see' attitude towards the change. People that are actively promoting the new architecture should be recognized for their efforts. If things don't succeed, the people with the 'wait and see' attitude should suffer the consequences, not the people that were willing to change something.

- **Learn from the mistakes**. This is different from blaming people or technologies. If something goes wrong, it is important to know what you can do to prevent it the next time. Nothing more, nothing less.
- **Look for a sponsor**. It is important for all types of initiatives (strategic, departmental, and IT driven) to have a corporate sponsor. Otherwise, the previous goals can't be reached.

Summary

In this chapter, we looked at costs and benefits of SOA for different stakeholders and different strategies. In strategic SOA, the perspective of the business case is from the entire enterprise or company. If the SOA initiative is IT-driven, the business case is defined in terms of IT goals, costs, and benefits. A tactical or departmental SOA is evaluated in terms of costs and benefits for a department.

The roadmap that you create also depends heavily on the type of initiative: strategic, IT driven, or departmental. Apart from objective criteria such as cost and benefit, time to complete the project, and ability to repeat the process, perception is an important factor that determines the ability of an organization to mature.

In the next chapter, you will learn about governance of an SOA: life cycle of services, tooling you can use, and versioning of services.

8
Life Cycle Management

Now that you know how to plan and realize a Service Oriented Architecture, it is time to take a look at the life cycle of services in an SOA. Controlling and communicating the life cycle is important in your organization. Consumers need to know the stage of a service, to decide whether they can use it. Providers need to keep track of versions and support changes that are requested by consumers, without creating chaos or a big financial burden caused by supporting too many versions at the same time. Tooling can help keep track of the services in your organization, including their stage and version. At the end of this chapter, you will be able to control the service life cycle and versions in your SOA and understand the role tooling plays in this process.

Service stages

A service goes through several stages; it has a life cycle. The following figure shows the various stages of this life cycle:

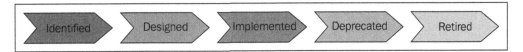

Life Cycle Management

You have already read about most stages throughout the book; you read about the identification and design of services in *Chapter 3, Service Identification and Design* and *Chapter 7, Creating a Roadmap, How to Spend your Money and When?*. In *Chapter 5, The SOA Platform, Chapter 6, Solution Architectures,* and *Chapter 7, Creating a Roadmap, How to Spend your Money and When?* you learned about the implementation of services. Apart from identifying, designing, and implementing a service, you also need to take into account the possibility of cleaning up services. Services can become obsolete, because they don't conform to the requirements anymore, because there are better alternatives or because nobody is using them anymore. The stages deprecated and retired are used for this. The following table explains the different life cycle stages of a service and who is involved in reaching that stage.

Stage	Description	Role
Identified	The service is identified; the organization is aware that it is needed. The approach to identification can be either top-down, bottom-up, or meet in the middle, as you learned in *Chapter 7, Creating a Roadmap, How to Spend your Money and When?*.	**Architect**: Top-down (and meet in the middle) identification of service is based on the process or user interface requirements. **Developer**: Bottom-up identification is based on the existing capabilities.
Designed	The service interface (operations) and contract are known and documented. A developer can create a mockup of the service based on the design by tooling, and clients can be built based on the design.	**Architect**: Top-down design of services based on the process or user interface requirements. **Developer**: Bottom-up (and meet in the middle) design based on existing capabilities.
Implemented	The service is available for consumers to use in production systems.	**Project**, or the service is bought from a **supplier**. **Administrator**: Deploy the service and makes it available.
Deprecated	The service is a candidate for replacement or is obsolete. Current consumers can keep using the service for now; new consumers should use a replacement or find other alternatives.	**Service provider**: Decides to move to this state.
Retired	The service is no longer available for consumers.	**Service provider** decides and the **administrator** undeploys the service.

There are no approval states in this life cycle. Within your organization you need to decide who is responsible for what type of actions and who needs to approve those. For example, you could decide that since you have already created a business case (see *Chapter 7, Creating a Roadmap, How to Spend your Money and When?*) for the realization of the SOA, you don't need to approve identified services explicitly. If something is identified and later you decide you don't need it after all, you can either delete it, or retire it straight away. Another approach is to approve the services in the step *define the solution in detail* (see *Chapter 7, Creating a Roadmap, How to Spend your Money and When?*), as part of the approval of the project architecture.

Keep details out of the life cycle

Beware of adding too many details of the software development and release management in the life cycle of the services. It becomes tedious and outdated very quickly. The only message it needs to convey to the service consumers is, can these services still be used?

Versioning of services

During the life cycle of a service, the service changes because consumers have change requests, laws and regulations change, and errors need to be fixed. First, you learn about versioning of services, and then the relationship with the different stages of a service is investigated. A common way of keeping track of these changes is using **version control**. Version control is the management of changes to documents, software, and artifacts. Changes are identified by a number or letter code; a *version* or *revision* number. Now when do you give your document, data model, or service a new version number? And what type of **versioning scheme** are you going to apply? Usually, you make a distinction between minor and major versions of a change. How does that work in a service? As you have read in *Chapter 2, The Solution* a service consists of an interface, a contract, and an implementation. All these aspects of a service can change. Let's look into the different types of change and how this affects the version of your services.

Type of change – contract, interface, and implementation

Let's revisit the `BreakfastService` example from *Chapter 2, The Solution* and see what the impact is for administrators and consumers when something changes. To refresh your memory, the example was about a diner that offers breakfast. The menu lists all their services. The **contract** of the service states the quality, price, availability, order time, and so on. The **interface** is the way we interact with a service. When ordering breakfast we interact with Jane, our waitress, and the menu that is in English and Spanish. The **implementation** of the service is the cooking of the service, and the serving and eating of it.

Changing the contract

The contract of the service states:

- Ingredients are all local and natural
- Breakfast might contain gluten
- Breakfast can be ordered from 7 a.m. to 1 p.m.
- Breakfast costs $9.95
- Payment by credit card or cash is accepted
- Currency that is accepted is in dollars
- Time between ordering breakfast and the delivery time to the table is 5 minutes to 10 minutes
- Complaints should be delivered to the manager by telephone

Prices of the ingredients increase every year, so after the first year the breakfast place is in business, the cost of the breakfast is increased. This is a major change in the contract, so the owner creates a new menu with the new prices, effectively creating a new version of the service.

The waitress informs the regulars (customers that visit the diner every week) about the increase in advance. Other customers find out when they visit the breakfast place.

After having been in business for a couple of years, the owner of the breakfast place notices that a lot of tourists from Europe and Asia visit his breakfast place. They are suffering from jet lag and have different breakfast requirements. They would rather have something light and pay less for the breakfast. The manager decides to change something in the contract: not all breakfasts cost the same anymore; it depends on what you order. Now this is good news for customers who want to eat less: they don't have to pay for something they did not order. However, existing customers who were used to the "all inclusive" breakfast concept and eat more won't appreciate the change.

Obviously, the owner also has other options, not just changing the service for everyone at once:

- Change the contract for everyone, everybody pays a la carte
- Add the "light" breakfast option to the menu as an additional menu for a fixed lower price of $4.95
- Offer an a la carte option next to the all-inclusive breakfast

After some research, he decides to use the last option, in effect leaving the old contract intact by *adding* an a la carte option to it.

Note that in both examples nothing has changed about the interface, you still order what you want to eat for breakfast, and the implementation has not changed either. The same cook is preparing the breakfast, the same ingredients and kitchen utensils are used, the same cooking method is applied, and so on. The change was in the *contract* of the service. The first change (increase in price) affected all the customers in the same way. The second change was more complicated, it was an improvement for some customers but the owner did not want to scare away the other group. Obviously, the owner does not use version numbers in his menu, but he did create a new version of the menu. The way this was communicated was not with a version number but with an effective date and an announcement to the customers.

Changing the interface

Apart from the contract, the interface can also change. As you have read before, a lot of customers are from Europe and Asia. For these people, it is sometimes hard to speak English. So the owner of the diner decides to print the menu in multiple languages: Spanish, French, Japanese, and Chinese. He also hires some waitresses and waiters that speak multiple languages.

This change has no impact on the current customers; English is still supported as a language to order the breakfast in.

After a while, the waitress who speaks French quits her job and the owner decides not to replace her, because only a small number of customers speak French. This change has an impact on the current customers who speak French; they will have to switch to another language that still is supported.

Changing the implementation

After a couple of years, the owner of the diner decides to hire some new kitchen staff and replace some of the kitchen tools. The new people improve some of the processes in the kitchen, thus creating a more efficient operation. The customers notice that a dish is served a little faster than in the past and that fewer meals arrive cold or over-cooked as a result of the improved operation.

Life Cycle Management

Versioning schemes

You want to keep track of changes to a service, using version control. You don't want service consumers to accidently use the wrong version. This can cost money or cause errors to occur. In the case of an IT service, you don't want to break the code of the service consumers. The types of change that can occur in the `BreakfastService` also apply to IT services; you can change the interface, the implementation, or the contract.

The service as a whole is the unit of interest for the service consumer; therefore you need to version the service as a whole. This means that you change the version of the service if any of the parts of a service change, whether this is the implementation, the interface, and/or the contract. As a consequence, there is no need to version the contract, interface or implementation separately.

Version the service as a whole

Version the service as a whole and you need to version the underlying files. There is no need to version the contract, interface and implementation separately.

The following diagram illustrates this for `OrderService`. This service was introduced in *Chapter 1, Understanding the Problem?* and *Chapter 2, The Solution*. Every time a change is made to a file, this is recorded in the version control system. This has no impact on the version of the service. Once you decide to release the change into production, you determine the new version of the service as a whole.

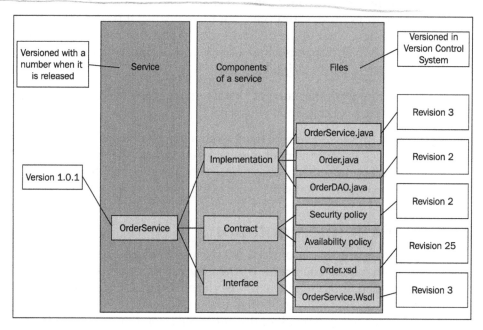

The diagram shows OrderService with a version 1.0.1. It consists of an implementation, contract, and an interface. These are not versioned separately, because this is of no interest to the consumer. Three Java files make up the implementation. These are versioned in the version control system, because the service provider needs to keep track of the changes they make. The contract consists of two policy files: a security policy and an availability policy. These are versioned in the version control system as well. The interface consists of an XSD and a WSDL. These are versioned in the version control system.

Versioning and life cycle stages

There are several things you can do when the version of a service changes, as you learned with the change of contract of BreakfastService:

- You can replace the current version with the new version
- Let the new and current (or old) version co-exist (for a limited time period)

Apart from deciding what to do with the *old* version, you also have to decide what to do with the version number. This depends on the impact of the change; to determine whether a change is minor or major, you have to look at the impact the change has on its current consumers. For example, adding an operation or a field has little impact on current consumers. If you want to make a major change, it is good practice to create a new major version of the service, and to support consumers who want to keep using the previous (deprecated) service for a certain time period.

The following table shows a common versioning scheme that works well for both consumers and providers:

Change type	Minor version	Major version	Previous version
Major change	To 0	Increase by 1	Keep it (stage is deprecated)
Minor change	Increase by 1	Stays the same	Replace it (stage stays implemented)

Let's look at an example; suppose your organization offers OrderService and uses the convention [major version].[major version].[minor version]. The current version is 1.0.0. This means the major version is 1.0 and the minor version is .0.

Now if you make a major change, you increase the major version and keep the previous version available to consumers for a little while. This results in two services:

- OrderService 1.0.0 (stage *deprecated* with a planned end date)
- OrderService 1.1.0 (stage *implemented*)

Life Cycle Management

If the change is minor, you increase the minor version and discard the previous version. This results in one service:

- OrderService 1.0.1 (stage *implemented*)

Supporting two versions has advantages for both the consumers and for the providers. Consumers can plan the migration to the new version, and planning the upgrade for the provider is also a little easier because not everybody needs to test the new service at the same time.

> Note that you will keep track of all the files that you use during development in your version control system. The version number that is of interest here is the version number that you communicate as a whole to the service consumers when the (new version of the) service is released.

Making the version explicit for service consumers

When you are using a WSDL to describe your interface to your consumers, you can make the version of the service explicit by putting the (major) version number in the namespace and in its endpoint.

A namespace in a WSDL or XSD is used to differentiate between elements, and it enables the document to reference multiple external specifications, including the WSDL specification, the SOAP specification, and the XML Schema specification.

By using the version in the endpoint, it is also easier to support two versions of the same service on your server.

Let's see how this works with a WSDL for `OrderService`:

```
<wsdl:definitions name="OrderService-1.0"
  targetNamespace="http://vennster.nl/CRM/OrderService-1.0"
  xmlns:tns="http://vennster.nl/CRM/OrderService-1.0"
  xmlns:xsd="http://www.w3.org/2001/XMLSchema" xmlns:wsdl="http://schemas.xmlsoap.org/wsdl/"
  xmlns:soap="http://schemas.xmlsoap.org/wsdl/soap/"
  xmlns:msg="http://vennster.nl/CRM/Messages-1.0">
  <wsdl:documentation>
    The Order will create an order for multiple orders
    Version history
    V1.0.0 Initial service description
  </wsdl:documentation>
  <wsdl:types>
  ...
```

```
      </wsdl:types>
      <wsdl:message>
...
      </wsdl:message>
      <wsdl:portType>
..
      </wsdl:portType>
      <wsdl:binding>
...
      </wsdl:binding>
      <wsld:service name=OrderService-1.0
        <wsdl:port name="OrderServicePort"
            binding="tns:OrderServiceSoapHttpBinding">
        <soap:address location="http://vennster.nl/CRM/OrderService-1.0"/>
        </wsdl:port>

      </wsdl:service>
    </wsdl:definitions>
```

The highlighted parts show the version in the namespace and in the endpoint (`soap:address`). In this case, the major version is in the namespace (1.0 and the endpoint); the minor version is in the documentation (1.0.0).

With REST services you can make a distinction between versions in a similar way. Basically you have two options:

- Put the version in the URI of the service, for example `http://vennster.nl/crm/api/v1/orders`
- Put the version in the vendor MIME media type, for example `application/vnd.vennster.crm.orders-v1+xml`

> **Multipurpose Internet Mail Extensions** (**MIME**) are used to identify the type of representation that is in the body of an HTTP request or HTTP response. MIME types are sometimes referred to as **CONTENT-TYPES**. The MIME type has a major type and a subtype, separated by a slash.

The major MIME types are text, video, image, audio, and application. Application can refer to a number of formats: `application/xml`, `application/pdf`, `application/octet-stream`, and so on. For vendor specific commercial use, `vnd` is used as a prefix, followed by the name of the company and the domain for example, `application/vnd.vennster.crm`. For personal non-commercial use, `prs` is often used. For experimental or non-standard types you can use `x`.

Putting the version in the vendor MIME media type, has the disadvantage that user agents such as browsers, wget, and so on don't understand the MIME type. So you might not be able to display the resource correctly. The advantage of putting the version in the MIME type is that it has less impact on the client code.

To make the version explicit in a service, you can implement an operation getVersion that returns the version of the service (both the major and the minor version). This operation can also be used as a heartbeat operation by monitoring tools.

> **Versioning tips**
>
> Support the current version and the previous version in case of a major change.
>
> Use major and minor versions. Minor versions can be put in the documentation. Major versions can be expressed in the namespace and endpoint in case of WSDL or in URI, or MIME type in case of REST.
>
> Implement a getVersion method in your service.

Communicating change

In the previous paragraph, you learned what type of change could occur in a service and what versioning schemes you can apply. These changes have some impact on the customers or service consumers. To make sure that service consumers can adjust to the new version of the service, you have to take the following steps:

- Determine if the change is major or minor
- If the change is major:
    - Change the state of the service to *deprecated* and determine the "end of life" date;
    - Create a new version of the service with the state *identified*
    - Announce the change to all current clients
    - Design the new version of the service and change the state of the new service to *designed*
    - Communicate the new design to clients who want to migrate
    - Realize the new version of the service and change the state to *implemented*
    - When the "end of life" date is reached, remove the old version

- If the change is minor:
    - Design the new minor version of the service
    - Announce the change to all current clients
    - Realize the new version of the service
- Communicate the situation to all current clients and prospects that have indicated interest in the service

There are different ways of communicating these changes to your clients: you can announce it in a meeting, you can send emails, or you can update a central registry that describes all the available services.

Changing the namespace and endpoint of the service is a good way of communicating the change at *runtime*. The client calls a service using the namespace in its code, as you can see in the Java example given as follows:

```java
public class OrderServiceClient{
  public static void main(String[] args) throws Exception {
    URL url = new URL("http://vennster.nl/CRM/OrderService-1.0?wsdl");
    QName qname = new QName("http://vennster.nl/CRM/OrderService-1.0/", "OrderService-1.0");
    Service service = Service.create(url, qname);
    OrderService orderService = service.getPort(OrderService.class);
    System.out.println(orderService.orderProduct("ipod"));
  }
}
```

Now let's look at tooling support for versioning and life cycle management.

Tooling

There are two types of tools that help in keeping track of the services that are provided and used in your organization: a registry and a repository. The **registry** lists the services and its features and has an interface to search for services and to add information about services. A **repository** holds the actual service artifacts, such as WSDLs, policies, XSDs, and so on. It's like a library, the registry is the catalog that lists all the books and other things you can borrow. You can search it, find information about the books and CDs and add items to it. The repository is the shelves where the books and CDs are stored.

Life Cycle Management

There are two use cases for searching in a registry: runtime discovery of services and design time discovery of services. Runtime discovery of services means that a service consumer looks for a service, based on certain metadata. The registry returns a number of potential candidates. The consumer inspects the web service description and then binds to the service provider of the server that is the best fit.

The following figure shows the conceptual model of runtime discovery as it is used in **Universal Description Discovery and Integration (UDDI)**, a standard for service registries.

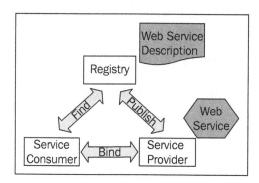

Runtime discovery is hardly ever used in environments where SOAP or ebXML are used. The main reason is the overhead that is involved, apart from searching for the right web service, the client needs to generate a service consumer that is compliant with the WSDL of the service. One of the examples that shows how little it is used, is the fact that IBM and Microsoft offered a public UDDI registry that could be used for runtime discovery, but they have since stopped this effort.

Design time searching is a more common use case. Often prospective or current clients are looking for a specific service or for specific information about a service. Think for example about a project that wants to use `CustomerService`. The project first of all wants to know if the service is implemented already. They need to know the conditions of use and the interface. A registry is a very useful tool in that case. Once they decide to use it in the project, they will have to go to the repository to get access to the artifacts like the WSLD, test suites, and so on.

The biggest difference between runtime and design time service discovery is with design time use of the registry, the binding of the consumer to the provider is done beforehand, during coding of the application; you know what service you are going to call. You have seen this in the previous code sample, the service address and qualified name are known at the time you are building your application. With runtime discovery, the consumer doesn't know in advance what services are available and it is decided at runtime what service to call.

Standards

There are several standards for service registries and repositories. The three main standards that are associated with a certain type of service standard are:

- **UDDI**: The acronym stands for Universal Description, Discovery and Integration. It is a standard that is maintained by OASIS. It defines a set of services to support the description of web services providers; the web services themselves, and the technical interfaces that are used to access these services. It is mainly associated with environments where SOAP and WSDL are used.

- **ebXML RegRep**: This specification is also maintained by OASIS. It defines interoperable registries and repositories with an interface that enables submission, query, and retrieval of contents. It actually consists of two specifications: ebXML Registry Information Model OASIS Standard (ISO 1500-3) and the ebXML Registry Services Specification OASIS Standard (ISO 1500-4). It is based on ebXML, an XML standard that enables an electronic marketplace and is focused around specific business processes.

- **Atom Publishing Protocol**: This specification is maintained by IETF. It is an application level protocol for publishing and editing web resources using REST. This means it is based on HTTP and XML. The protocol defines interfaces for retrieving (collections of) resources, discovery and description of collections of resources, editing, deleting, and creating resources.

Registries are widely used within enterprises for design time use; to keep track of the services, the contracts, and the interface. It is very useful in the process of service identification to determine whether the service is already available, but also later when it is implemented to keep track of the state (life cycle stage) of the service.

Often, an ESB is used to hide the location and specific interface of service in the organization instead of a registry, thus making runtime discovery obsolete.

Instead of buying a service registry or service repository, you can also create your own using a Wiki or your company intranet.

Information needed

Not only if you create your own registry, but also when you use a tool you buy on the market and need to configure it, it is important to realize what information about your services you need to record. A registry helps service consumers in:

- **Finding services**: Potential clients need to know what services are available, how to use them, and what the conditions of use are.
- **Troubleshooting**: Whenever existing consumers experience problems it should be clear who can be contacted to solve the issue.
- **Change process**: If you need a change to the service, it should be clear who to contact.

Find services

To help in the design process of potential consumers, the following functionality should be offered by the service registry/repository:

- Search for artifacts and service descriptions on certain attributes.
- Create taxonomy; you learned in *Chapter 3, Service Identification and Design* and *Chapter 4, Classification of Services* that there are different categories of services. It helps to find a service if this taxonomy is reflected in the registry/repository.
- Store the service owner. If future consumers have questions or there is a discussion about requirements, it is important to know who has the final say.

Troubleshooting

To help the troubleshooting process, the registry/repository should contain the following information:

- **Administrator of the service**: If something goes wrong, the client needs to know who can be called.
- **Consumers of the service**: If a service is down, the administrator needs to know who is going to experience problems so they can be warned in advance (proactively).
- **Version of the service**: If something is wrong with the service (for example, a bug) it is important to know what version of the service is used by whom.

Change process

To support the change process the following information is needed:

- **Owner of the service**: This is the person who decides what is going to be implemented, when, and how much budget is available.
- **Consumers of the service**: They need to be consulted about changes that are planned.
- **Version of the service**: That is currently active and by who it is used.

The following table shows some of the information that needs to be stored in a registry. The list is not exhaustive, and you can expand it to suit your needs:

Attribute	Type	Description
Identification	Alphanumeric	Unique identification of a service.
Functional description	Alphanumeric	Functional description of the service, including its operations.
Type	Choice	Event, process, service, data element (CMD), transformation.
Version	URI or MIME type	See *Versioning Schemes* given earlier in this chapter: namespace or MIME type.
State	Choice	Identified, designed, implemented, deprecated, retired.
State Date	Date	Date the state was set.
Predecessor	Service identification	In case of a new version of a service you can point to the previous version here.
Successor	Service identification	In case of a new version, you can point to the newer version in this field.
Test suite	References	References to one or more test suites, preferable tests that can be run automatically.
Consumers	References	References to applications, processes, services that consume this service.
Contact data	Reference to owner and administrator	Contact data of the owner and the administrator of the service, for example email address, phone number, and so on.
Security (availability, confidentiality, reliability, and so on)	Reference	Reference to policies that apply.
SLA	Reference	Reference to SLA.
Technical artifacts	Reference	Reference to WSDL or technical design.

Life Cycle Management

The references mentioned in the previous table are references to the repository or some external source.

Registries and repositories in your IT landscape

You have read about the relationship between ESB and registry/repository briefly in the previous paragraph. But there are more tools in your organization. The following figure shows how the main tools most organizations use to govern their IT assets, both design time and runtime relate to a registry/repository. The numbers represent different tools, the letters represent information types and the arrows show what tools use this information.

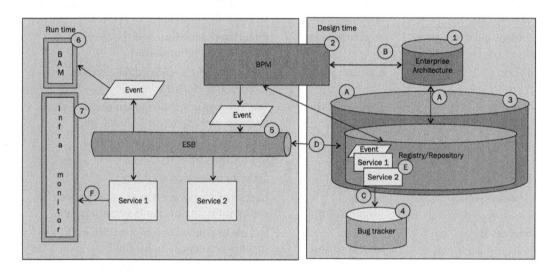

Enterprise architecture tools

In architecture modeling tools, there are often multiple models, describing the to-be situation, the current situation, and situations in between. Descriptions of models of the future situations can lead to the identification of new services that need to be developed. Descriptions of the current situation give insight into the dependencies between processes and existing services. Process descriptions in architecture models are mainly used to track organizational goals to processes, describe improvements, and define capabilities in an organization. As is shown by arrow "A", information in the registry about services is used to describe the current situation in the enterprise architecture modeling tool. New services that are identified in the enterprise architecture model are registered in the registry, as well as the processes that (will) consume these services.

Business Process Management tool

A BPM tool, or the older term, "workflow" tool also holds process descriptions just like the enterprise architecture modeling tool. These models are used to actually execute the process. Some of these BPM tools also support a higher level, more abstract way of modeling, in fact creating some overlap between enterprise architecture tools and BPM tools. Sometimes these tools offer synchronization options, for example by exporting the processes from the modeling tool into the BPM tool or vice versa, as is shown by arrow "B". Arrow "A" shows that the same information is shared between a BPM tool and the registry/repository, as between the enterprise architecture modeling tool and the registry/repository. Executable processes can also be published in the registry, as business services.

Architecture tool versus business process management tool

Use the architecture tool of your organization to identify future services and publish these with the state "Identified" in the registry/repository. Use the BPM tooling to describe executable processes. Publish these to the registry/repository as soon as they are designed with the state "Designed". Update them to "Implemented" as soon as they are in production and being used by the organization.

Configuration Management Database

Configuration Management Database (CMDB) is the same as a service registry or repository, with one difference that it contains information about all the components of Information systems in your organization. The term stems from ITIL and helps you to understand the relationship between components and track their configuration.

ITIL stands for **Information Technology Infrastructure Library** and is a set of practices for IT service management.

In fact, a registry/repository contains only a subset of what CMDB contains, that is the information that is relevant to the service consumers. Logically, the service registry or repository is part of your CMDB, but just for services and focused more on the consumer than the provider. CMDB and registry/repository tooling both offer the same type of functionality, that is options to automatically harvest items from systems, interfaces to add and edit information, and so on. You might wonder if you need a service registry/repository if you already have a CMDB in your organization. If CMDB contains the information that is described earlier in this chapter and the clients in your organization can easily get to this information, you don't need a registry/repository. But often CMDB is used more for the service providers, so you need to arrange for information specifically targeted at the consumers.

Life Cycle Management

Bug and issue tracker system

This tool is used to keep track of changes, bugs, and issues that arise with functionality that is in use, or is being developed. As you can see in Arrow "C", information about services is used in this tool to determine the correct functionality, impact on consumers, and so on.

ESB

You read about the ESB functionality extensively in *Chapter 5, The Soa Platform* and *Chapter 6, Solution Architectures*. An ESB can route service requests from service consumers to the correct service provider. This way, part of the binding of the client to the service is done by the ESB instead of the registry/repository. The address of the service on the service bus is published in the registry so that clients know what to call. These services are *public* and available for consumers. The services that are called by ESB are stored in the registry/repository as well, but these services are private, and not to be called by any other service consumers. The following image shows that services that are created on the ESB are published to the registry. The description of the services that are called by the service bus is imported by the ESB from the registry. This can often be done automatically from the ESB, depending on the standards and brand/suite you use. Arrow "D" in the previous figure also shows this relationship.

The following diagram shows the relationship between a registry/repository and Enterprise Service Bus. The public services, or the services that are exposed to service consumers can be published in the registry/repository (either by a pull or by a push mechanism). The description of the services that are called by the enterprise can be imported by the ESB from the registry/repository, if a formal description exists. This would not be the case if the ESB puts a message in a file (file adapter).

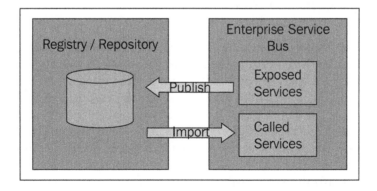

Business Activity Monitoring

Business Activity Monitoring (BAM) is also discussed in *Chapter 5, The SOA Platform* and *Chapter 6, Solution Architectures*. It enables you to monitor business processes and events. It is based on events or alerts that are generated by processes and services. There is no direct relationship between BAM and the registry or repository.

Infrastructure monitoring

Tools that monitor the health of services and servers have no direct relationship with the repository or registry. It is important that services that are published in the registry as "implemented" or "deprecated" are monitored by the monitoring tools and that the contract is used to determine what the desired performance and behavior is.

Summary

In this chapter, you have learned about the life cycle of a service, and what types of changes in a service can lead to a new version of the service. You have seen that you need to communicate and keep track of the services and versions using a registry or repository. This tooling can be purchased or you can create the tools yourself. Finally, the attributes you need to store in the registry and the position of the registry/repository in your organization was discussed.

In the next chapter, you will learn about the governance processes that will keep your SOA under control.

9
Pick your Battles

You have learned in the previous chapters how you can start implementing an SOA in your organization. It is important that you keep your eye on the ball during the realization and use of this architecture. This chapter describes how to make sure you don't lose track of the goals you have set. An important part of creating a successful SOA is that you allow the organization and people to learn, without losing money or motivation: you have to pick your battles! In this chapter, you will learn this from four perspectives:

- The architecture process
- The development process
- Operations
- Change management

There is an official term for picking your battles: governance and SOA governance. Let's look at that first.

Governance

Picking your battles means that you focus on the important things: on the result. Think, for example, about tying shoes. You have been taught to tie your shoes one way, your spouse has been taught another way. Both ways work equally well: neither of you trip over your shoes, the ties look the same and they don't get loose during the day. So the way your spouse ties his or her shoes, has no impact on the result; it is just a matter of habit and taste.

The same applies to activities within your organization. The way you implement a service has to adhere to certain rules to ensure quality. But within these guidelines it doesn't concern anybody, except the team. Picking your battles is important for several reasons:

- You can't control every project or activity in your organization in detail; large organizations have a lot of projects and changes. It is important to focus on guidelines and the result, and not waste time and energy on minor things.
- Change takes time and certain preconditions have to be met to be successful; it is difficult for people to change their ways, and even more difficult to do that with a group of people. This takes time; you can't change everything at once. It is important to focus energy on efforts that have a bigger chance of success and to minimize the impact of projects that are not in line with the strategy.

The formal term for picking your battles is governance. There are several definitions and books discussing governance and SOA governance. Sometimes both these definitions may seem too vague or complex. But if you think about the example listed previously, it becomes clearer. The following definition fits nicely with the term 'picking your battles':

> "**Governance** *is the process of making correct and appropriate decisions on behalf of the stakeholders of those decisions or choices." -From Service Oriented Architecture Governance for the Service Driven Enterprise, Eric A. Marks, 2008.*

The important part of this definition is that you have to make correct and appropriate decisions. Governance is about choices: about what is important and what is not. Importance is not determined by one project, or one supplier, but the stakeholders who are supposed to make these decisions and choices: the board, managers, and team leads.

The purpose of governance is to exercise control over what happens in your organization. If you apply this to your SOA endeavor, you can use the following definition for SOA governance:

> *"SOA governance refers to the processes used to oversee and control the adoption and implementation of service-oriented architecture (SOA) in accordance with recognized practices, principles and government regulations." -From Techtarget* (http://searchsoa.techtarget.com/definition/SOA-governance).

People debate about the difference between governance and management, the scope of SOA governance, and the proper definitions. This chapter takes a more practical approach; it describes important steps for your organization and key success factors that will help you control your effort. You can decide to use a different definition for your organization if that is a better fit, as long as you pick your battles: make the right decisions and in effect, exercise control.

Architecture process

The architecture process plays an important role in controlling the SOA in your organization. In *Chapter 1, Understanding the Problem?*, you learned about different architecture results: target enterprise architecture, reference architecture, and project architecture.

The meet in the middle approach was introduced and explained in the section *Approaches* in *Chapter 7, Creating a Roadmap, How to Spend Your Money and When?*. Using this approach, the services are identified top down. The design and realization is done bottom up. There are two distinct ways a project can start: because an ad hoc business need is going to be implemented, or because a planned feature is next on the roadmap. Let's see what that means for the architecture process in relation to making decisions about your SOA.

Ad hoc business need

When there is an ad hoc business need, a project is defined in your organization. An ad hoc business need is something that comes up in your organization and is not planned on your organization's strategic roadmap. It is important that this ad hoc business need does not interfere with the realization of your architecture and strategy. The following figure shows how you can incorporate the realization of this ad hoc business need into your achitecture process. This way it does not interfere and can even contribute to the target enterprise architecture of your organization:

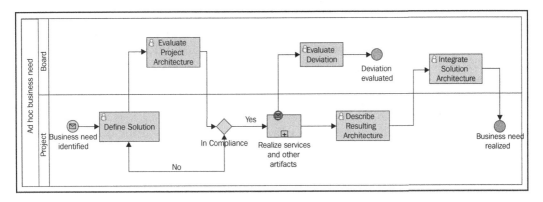

The figure shows the following steps:

1. **Define the solution**: The project defines the solution and describes this in a project architecture document.
2. **Evaluate the project architecture**: The board evaluates the project architecture.

3. **Realize services and other artifacts**: This is the start of the realization phase of the project.
4. **Evaluate deviation**: During the project, issues concerning the principles and guidelines that apply will come up. These deviations from the target (enterprise) architecture are discussed with the architecture board and the board decides what to do with the deviations.
5. **Describe the resulting architecture**: Once the project is finished with the realization, the result is described in a project architecture document.
6. **Integrate solution architecture**: The board integrates the relevant elements of the resulting architecture in the solution architecture.

If the project is in compliance, it can start with step 3. If it is not in compliance, the architecture board can decide to ask the project to change certain parts in the architecture, in effect starting with step 1 again.

Note that this process fits seamlessly in the overall process that was explained in *Chapter 7, Creating a Roadmap, How to Spend Your Money and When?*, in the section *Organize your SOA effort*. It is part of the steps **Realize feature** and **Evaluate feature**. A number of steps warrant a little more explanation.

Define the solution

In the project architecture document, the project explains how they will adhere to the principles and guidelines of the enterprise architecture and what part of the target architecture the project will realize. In case of an ad hoc business need, the latter is often minimal. Assuming the solution architecture of your organization is based on services, a section of the architecture document should be dedicated to what services the project is going to consume and what services the project will realize. It is important that the services that are realized in the project adhere to guidelines that are established in your organization. The project needs to adhere to the classification that you have learned in *Chapter 4, Classification of Services*, or a classification that you have chosen in your own organization. If the project plans to deviate from the guidelines, this should be listed and explained in the project architecture as well. As you can see, this step is part of the **Define the solution** step that was described in *Chapter 7, Creating a Roadmap, How to Spend Your Money and When?*, in the section *Organize your SOA effort*, as part of the **Realize feature** step.

Deviations

As you have seen in the figure, deviations can be identified at the start of the project, and also during the realization of the services and other artifacts. The architecture board needs to evaluate these deviations and decide what to do with them. There are four possible outcomes for each deviation:

1. The deviation is approved, but needs to be fixed in the future. A date or release in which the deviation is removed is part of the approval.
2. The deviation is approved and considered a permanent solution for this project.
3. The deviation is approved and considered an improvement of the target architecture. The deviation becomes part of the target enterprise architecture.
4. The deviation is declined because of the risk for the organization, the impact of the deviation for the organization, or compelling organization-wide business reasons.

In an SOA, deviations from the guideline that a service should be idempotent could occur in certain off-the-shelf software. This would be an example of the second case, because the project can't change the off-the-shelf software without losing the support and other benefits. However, it is not considered an improvement to the target architecture.

Integration in the solution architecture

Once the project is finished, the architecture end state is described and explained to the architecture board. The architecture board evaluates the result and updates the enterprise architecture accordingly. The following changes are made:

- The current situation is updated with the project result. Relevant services and components are modeled and/or marked implemented.
- The principles and guidelines are updated with the deviations that are considered an improvement.
- Design decisions that are relevant for other projects are recorded.

This step is part of the *Integrate solution* step that we described in *Chapter 7, Creating a Roadmap, How to Spend Your Money and When?*.

Planned feature

The other type of project is a project that is started based on your organization's roadmap or portfolio. You learned in *Chapter 7, Creating a Roadmap, How to Spend Your Money and When?*, how to create such a roadmap. Let's revisit the architecture steps and compare them with the ad hoc business need process.

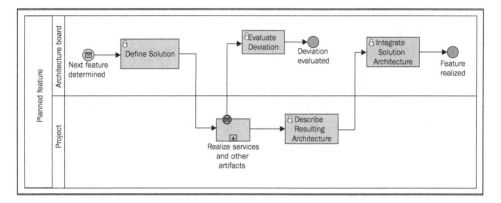

The steps are as follows:

1. **Define the solution**: The board defines the solution and describes this in a project architecture document.
2. **Realize services and other artifacts**: This is the start of the realization phase of the project.
3. **Evaluate deviation**: During the project, issues concerning the principles and guidelines that apply will come up. These deviations from the target (enterprise) architecture are discussed with the architecture board and the board decides what to do with the deviations.
4. **Describe the resulting architecture**: Once the project is finished with the realization the result is described in a project architecture document.
5. **Integrate solution architecture**: The board integrates the relevant elements of the resulting architecture in the solution architecture.

As you can see the only difference from an architecture perspective is the way the project is started. As this project is part of the realization of the strategic roadmap, the architects can define the solution in advance; they know when it is started and have a say in the scope. With the ad hoc business need, it is a trigger coming from the organization, so the architect board does not know the scope and solution. Make sure that the solution is a high-level description with an emphasis on guidelines and principles. It should provide enough guidance for the project to base their detail designs on. It is perfectly OK if you still have unresolved issues or questions. The rest of the process is the same.

Pick your battles

There is a natural conflict of interest between the architecture board and a project. The reason for defining a project is that your organization wants to monitor time, money, and results in a well-defined manner. The architecture board is responsible for the long time impact of choices, and needs to make sure that all projects contribute to the overall goals of the organization. Something that saves money for the organization as a whole can cause the project to become more expensive, or take longer. In the following table, common SOA issues that cause friction between projects and your architecture board are listed. Obviously there are issues that occur in all architecture types, but these are not relevant for this discussion about SOA governance.

Issue	Architecture board	Project
Reuse services	<ul><li>Increase data quality</li><li>Less duplication of functionality</li><li>Saves money</li></ul>	<ul><li>Dependencies outside the project are hard to manage</li><li>Takes time to investigate</li></ul>
Create reusable services	<ul><li>Saves money for the entire organization</li></ul>	<ul><li>More cost in this project</li><li>Takes time to investigate</li></ul>
Use an **Enterprise Service Bus** (ESB)	<ul><li>Services are easier to change later</li></ul>	<ul><li>More cost in this project</li><li>Takes time to realize the ESB components</li></ul>

The friction between long-term goals and projects is not a bad thing; it is designed to occur. It is important that this friction is balanced; if the architecture board has too much influence, this has a negative impact on the success of projects. If the projects have too much influence, this has a negative impact on the sustainability of the endeavor. Of course, this also is true in other architectures. But because SOA is about services that are used by service consumers, architecture becomes more important to make sure that the services are actually used, and not just rebuilt every time they are needed in a project.

Architecture has to show it has a positive influence on the quality of the result and projects have to show they have a positive influence on the organizational goals. If you evaluate solutions that projects propose, make sure that you focus on the business case and only try to enforce guidelines and principles that are based on the company strategy. Don't interfere with things that only impact a specific department, or have no impact on the architecture as a whole.

> **Architect tip**
> Focus on the business case and only declare a project 'not in compliance' if there are negative consequences for the organization as a whole. The target architecture is a means to an end, not the goal. Talk with the project about possible improvements and find out how feasible they are within the limits of the project.

Let's look at an example. Suppose a project proposes to use REST services instead of SOAP services in their project. The company has decided a couple of years before that SOAP services are the standard to use for services.

When they evaluated the proposed solution by the project, the architecture board took the following aspects into account:

- Service orientation is a key value in the company's strategy. REST services support this value, they are first class services too.
- Standards change and the organization can use the ESB to translate from REST to SOAP, if needed. That way, current and future service consumers can use either type.
- The developers in the project explained to the architecture board the advantages of using REST for their project. It is a frontend project, where REST is more flexible and common than SOAP.

Instead of delaying the project by denying the proposal to use REST, the architecture board decides to give the project some positive advice. They offer to help with the design of the services and a versioning scheme. After the project was finished, the board decided to add REST services to the list of SOA standards, because the results were positive for both the project and the organization as a whole.

Development process

Services that are identified in your organization are either used or created in the development process. The guidelines and principles that are defined in architecture come to life during the development process.

The process in an SOA is a little different from traditional projects in a silo, that is, they are in an isolated environment, less dependent on the rest of the organization. It is, however, very similar to any integration project. So if you are familiar with integration projects, you won't have a lot of trouble working in an SOA environment, as far as development is concerned. The following figure shows the development process for a service.

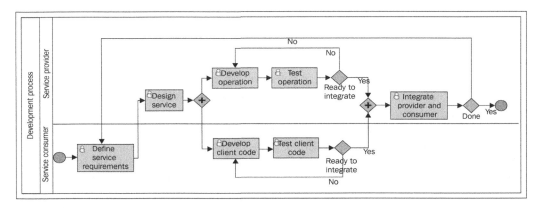

1. **Define service requirements**: Usually development of a service starts with defining the service requirements. Often the service has already been identified. What is not known yet are the operations. Gathering requirements from the first consumer(s) will help you get the right input for the design, together with the architectural constraints that were described in the architecture document.

2. **Design the service**: Once you have the requirements from one or more consumers, you can start designing the service. This means you define the operations and the parameters of the operations. Thinking about the contract (load, security, and so on) is also part of it, as well as designing the implementation. After this step, the service moves from stage identified to design.

3. **Develop operation, test operation, develop client code, and test client code**: Once the design is done, both the service consumer and the service provider can start working in parallel. They both develop code and make sure it is working (test it).

4. **Integrate provider and consumer**: The client code is integrated with the provider, once both have working software. If the feature or service is done, the project ends. If the project is using a more iterative or agile approach, the project iterates a couple of times over the requirements; design and implementation steps for the same service or feature.

Pick your battles

Often projects implementing services fail because they fail to look at the requirements of the service consumers. This leads to overly generalized services that are difficult to use. Think, for example, about a CustomerService. Projects that create services independently of (future) consumers, design operations such as getCustomer(id), searchCustomer(SearchCriteria), and updateCustomer(Customer). This leads to a lot of work for the service provider; they need to implement these operations. It is, however, also a lot of work at the consumer side. Think, for example, about an application that wants to update the address of a customer. In order to do that, they need to get the entire customer object, replace the address (or append it?), and call the updateCustomer(Customer) operation. It would be much more convenient to have an operation move and just pass the new address and the customer ID to the service.

Service provider tip

Only design and realize services and operations that are needed by one or more specific consumers. Make sure the operations and parameters are useful for more than one consumer.

On the other hand, consumers have very specific needs and sometimes ask for features or operations that interfere with the use of the service by other consumers, or which would result in an explosion of the number of operations in a service. For example, a consumer might want to update the address and the marital status of a customer at the same time. This is very convenient from this service consumer's perspective. But the marital state of the customer is not something other departments use. So this service is not reusable enough to warrant a separate operation. In this case, the service consumer needs to update the marital status and the address in two separate calls.

Service client tip

Discuss your requirements with other departments and service consumers, to discuss the best way to use the services.

This might seem like the responsibility of the service provider at first. But your organization will greatly benefit if everybody sees services as something they share with the rest of the organization. It often helps to see how other departments use the functionality and data from the service, to understand the changes that are needed. When you start using an enterprise wide service such as the `CustomerService`, some of the business processes in your department will change. Instead of asking your customer for their address you will already have access to it, using the service. Obviously, there will be data and functionality that you use, that is not available from `CustomerService`; functionality and data that are specific to your department. Instead of adding this to the shared service, you need to handle the difference between shared and specific functionality as a service consumer. Talking to other departments to find out how they handle this, helps you in formulating requirements for service. Other departments can also explain how much time it takes to realize the integration and other details that are not the focus of the service provider.

Operations

After the service and service consumer have been realized, they need to be installed and monitored in the acceptance environment and, more importantly, in production. The success of your SOA not only depends on the way it is developed, but even more on the way it is operated as well. Operations are the most difficult part of an SOA. Reasons for this are as follows:

- **More real time dependencies between components**: In traditional environments, functionality is duplicated. If the server that runs your ERP system goes down, the marketing department can still use their CRM application. But in an SOA, if a service goes down, multiple consumers will suffer the consequences. So changing hardware or restarting a server potentially has a high impact on the operation of your business. It is important to think about this in advance and have contingency plans ready.

- **Services are the element of control, not a whole application or technology layer**: In the past, operations monitored applications or layers. Operations were responsible for the database layer or for the ERP application. Releases for such applications are scheduled regularly, for example, every three months, and usually containing a lot of different changes. With services, the units you monitor and control are smaller. This means that more releases are scheduled. The advantage, however, is that these releases are smaller, making it easier to control the impact.

Pick your Battles

- **More enterprise-wide infrastructure components to monitor**: In traditional environments, there are a few of these components, such as e-mail. In SOA there are more of these services. Examples are an Enterprise Service Bus, a Service Registry, and Business Process Management tooling. These components require more work, because they impact more users, are more prone to be the target of security-related attacks and have to withstand heavy load.

- **No user interface to monitor the services**: Traditional applications have a GUI, making it easy to check if everything is up and running. Services don't always have a user interface. For example, the `CustomerService` that is used by other systems does not have a GUI. So when it's down or something goes wrong, the error is detected by people using the GUI of the service consumer. This makes it harder to detect the real cause of the problem for operations. This can be solved by using tooling that alerts operations when performance deteriorates or when services are down.

- **Error handling and 'lost messages'**: Some of the communication is asynchronous. Sometimes an error occurs. This can go unnoticed for weeks at a time, because there is no visible error for the user. The faulted message is 'waiting patiently' in the error queue. Operations have to make sure they monitor all the asynchronous communication vigorously and have procedures and guidelines in place to detect these problems. Service providers have to comply with these guidelines and offer proper error handling for these types of error.

Operations in IT are like choosing transportation: a rowing boat is less complicated to maintain and operate then a sailboat. But if you want to be fast, go far and don't want to be taken over by the waves, you better take a sailboat. It's worth the effort, time, and money. The same applies to SOA. It is not free, it comes with a cost: it is more complex and takes more time to set up than a traditional silo IT environment. But in your business case you have determined that the benefits outweigh the cost. You have to make sure that the consequences are taken into account in the execution of the business case: measures should be taken to solve the issues listed previously.

Another thing that needs to be decided is the financial aspect of a service. In traditional silo environments, it is often easy to allocate cost to a specific department. In SOA, this becomes harder for the following reasons:

1. Some costs depend on usage (or number of service calls), others on complexity.
2. Not everyone starts using the service at the same time, so a disproportionate part of the financial burden is put on the first consumer.
3. You want to reward departments for using services, not 'punish' them for using services.

Depending on the type of goals you are trying to accomplish, you need to come up with a financial scheme for the realization and maintenance of your services. It is an important decision to make, because it will greatly influence the perception your service clients have about the cost of SOA. There is not one correct scheme to solve this, the type of business case (strategic, IT driven, departmental) is an important factor that determines how you want to solve this.

Pick your battles

As you have seen now, operations play a big role when your organization moves to an SOA. Often this isn't acknowledged until the very last moment; when you are about to deliver the software for installation. This leads to delays in delivery and a lot of frustration between the different stakeholders.

Common issues that occur between operations and projects are given in the following table:

Issue	Project	Operations
Releases	Release new features as soon as possible to minimize time to completion	Releases based on time intervals to maximize stability and predictability
Access to services	Offer access to services to minimize rework and satisfy business requirements	Access restricted to ensure security policies and minimize risks
Procedures	Minimize the procedures involved with releasing and using services to maximize flexibility	Adhere to strict procedures to maximize stability
Access to infrastructure	Have access to and manage as many environments (development, test, and so on) as possible to maximize flexibility	Minimize access to the test and acceptance environments to maximize stability and control

Pick your Battles

Like friction between the project and architects, the friction between operations and the project have a purpose. People in operations are responsible for keeping the IT up and running in your organization. If something goes wrong, they are the ones that get called in the middle of the night and need to fix it. For that reason they focus on stability. The projects in your organization are responsible for making changes. They are the ones that get called on by the business if the needs are not met. For that reason they are focused on changes and innovations. Without operations, your IT would fall apart because new services and technologies are incompatible, not tested, and nobody knows how it works. Without projects your organization would slow down and less innovation would occur, making it hard for your organization to compete.

> Operations tip
> Prepare for SOA by adjusting your procedures and policies regarding access and release management when the project is started (long before it goes live).

Think, for example, about a company that wants to use a Cloud solution for their recruitment process. One of the requirements of the HR department is that the e-mail and calendar services of the organization are used. This has several advantages:

- The mails from the HR department don't get scattered around over multiple mailboxes, there is one place where all e-mail communication is stored
- Availability for job interviews with job applicants can be based on the calendar they already use
- No extra e-mail address and account details to remember
- Features of the mail and calendar services, such as mobile access that are available from the corporate mail service, are automatically available for the recruitment mails

When first confronted with this requirement, operations reacted negatively to the request. Opening up the e-mail and calendar services would mean opening up a vital infrastructural service in the network of the organization.

After some research, however, they came to a different conclusion. The solution they were using in the organization supports web services that are secure and take into account access from outside of the network.

They decided to go ahead and created a new policy for access to the web services and also changed the procedure for upgrades of the mail and calendar services to include tests with the web services. The Testing and Acceptance environments were updated to include the web services.

[Project tip

Involve operations at the start of the requirements gathering process. This way they can provide input for the new services and prepare for the changes.]

Change management

Once something has been realized and is in production, change requests will start to come in. You learned about life cycle management of services in the previous chapter. Apart from the life cycle of services, there are other aspects to take into account when you look at the change process in an SOA. Basically, there are two major differences compared to silo architectures:

- More and other types of users (service clients) need to be involved. Traditional applications cater for all the needs of a specific department. Think of a **Customer Relationship Management** (CRM) application. If something needs to be changed in the application, the impact of the change on sales or customer relations department is discussed. But in an SOA, services are shared by multiple departments. The back offices also use the CRM services. If something is changed, not just the sales department needs to be consulted, but all the departments that make use of the services. This includes projects that are not in production yet.

- The unit of control of a change needs to make sense to the clients of the services. Often in large organizations there are different change managers for different types of applications. For example, there can be a change manager for office automation, and a change manager for middleware. This is difficult for prospective services clients. Remember the cloud provider that wanted to use the exchange services for the recruitment process. They had to apply for a change at the office automation change manager for using the web services from the mail and calendar services. They had to apply for a change with the middleware change manager because the services needed to be exposed on the Enterprise Service Bus. One of the changes could be granted, and the other one could be denied. This is very frustrating, and causes departments and projects to look for different solutions. It is very important that changes are evaluated from the consumer point of view, as a whole. Internally, a breakdown is created to evaluate the impact the change will have.

[Change tip

Hide implementation details in your demand or change management as much as possible. Make sure you talk about changes in terms of requirements and business needs. Evaluate the results as part of the business processes.]

Pick your battles

Change management in an SOA can be difficult, because users tend to disagree with each other on priorities and direction of changes. Also, getting projects and users involved is difficult. Projects tend to minimize external dependencies. If a change they need on a service is not part of the project scope, they tend to reject responsibility for it and don't want to spend resources on it. Users often find services abstract and fail to see the relevance to their process. Last but not least, sometimes departments and users want changes to make their own work easier, causing difficulties later in the process.

This can happen, for example, when an organization decides to create a CRM service. All other departments use the data from the CRM service in their applications. Applications can either call the CRM service directly using a web service or synchronize their application with the CRM system. So far, all the users are happy. It is agreed that changes in customer data are made in the CRM system. Now, the problems start. Users from a back office application are used to keeping their own records about customers. They don't want to depend on other departments for that. They apply for a change to the synchronization feature, to make it two-way. The change board does not want that for several reasons:

- The source of the data will become unclear, if everybody can change customer data. The advantage of having one source in the company is that the quality of the data increases. If everybody can change the data, this is no longer true. People will start changing the data back and forth.

- Technically it will become more complex; two-way synchronization is more complex than one-way synchronization.

The change would make the work process for the department that requested the change easier. But for the organization as a whole, it would mean that the quality of the customer data would deteriorate and that other departments would suffer the consequences. Instead of agreeing to the change, an analysis of the data the department needs is done. It appears that a majority of the data is only used by the specific department. There is no need to synchronize this data with the central CRM system. Two fields remain: the e-mail address and telephone numbers of customers. These are available in the central CRM service and used by several departments. The change board and the key users agree to maintain the rule; the CRM system is used to update data. The department gets access to the user interface so they can change the e-mail address themselves. The application keeps track of who changes what. After three months, the quality and stability of the e-mail address and telephone number is evaluated. The result is good; the department does not make a lot of changes. The changes that are made are valid and the quality of the data improved.

You have seen in the previous example that the friction between an individual service client and the change board occurs because they both have different interests. The change board looks at the impact for all the departments and the overall organization. The individual departments know their own processes best. Therefore, it is very important that all departments are involved in the change process.

Summary

In this chapter you learned about the processes that are involved in governing the SOA endeavor in your organization from different perspectives: the architectural point of view, the development point of view, the operations perspective, and the change process point of view. From each point of view there are things that are different compared to traditional silo organizations. You learned for each point of view the important battles. In the last chapter, you will learn how these processes fit in with existing processes within your organization.

10
Methodologies and SOA

You have learned about SOA from the perspective of architecture and learned how to plan and realize an SOA using a structured process that results in a concrete roadmap. In this chapter you will learn how popular processes, that are used in IT projects such as **BiSL (Business Information Services Library)** for information planning and functional requirements, ASL for application management, and PRINCE2 for project management, fit in an SOA environment and SOA roadmap.

This chapter provides:

- An overview of existing, popular processes that are often executed to manage the IT landscape of an organization
- An example of a methodology for every process that is discussed
- The impact that SOA has on these processes

The following processes are discussed:

- **Demand management**: The process of managing and prioritizing the functional demands of the organization, its clients, and its end users. These demands need to be translated into concrete projects to realize them.
- **Project management**: The process of managing the realization of IT solutions such as applications and services.
- **Software development**: The process of designing, developing, testing, improving, and delivering software components.
- **Application management**: The process of monitoring and maintaining the organization's applications technically and functionally on the behalf of its end users and clients.
- **IT service and operations management**: The process of technically monitoring and maintaining the IT assets and infrastructure of an organization, and providing IT services to end users.

These processes can be implemented within a single organizational unit, spread across departments of an organization, or spread across organizations if IT services are outsourced.

The methodologies that are discussed as examples are generic and can be applied to SOA and non-SOA environments alike. Methodologies often provide blueprints for processes, best practices, and a common language and definition for stakeholders. There is overlap between methodologies, as they tend to describe processes of bordering topics. For example, methodologies for application management might describe processes that belong to IT service and operations management, and vice versa.

> The methodologies chosen as example are ones that are popular in the Netherlands and/or Western Europe. As a cultural side note, the Dutch as well as some other Western European countries are very much oriented towards structured processes and rigid documentation and therefore embrace methodologies easily for better or for worse. Popularity and application of such methodologies differ as per continent and region.

Demand management

Demand management is responsible for realizing, maintaining, and improving the information and functional needs of an organization from a business perspective: clients and end users. This is called the **demand side**, as opposed to the **supply side** of an organization that is formed by IT operations, vendors, suppliers, and so on. You can read more about demand management, its definition, and related subjects on the website of the ASL BiSL Foundation (http://www.aslbislfoundation.org).

Demand management collects and prioritizes:

- Demands and wishes for new solutions to support the organization's goals and strategy
- Issues and bugs of existing solutions
- New rules and regulations that apply to the organization and need to be implemented

Demands are analyzed and for those demands that need to be realized the following activities are started:

- Demand management initiates projects to realize new solutions, or change existing ones. Solutions can be IT solutions such as applications or non-IT solutions such as new working instructions or setting up a new department. Closely-related projects can be bundled into programs. Programs and projects are managed through portfolio management, which is part of demand management, or is a separate responsibility within the organization.
- Demand management asks application management or IT service and operations management to change existing applications or the existing technical infrastructure to solve issues.

Business cases can be created during analysis to decide whether demands should be realized. Whether demands should be realized generally depends on funding (who has the money to realize solutions) and politics (who are influencers, who have the power to decide that demands should be realized). Demand management verifies demands that are realized on correctness and completeness.

Demand management can be a centralized function within an organization, decentralized among different departments and managers, or be a mixture of the two. In the latter case, demands are managed centrally or departmentally based on criteria such as importance, impact, scope, cost, and so on. In a centralized model, end user groups and departments need to be represented by stakeholders in the demand management organization. Demand management is generally not outsourced.

Methodology

BiSL is an example of an IT demand management methodology. It provides a framework that divides demand management processes into the following levels:

- Strategic processes
- Management processes
- Operational processes

BiSL describes the processes within these levels, their hierarchy, and the relations between them. Examples of demand management processes described by BiSL are:

- Supply chain management (strategic)
- Relationship management with end users and their organizations (strategic)
- Financial management (management)
- Contract management (management)
- End user support (operational)
- Change management (operational)

 Organizations that use BiSL for demand management often use it together with **ASL (Application Services Library)** for application management and **ITIL (Information Technology Infrastructure Library)** for IT service and operations management.

See http://www.aslbislfoundation.org/en/bisl for more information on BiSL.

Impact of SOA

Traditionally, demand management has focused around applications and the business processes that applications implement such as creating new applications, replacing applications, and changing existing applications to suit the needs of end users. Such applications appear quite independent of each other since data and functionality is duplicated. In an SOA, services are used to create composite applications and business processes so that functionality only needs to be created once and changed in one place. The demand management processes need to be tuned to reflect this way of creating solutions and focus on creating reusable services.

In *Chapter 7, Creating a Roadmap, How to Spend Your Money and When?*, section *Organize the SOA Effort*, you learned what activities are needed to plan and realize an SOA. These activities should be included in the demand management process; some examples are as follows:

- Parts of a new solution that is realized for a specific consumer could be valuable to other consumers as well. This might mean that additional work needs to be done in the project to create reusable services. Launching customers that sponsor the solution should be rewarded for creating such reusable services and not be punished with higher costs and having to deal with more dependencies and other consumers. Vice versa, when demand management initiates a new project to create a solution, the service registry and repository should be inspected to look for already existing services that can be used in the new solution.

- Changes to existing applications might involve changes to services that are used by other consumers as well. Especially when changes are initiated on behalf of one specific consumer, it is important to analyze the impact of changes as these might affect other consumers. As you have learned in *Chapter 8, Life Cycle Management*, a registry and repository, in which service dependencies are documented, is a helpful tool for impact analysis.

- Suppliers such as software and application vendors that are managed through demand management need to deliver solutions that fit in an SOA environment. For example, a vendor of packaged applications might need to offer services in its applications so that these can be integrated with other applications and processes in your organization.

- Life cycle management needs to deal with service versioning besides introducing, changing, and deprecating applications.

Link demand management and enterprise architecture

It is important that demand management not only looks at the specific interest of a particular customer but also takes into account enterprise-wide benefits. Demand management and enterprise architecture should work together to make sure that solutions are both valuable to end users and customers, and are created in such way that the enterprise-wide benefits of SOA are realized. Demand management is focused on the first, while enterprise architecture is focused on the latter. Make sure that demand management and enterprise architecture processes are implemented in such a way that they communicate with each other.

Project management

Project management is the process of delivering well-described solutions managed using activities such as planning, budgeting, prioritizing, communicating and influencing stakeholders, and assembling and managing the project team. The solution that needs to be delivered by the project isn't necessarily a piece of software, but can also be the creation of a new department for example. Demand management initializes projects.

Projects are bounded in scope and time as opposed to continuous processes and activities such as human resource management and customer relationship management within organizations.

Project managers are responsible for delivering the specified solution within certain constraints such as budget, and are allocated resources to achieve this goal. Projects can be managed from the demand side (for example, customer) as well as the supply side. The overall project responsibility and acceptance of the realized solutions are demand-side activities.

Project managers can roughly influence the following aspects to steer the project:

- Quality of the solution
- Cost of the solution
- Time that it takes to realize the solution

Methodology

PRojects IN Controlled Environments 2 (PRINCE2) is a project management methodology that is popular among others in Western Europe and originates from the UK. PRINCE2 can be used to manage IT projects as well as other types of projects and follows a process-driven approach to manage and complete a project. The following figure that is taken from the PRINCE2 Wikipedia page shows the processes involved in PRINCE2 in blue.

Chapter 10

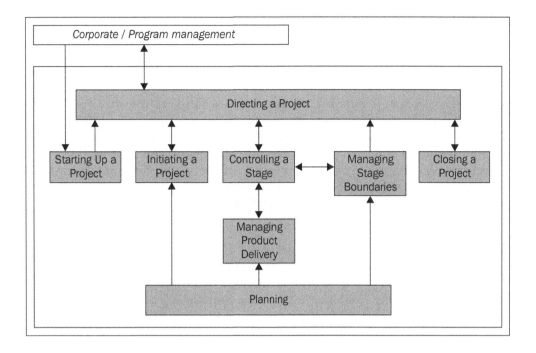

A project managed by PRINCE2 defines products that need to be delivered. An important aspect of PRINCE2 is that a project is broken down into multiple stages that deliver (parts of) products based on work packages.

PRINCE2 not only describes the process activities that need to be executed, but also:

- Artifacts that need to be created during the project such as a project brief, **project initiation document** (**PID**), business case, and so on.
- Stakeholders that need to be identified and groups that need to be created such as a project board, (executive) sponsor, project manager, and team managers. The responsibilities of these stakeholders and groups are also defined.
- Agreements that need to be defined by project stakeholders such as how project issues should be escalated and how the project will be evaluated.

It is important to scale and implement PRINCE2 for your particular project needs since the methodology can be overkill for smaller projects due to the artifacts and activities that it prescribes. (See http://www.prince2.com/ for more information.)

[247]

Impact of SOA

There can be tension between the benefits that SOA wants to achieve on the level of departments and organizations as a whole versus the often more local goals of projects.

For example, consider an organization that executes a project to realize a new financial application. Project management of the new application wants the application implemented as soon as possible, for the lowest price, and best quality for the direct end users in the financial department. The organization's architects propose that the financial application can act as implementation for a new `FinancialService` that will provide value for other departments in the organization as well. This would mean that the project needs to execute additional activities such as the following:

- Develop a reusable service according to the service design principles instead of developing more specific, and tightly-integrated business logic. When using PRINCE2, a business case that determines the added value of a reusable service can be included in the **Starting Up a Project** (**SU**) phase. This was discussed in *Chapter 7, Creating a Roadmap, How to Spend Your Money and When?*, in the section *Business case: Benefits for the different stakeholders*. Best-practices for creating reusable services that you learned in previous projects can be collected in this phase.

- Define and negotiate service contracts with the future consumers of the `FinancialService`. These (future) consumers should be involved in the PRINCE2 process **Directing a Project** (**DP**) so they are informed and are able to provide input for the services they will reuse. Details such as service operations, inputs, and outputs can be further defined when executing a stage.

- Update the service registry and repository as discussed in *Chapter 8, Life Cycle Management*, in the section *Service Stages*. In PRINCE2, this activity can be added to the work package delivery in the process **Managing Product Delivery** (**MP**).

- Make sure that the operational procedures and information of demand management, application management, and IT service and operations management are updated to deal with the new consumers of the services besides the end users of the financial application. In PRINCE2, this should be a part of the **Managing Product Delivery** (**MP**) and **Closing a Project** (**CP**) processes in which products such as services are handed over.

This example shows that you can keep using a familiar project management methodology such as PRINCE2 when realizing an SOA. In case of PRINCE2, the work package breakdown might result in more work packages since you will focus on services and service operations instead of entire applications. Next, the project will need to deliver additional artifacts and execute additional activities such as updating the registry and repository and communicate with future consumers of services that are delivered.

Projects should be rewarded for using and creating services

Reward projects for consuming existing services and creating usable services for other consumers in their projects, when it benefits the organization. Rewards can be delivered in different formats: visibility and praise by the organization, extra budget for creating services, priority treatment of issues, and requests for support.

In PRINCE2 terms, consumption of existing services and creation of usable services should be part of the business case during the **Initiating a Project** (**IP**) process.

Software development

The process of software development spans a number of activities:

- **Requirements management**: Gathering demands, wishes, and constraints for your project and prioritizing them. Finding out what end users and the business want, what laws and regulations apply for your project, and what architecture guidelines are relevant. Requirements can be functional, as well as non-functional (response time, availability, and so on). Requirements need to be communicated to designers and developers. Based on these requirements testers can create test plans, and code can be designed and developed.

- **Solution architecture**: Create the solution architecture for the project based on the requirements and relevant reference architectures. Possibly have the solution architecture validated by the organization's architecture board.

- **Design**: Design the software and hardware solution based on the requirements and solution architecture.

- **Development**: Develop the software based on the design. Development includes the creation of unit tests, and testing the software based on these tests.

- **Testing**: Test the software using integration, user, and acceptance tests.

- **Delivery**: Package the software and deliver it to IT service and operations management for deployment to the acceptance and production environment.
- **Maintenance**: Changing software that is in production to solve bugs or add new features. This can also be seen as a particular type of development activity. Maintenance is often initiated through demand management.

 Dedicated methodologies and frameworks exist for each of these activities. For example, **TMap** is a dedicated framework for testing.

Methodology

Development methodologies can be roughly divided into the following categories:

- **Waterfall methodologies**: In waterfall methodologies, a project phase such as requirements management or design is completed and documented in its entirety before moving on to the next project phase. This is also called **Big Design Up Front**. An example of a waterfall methodology is **System Development Methodology (SDM)**.
- **Agile methodologies**: Used in this chapter to denote methodologies that are iterative by nature, meaning that there is not one big flow of sequential phases for the whole project, but several smaller iterations in which all phases are executed to realize part of the solution. These iterations continue until the project is finished. The focus in agile methodologies is on delivering working software over other artifacts. Examples of agile methodologies are **Scrum**, **Extreme Programming (XP)**, and **Kanban**.

Waterfall methodology is easy to understand due to its simple and structured approach. The downsides of waterfall methodologies are that it is difficult to respond to changes during the project and that working software is delivered and demonstrated to end users late in the project cycle. This greatly increases the chances that the project does not deliver what is needed since it is extremely difficult to get all requirements, architecture, and design right the first time. It also means that errors in the requirements or design phase, and changing demands from users and the business are expensive to mediate since they are only discovered at the end of the project during testing.

Due to these drawbacks agile methodologies have been introduced during the last decades that are now the de facto way to develop software. Agile methodologies take into account that requirements evolve in time, and change during the project. Such changes can be incorporated in new iterations of the project.

There are several methodologies that are related to agile methodologies such as prototyping and **test-driven development (TDD)**.

Chapter 10

Impact of SOA

By nature, agile software development fits better with SOA than waterfall methods since SOA focuses on smaller building blocks (services) that can be developed independently rather than large systems that need to be developed as one monolith. Services are logical features to choose as a work package for iterations in agile development.

Big waterfall type projects will counter effect some of the advantages of SOA such as flexibility and responsiveness to change.

> When using PRINCE2 and Scrum in an SOA environment, it is important to define work packages based on the main units of work in an SOA: services, service operations, and processes. In PRINCE2, this is typically done during the **Controlling a Stage** (**CS**) process. Do not determine all stages and work packages for the entire project beforehand, but plan and define work packages gradually during the project.

Application management

Application management is about changing existing applications, or solutions, in a structured way to solve errors, implement new functionality, or implement new rules and regulations. Creating new solutions is out of the scope of application management.

Changes that application management needs to realize come from demand management or directly from end users when demand management does not need to be involved (for example, errors that can easily be pinpointed and for which the fix has only local impact) or smaller organizations that haven't implemented demand management separately. Application management is on the supply side of IT and can be outsourced.

Examples of activities that are part of application management are:

- Changing a financial application to support IBAN bank account numbers besides country-specific bank account numbers
- Creating a new web page for the organization's website in the CMS application, or changing text labels of the HRM system
- Correcting customer information in the database of the CRM application
- Changing configuration items of applications such as timeout values and Web Service endpoints of services that are invoked
- Changing security settings in applications such as user accounts

[251]

- Correcting exceptional behavior in process instances (for example, reversing process steps)
- Changes to application software to fix faults, improve software quality, or implement new functional or technical demands
- Helping and instructing end users of applications
- Inspecting log files, audit information, and so on to answer end user questions

Often, application management involves configuration and functional changes to applications, but can also require software development activities or help of IT service and operations management. Since application management requires expertise and knowledge of the applications, application management is usually implemented in a decentralized fashion or clustered in sets of applications that cover a certain functional domain.

Methodology

Application Services Library (ASL) is an example of an application management framework. It provides process blueprints and best practices for management, maintenance, and change of IT applications.

ASL contains six sets of processes that are divided into a strategic, tactical, and operational layer:

- **Application Cycle Management processes (strategic)**: Processes that deal with the long-term view and management of applications such as their life cycle, future demands, the overall portfolio of applications in an organization, and the future developments in IT.
- **Organizational Cycle Management processes (strategic)**: Processes that deal with the long-term view and management of the organizations involved in application management such as following IT market trends, developing the right skill set in your organization for application management, and interacting with consumers of applications.
- **Management processes (tactical)**: Purpose of these processes is to coordinate the operational processes, and change and improve them overtime as needed. Management processes include planning and control, financial management, quality assurance, and managing service levels.

- **Service Organization processes (operational)**: Processes that support the daily use of applications by customers and end users. The processes include incident management, guaranteeing the availability and continuity of applications, and managing the configuration of applications. These processes are also described by ITIL (the IT service and operations management methodology that is described later on in this chapter).
- **Development and Maintenance processes (operational)**: Processes that define how software changes are realized such as analysis, design, realization, and testing. These processes overlap with software development methodologies.
- **Connecting processes (operational)**: Processes that tune the latter two types of operational processes: service organization, and development and maintenance processes. Connecting processes include release management and change management.

See http://www.aslbislfoundation.org for more information.

Impact of SOA

As was discussed for demand management, solutions might use services that are used by other solutions as well. Application management cannot change a service for a particular consumer without investigating whether other consumers use the service. Application management needs to have insight in the service dependencies for the solutions they are responsible for. In case services need to be changed that are also used by other solutions, the application managers of these impacted solutions need to be consulted.

Besides managing applications and processes, the need arises in an SOA environment to have managers that are responsible for the management of services as well.

Traditionally, most applications had their own dedicated consoles for managing the application. SOA introduces new middleware components such as an ESB and BPM platform that are used to support several solutions. Application managers need to be trained to use the management consoles these tools offer and need to know what and how settings can be changed: a service endpoint might be changed in the ESB console, while a process step might be reversed in the BPM console.

SOA and BPM enable better integration between various organizations through services and process automation. Business processes are executed as a chain of various services. Application managers need to know the context in which their services are used to properly manage them. The context can refer to business processes, composite services, user interface that consumes the services, and so on.

IT service and operations management

IT service and operations, or technical management is responsible for maintaining and proactively monitoring the technical infrastructure on which IT solutions run, and helping end users of the technical infrastructure (phones, laptops, devices, software, and so on). IT service and operations includes the following services and activities:

- Maintenance of basic infrastructure such as connectivity and networking, storage, devices such as smart phones, laptops, desktops, and servers
- Maintenance of office automation such as client machines for employees, mail, word processing, browsers, and so on
- Maintenance of middleware on which applications run such as databases, message-oriented middleware, ESBs, and so on
- Advising projects with regards to IT infrastructure, capacity planning, and IT guidelines
- Helping projects in the delivery of software from development to production

IT service and operations handle requests from demand management or application management to solve issues such as networking issues or performance problems that are caused by the technical infrastructure. IT service and operations also initiate projects and activities on their own such as the replacement of aged hardware, rollout of software updates, and so on.

Organizations can either have their IT infrastructure on-site, hosted at a hosting provider (or Cloud), or a hybrid mix of these. An IT operation is on the supply side of IT and can be outsourced.

Methodology

Information Technology Infrastructure Library (ITIL) is a popular framework for IT service management (and more) that approaches IT service and operations management from the customer side: the services that the business needs from IT.

ITIL provides best practices, checklists, and other instruments for IT service and operations management. The phases in ITIL cover a set of proceses and actvities. The most important are:

- **Service strategy**: Aimed at developing and improving the IT organizations and services they offer in the long term. This includes processes such as portfolio management of IT services that are offered, financial management of those services to make sure that services offered are cost-effective, and relationship management with customers and the business.

- **Service design**: Aimed at creating IT services that customers need and are delivered the way customers have agreed upon with the IT supply organization. This includes processes such as management of service levels (and agreements), maintaining and evolving the service catalogue describing the IT services, and maintaining availability and continuity of IT services.

- **Service transition**: Aimed at taking new IT services into production in a controlled way with minimal disruption of existing IT services. This includes processes such as managing releases and deployments, change management, evaluation of changes, and configuration management of IT services.

- **Service operation**: Aimed at the day-to-day monitoring and maintenance of IT services so that these services are delivered to customers as agreed upon. This includes processes such as incident management, access management (for example, granting access rights to users of IT systems), communication with customers about issues, events, and so on, and providing and maintaining a service desk facility for customers.

- **Continual service improvement**: Aimed at improving the offered IT services in a continuous fashion. Examples of improvements are increasing the quality of the IT service, and delivering the same IT service cheaper to customers. Metrics of current IT services are collected to be able to analyze these services and suggest and realize possible improvements.

See `http://www.itil-officialsite.com/` for more information.

Impact of SOA

The introduction of SOA in an organization often means the use of new middleware products such as an Enterprise Service Bus, BPM platform, or Business Rules Engine that either runs on premise or in the Cloud. These new middleware products need to be managed by IT service and operations which requires training of existing staff, hiring new employees, or outsourcing of management of these components to other companies. Several of the building blocks that are named in *Chapter 5, The SOA Platform*, such as an ESB run services that are used from several primary processes making these middleware components crucial for the day-to-day operations of your organization. Good administration and maintenance by IT operations of these components is therefore vital.

Another challenge for IT service and operations besides new middleware is the changing structure of the application landscape and the dependencies between software components such as explained in the previous chapter.

The processes of IT management such as described by ITIL can still be used to manage an SOA environment but need to be changed at some places to effectively manage services:

- The process of relationship management that is part of service strategy should take into account that services are used by multiple consumers that are possibly outside your own organization. Reuse can result in a change of financial management of IT services since costs can be shared by all service consumers; possibly on a pay-per-use basis.

- As part of service design phase, IT service and operations need to provide access to the registry and repository for (future) service consumers so clients can inspect and use SLAs and interface definitions of services. The new middleware components should be configured so that metrics and other operational data is collected and presented to service consumers. For example, by providing BAM dashboards and publishing metrics provided by ESBs such as average response times of services, availability of services, and so on.

- IT services and operations will need to deal with more, but smaller releases during the service transition phase. For example, instead of a single deployment slot per month used to deploy and upgrade entire applications you might need a weekly deployment slot to deploy and update smaller services. IT services and operations should be flexible enough to deal with a higher frequency of new and changed services. This requires a focus on integration and an understanding of the dependencies between services and their consumers and requires a versioning strategy such as discussed in *Chapter 8, Life Cycle Management*. Apart from the frequency, the type, and form of artifacts also changes. Instead of very elaborate functional and technical designs of entire applications we might require an update of the registry and repository and refer to that.

- To guarantee the quality of the service operation phase, operators and administrators need to be trained so that they can operate and manage the new middleware components such as an ESB. As part of incident management, operators need to verify if problems that a service consumer experiences also apply for other consumers that haven't reported such problems yet. As discussed earlier in the book, the heartbeat operation of services can be used to create a dashboard that proactively and periodically polls if services are still available.

Summary

You have learned in this chapter how you can tune your existing methodologies to make sure your SOA endeavor is going to succeed and will be sustainable. The existing methodologies for demand management, project management, application management, and IT service and operations management can still be applied. The major difference is the number of stakeholders in each of these processes, and the unit of work we are talking about: services instead of applications.

Index

Symbols

.NET Messaging (NMS) API 119

A

actor type, service 93
ad hoc business need 225, 226
Advanced Message Queuing Protocol
    (AMQP) 119
agents 118
agile methodologies 250
Ant 157
Applicable Service Principles 88
Application Cycle Management processes
    (strategic) 252
Application Development Framework
    (ADF) 153
application management
  about 241, 251
  activities, example 251
  Application Services Library (ASL) 252
  methodology 252
  SOA, impact 253
Application Services Library (ASL)
  about..244
  Application Cycle Management processes
      (strategic) 252
  connecting processes (operational) 253
  development and Maintenance processes
      (operational) 253
  management processes (tactical) 252
  Organizational Cycle Management
      processes (strategic) 252
  Service Organization processes
      (operational) 253

approaches, SOA realization
  about 190
  bottom-up identification 192
  example, document management
      service 190
  meet in the middle approach 192, 193
  Top-down identification 191
architectural layer, service
  about 94
  business architecture layer 95
  information architecture layer 95
  technical layer 95
architecture
  about 19, 24
  definition, URL 19
  enterprise architecture 25-27
  layering 22
  models 23
  project architecture 29
  reference architecture 27
  requisites 24
  Service Oriented Architecture 30
  software architecture 29
  solution architecture 28
Architecture Capability Framework 27
Architecture Development Method
    (ADM) 26
architecture process
  about 225
  Ad hoc business need 225, 226
  deviations 227
  picking your battles 229, 230
  planned feature project 228
  SOA governance 229, 230
  solution architecture, integration 227
  solution, defining 226

Atom Publishing Protocol 215
autonomy 65

B

best of breed
  about 144
  versus comprehensive suite 144, 145
Big Design Up Front 250
BizTalk orchestration 166
BizTalk Server
  about 166
  messaging component 166
  orchestration component 166
bottom-up development 113
bottom-up identification 60, 192
BreakfastService 96
BTS. *See* BizTalk Server
bug and issue tracker system 220
Business Activity Monitoring
    (BAM) 123, 150, 152, 165, 221
business architecture layer 95
business case
  about 175, 176
  benefits 175, 176
  company, as whole 177, 178
  departmental benefits 185-189
  example, TMS (Too Many Systems)
    company 182-185
  example, TPIR (The Price Is Right)
    company 180-182
  example, WATB (We Are The Best)
    company 177-179
  IT 182
business faults 67, 68
Business Information Services Library
    (BISL)
  URL 28
Business Process Execution Language
    (BPEL) 123
Business Process Management (BPM)
    tool 219
Business Process Modeling Notation
    (BPMN) 122, 152
business risk 9
Business Rule Management Systems
    Suite (BRMS) 125, 161

Business Rules Engines (BRE) 125
business rules, Microsoft 167
business rules, Oracle 153
business rules, SOA platform
  about 125
  components 125
  examples 125
business service identification 59
Business-to-Business (B2B) 94
Business-to-Consumer (B2C) 94

C

call information 12
Canonical Data Model. *See* CDM
case management platform 123, 124
CaseService 102
CCS 11
CDM 134
change management
  about 237
  pick your battles 238, 239
channel, service 93
claim information 12
ClaimService 191, 193
Closing a Project (CP) 248
common systems solutions 28
company as a whole, business case
  about 177
  example, TPIR (The Price Is Right)
    company 180-182
  example, WATB (We Are The Best)
    company 177-179
Complex Event Processing (CEP) 150, 165
complex events 109
composite services
  about 89, 99
  and process services, differences 103
  composite logic, locating 99
  DocumentService as 98
  implementing 100-103
composition. *See* service composition
comprehensive suites
  advantages 143
  disadvantages 144
  versus best of breed 144, 145
Compression parameter 84

Configuration Management Database
    (CMDB) 219
connecting processes (operational) 253
consumers attribute 217
contact data attribute 217
content based routing 120
content framework 26
Content Management System (CMS) 11, 83
Continuous Query Language (CQL) 159
contract
  about 33, 117, 118
  of service states 206, 207
contract-first development 113
Controlling a Stage (CS) process 251
CSS 11
Customer Contact System. *See* CCS
customer information 12
Customer Relationship Management
    (CRM) application 237
CustomerService.getCustomer
    operation 135

D

database link 100
decision logic 125
decoupling 65
demand management
  about 241-243
  activities 243
  BiSL 243
  demand side 242
  methodology 243, 244
  SOA, impact 244, 245
  supply side 242
demand side 242
departmental benefits, business
    case 185-189
deployment tooling, IBM
  about 163
  deployment scripts 164
  from IDE 163
  from web interface server 164
deployment tooling, Microsoft
  about 168
  BizTalk Server 169
deployment tooling, Oracle
  about 156
  from console 157
  from IDE 156
  scripting used 157
deployment tools 146
deprecated stage 204
designed stage 204
design tooling, IBM
  about 162
  composite services 163
  services 163
design tooling, Microsoft 168
design tooling, Oracle
  about 154
  for business anlaysts 154
  for developers 154
design tooling, SOA platform 136, 137
development and Maintenance processes
    (operational) 253
development process
  about 230, 231
  pick your battles, 232, 233
development tooling, IBM 163
development tooling, Microsoft 168
development tooling, Oracle 155
development tooling, SOA
    platform 137, 138
deviations 227
Directing a Project (DP) 248
Document Management System (DMS) 139
duplication of data and functionality 10

E

ebXML RegRep 215
elementary events 109
elementary services
  about 89, 98
  implementing, ways for 98
enterprise architecture 25-27
Enterprise architecture tools 218
enterprise content management systems 11
enterprise continuum and tools 27
Enterprise Edition (JEE) 119
Enterprise Information Systems (EIS) 149
Enterprise Service Bus (ESB) 229
error handling, IBM 164

error-handling mechanisms 146
error handling, Microsoft 169
error handling, Oracle 158
ESB
  about 120, 220
  composite services 120
  content based routing 120
  routing 120
  transformation 121
  validation 120
Event Definition Language (EDL) 149
Event-delivery Network (EDN) 149
events, IBM
  about 158
  IBM Business Monitor 159
  WebSphere Operational Decision
     Management 159
event sinks 150
events, Microsoft
  Business Activity Monitoring 165
  Complex Event Processing (CEP) 165
  Message-oriented middleware 165
  Microsoft Message Queuing (MSMQ) 165
events, Oracle
  about 149
  Business Activity Monitoring (BAM) 150
  Complex Event Processing (CEP) 150
  Event Definition Language (EDL) 149
  Event-delivery Network (EDN) 149
  Java Messaging Service (JMS) 149
  Oracle Advance Queuing (AQ) 149
  Oracle Event Processing (OEP) 150
events, SOA platform
  about 118
  interface for 119
  publish/subscribe 119
  queuing 119
example, insurance company
  management processes 9
  operational processes 9
  supporting processes 9
examples
  insurance company 8, 9, 11, 17
  international software company 15, 16
  software company 18
  utility companies 14, 15

exception shielding 69
eXtensible Business Reporting Language
     (XBRL) 135
external events 109
Extreme Programming (XP) 250

F

faults, service
  business faults 67, 68
  faulty user input 67, 68
  preventing 67
  technical and software faults 67, 69
faulty user input 67, 68
feature by feature, roadmap 194
Federal Enterprise architecture (FEA)
  URL 28
foundation solutions 28
Functional description attribute 217

G

gap-analysis 58
gateway 118
Geek and Poke
  URL 44
getVersion method 212
governance. *See also* **picking your
     battles** 224
granularity, service 73, 74

H

Health Level 7 (HL7) 135
HR-XML standard
  URL 188

I

IBM
  about 158
  business rules 147, 161
  deployment tooling 148, 163
  design tooling 147, 162
  development tooling 147, 163
  error handling 148, 164
  events 146, 158

monitoring 148, 164
registry and repository 147, 162
runtime environments 160
security 147, 161
service composition 146, 159
services 146, 158
test tooling 148, 163
user interface 147, 161
IBM Business Monitor 159
IBM Business Process Manager 160, 161
IBM Rational Application Developer (RAD) 163
IBM WebSphere Application Server (WAS) 158
IBM WebSphere ILOG Decision Validation Services 161
IBM WebSphere ILOG Rule Solutions for Office 161
IBM WebSphere ILOG Rule Team Server 161
Idempotency, service 69, 70, 72
Identification attribute 217
identified stage 204
Identity and Access Management (IAM) tooling
  about 131
  authentication 131
  authorization 132
  identity management 131
ILOG BRMS 161
implementation
  about 33
  building 114
  changing 207
  existing software, using 114
implemented stage 204
industry solutions 28
information architecture layer 95
information service identification 59
Information Technology. *See* **IT**
Information Technology Infrastructure Library. *See* **ITIL**
input or facts 125
Insurance Administration System (IAS) 182, 183
Integrated Development Environments (IDEs) 137

interface 33
  changing 207
  proprietary interfaces 115
  types 115
  web services 115
internal events 109
interoperability, service 64
isolation, service
  about 63, 65, 104
  print service, example 65
IT
  about 8
  and business, mis match 9, 10
  data and functionality, duplication 10
  importance 8
  insurance company, example 8-12
  risk, managing 9
  software company, example 18
  strategies 17, 18
IT, business case
  example, TMS (Too Many Systems) company 182-185
ITIL
  about 219, 254
  activities 255
ITIL (Information Technology Infrastructure Library) 244
IT service and operations management
  about 241, 254
  Information Technology Infrastructure Library (ITIL) 254
  methodology 254, 255
  SOA, impact 255, 256

J

Java Enterprise Edition (JEE) 149
Java Message Service (JMS) 119, 159
Java Messaging Service (JMS) 149

K

Kanban 250

L

loose-coupling 65, 105

M

management processes 9
management processes (tactical) 252
Managing Product Delivery (MP) 248
mash up 128
maturity model
  about 197
  experience 199
  growing up 198
  live 198
  maintenance mode 199, 200
  Newlyweds 198
  SOA, starting with 198
Maven 157
MediationFlows 159
meet in the middle 192, 193
meet -in-the-middle development 113
Message Oriented Middleware (MOM) 119
messaging component 166
methodologies 242
Microsoft BizTalk Server
  about 169
  BTSTask command-line tool 169
  business rules 147, 167
  deployment tooling 148, 168
  design tooling 147, 168
  development tooling 147, 168
  error handling 148, 169
  events 146, 165
  monitoring 148, 169
  registry and repository 147, 168
  Scripting and APIs 169
  security 147, 168
  service composition 146, 166
  services 146, 165
  test tooling 148, 168
  user interface 147, 167
  Visual Studio 169
Microsoft Message Queuing (MSMQ) 165
monitoring, Microsoft 169
monitoring, Oracle 157
monitoring tools 146
Multipurpose Internet Mail Extensions
    (MIME) 211

N

NORA
  URL 28

O

OASIS
  about 36
  example, international software
      company 38-43
  order-to-cash business process 37, 38
  URL 36
Open Group Definition 88
operational processes 9
operations
  about 233, 234
  pick your battles, 235, 236
Oracle
  business rules 147, 153
  deployment tooling 148, 156
  design tooling 147, 154
  development tooling 147, 155
  error handling 148, 158
  events 146, 149
  monitoring 148, 157
  registry and repository 147, 154
  security 147, 154
  service composition 146, 150
  services 146, 149
  test tooling 148, 155
  user interface 147, 153
Oracle Advance Queuing (AQ) 149
Oracle BPM Suite 152
Oracle Business Process Manager
    (OBPM) 152
Oracle Enterprise Pack for Eclipse
    (OEPE) 155
Oracle Enterprise Repository (OER) 154
Oracle Event Processing (OEP) 150
Oracle Service Bus (OSB)
  adaptive messaging 151
  configuration framework 151
  security 151
  service management 151
  service virtualization 151

Oracle SOA Suite 152
Oracle WebCenter
  about 153
  Application Adapters for Oracle
      WebCenter 153
  WebCenter Content 153
  WebCenter Portal 153
  WebCenter Sites 153
  WebCenter Social 153
Oracle Web Services Manager (OWSM) 154
orchestration component 166
OrderService
  consumer 43
  contract 39
  implementation 43
  interface 40, 41
  provider 43
  reuse 44
OrderService.getOrderDetails
      operation 135
order-to-cash business process 38
ordinary events 150
organizational boundaries, service 93
Organizational Cycle Management
      processes (strategic) 252
organizational risk 9
organizational silos 13
Organization for the Advancement of
      Structured Information Standards.
      See OASIS
organization-specific solutions 28
output or decisions 125

P

PaymentService 191, 193
picking your battles 224
policies
  about 118
  agents 118
  gateway 118
policy information 12
portal 129
portlets 129
Predecessor attribute 217

PRINCE2 247
process by process, roadmap 194
process services
  about 89, 103
  and composite services, differences 103
  implementing 104
process silos
  about 13
  insurance company, example 17
  international software company,
      example 15, 16
  utility companies, example 14, 15
product information 12
products
  about 32
  elements 32
project architecture
  purpose 29
project management
  about 241, 246
  Closing a Project (CP) 248
  Directing a Project (DP) 248
  Managing Product Delivery (MP) 248
  methodology 246, 247
  PRojects IN Controlled Environments 2
      (PRINCE2) 246, 247
  SOA, impact 248, 249
  Starting Up a Project (SU) phase 248
PRojects IN Controlled Environments 2.
      See PRINCE2
proprietary interfaces 115
publish/subscribe 119

Q

QoS 62
Quality of Service. See QoS
queuing 119

R

reference architecture 112
  about 27
  advantages 27
  disadvantages 27
reference models 27

registry
    benefits 216
    bug and issue tracker system 220
    Business Activity Monitoring (BAM) 221
    Business Process Management (BPM)
        tool 219
    change process, supporting 217, 218
    Configuration Management Database
        (CMDB) 219
    Enterprise architecture tools 218
    ESB 220
    infrastructure monitoring 221
    in IT landscape 218
    process, changing 216
    service consumer, benefits for 216
    services, finding 216
    standards 215
    troubleshooting 216
registry and repository, IBM 162
registry and repository, Microsoft 168
registry and repository, Oracle 154
repository. *See* **registry**
Representational State Transfer (REST) 117
RESTful services 117
RETE algorithm 153
retired stage 204
retrieveData operation 84
reusability, service
    about 76
    example 78
roadmap
    about 193
    feature by feature 194
    process by process 194
    service by service 194
    system by system 195
routing 120
Rule Execution Server 161
Rule Studio 161

S

Scrum 250
**Security Assertion Markup Language
    (SAML) protocol 132**
Security attribute 217
security, IBM 161

security, Microsoft 168
security, Oracle 154
security, service 66, 94
security, SOA platform
    about 131, 132
    applying 133
    applying, in SOA 133, 134
    Identity and Access Management
        (IAM) tooling 131
Server Faces (JSF) 153
service
    about 31, 32
    administrator 216
    Applicable Service Principles 88
    classifying 76, 90
    client 77
    components 32
    composite services 89
    consumer 35, 77
    consumers 216, 217
    contract 33, 206
    defining 87
    designing 61
    drivers 31, 45
    elementary services 89
    example, lets have breakfast 33, 34
    example, ordering passport 35
    faults, types 67
    good or bad 82, 83
    granularity 73
    idempotency 69, 70
    idempotency and statefulness 70-72
    idempotent 63
    implementation 33, 206
    implementation, hiding 63
    information, passing from smaller service
        to larger service 107
    information, passing within
        services 105, 106
    interface 33, 206
    interoperability 64
    isolation 63
    isolation (autonomy) 65
    myths 45, 46
    Open Group Definition 88
    owner 217
    print service, example 65

process services 89
provider 35
retrieveData operation 84
reusability 76, 77
reusability, example 78-82
reused 36
security 66
service registry 36
solutions 31
storeData operation 84
value, providing 62
version 216, 217
service aggregation 97
service by service, roadmap 194
service classification
  about 89
  actor type 93
  architectural level 94, 95
  benefits 96
  channel 93
  combining 95, 96
  insurance company, example 90-92
  organizational boundaries 93
  security level 94
**Service Component Architecture
    (SCA) 151, 159**
service, components
  contract 33
  implementation 33
  interface 33
service composition 89, 97
service composition, IBM
  about 159
  IBM Business Process Manager 160
  IBM WebSphere Enterprise Service Bus
    (ESB) 159
  Java Message Service (JMS) 159
  Mediation Flow 159
  Service Component Architecture (SCA) 159
service composition, Microsoft
  BizTalk Server 166
  Windows Server AppFabric 166
service composition, Oracle
  about 150
  Oracle BPM Suite 152
  Oracle Service Bus (OSB) 150
  Oracle SOA Suite 151, 152

service composition, SOA platform
  about 120
  Business Process Management (BPM) 122
  case management platform 123, 124
  Enterprise Service Bus (ESB) 120
service consumer
  about 62
  versioning changes, steps for 212, 213
  version, making explicit 210
service, drivers
  cost reduction 45
  flexibility 45
  standardization 45
service identification
  about 55, 56
  bottom-up service identification 60
  top-down service identification 56
service orchestration 97, 100
**Service Organization processes
    (operational) 253**
service-oriented. *See* **SOA**
**Service Oriented Modeling and
    Architecture.** *See* **SOMA**
service provider 62
service registry 36
service registry, SOA platform 134
service repository, SOA platform 134
services, IBM 158
services, Microsoft 165
service, SOA platform
  about 113
  bottom-up development 113, 114
  contract 117
  contract-first development 113
  implementation 114
  interface 115
  meet in the middle development 113
  policies 118
  top-down development 113
services, Oracle 149
service stages
  about 203
  deprecated stage 204
  designed stage 204
  identified stage 204
  implemented stage 204
  retired stage 204

service states
  contract, changing 206, 207
  implementation, changing 207
  interface, changing 207
service versioning
  about 205
  contract, changing 206, 207
  contract, service 206
  implementation, changing 207
  implementation, service 206
  interface, changing 207
  interface, service 206
Simple Object Access Protocol (SOAP) 116
Single Point of Truth (SPOT) 183
SLA attribute 217
SOA
  about 31, 46, 47
  application landscapes, rationalizing 51, 52
  example, international software
      company 49, 51
  example, utility company 47-49
  features 47
  maturity model 197
  solutions 47
  standardization 53
SOA governance 224
SOAP-based services 116
SOA platform
  about 112
  business process management 113
  business rules 113, 125, 126
  case management 113
  design tooling 113, 136, 137
  development tooling 113, 137, 138
  Enterprise Service Bus 112
  events 112, 118, 119
  example, order to cash 139, 140
  Identity and Access Management 113
  implementation 112
  interface 112
  policies (contract) 112
  registry and repository 113
  security 131, 132
  service composition 120

  service registry 134
  service repository 134
  services 113, 114
  user interface 113, 127, 128
SOA realization
  about 171
  approaches 190
  business case, refining 174
  feature, determining 172
  feature, evaluating 174
  feature, realizing 173
  features 174
  goals and approach, identifying 172
  handle failure 173
  high-level solution architecture,
      designing 172
  initial business case, creating 172
  roadmap, defining 172, 174
  roadmap impact, determining 174
  solution, defining 173
  solution, delivering 173
  solution, implementing 173
  solution, integrating 174
software architecture 29
software development
  about 241
  activities 249
  agile methodologies 250
  methodology 250
  SOA, impact 251
  TMap 250
  waterfall methodologies 250
solution architecture
  about 28
  common systems solutions 28
  foundation solutions 28
  industry solutions 28
  organization-specific solutions 28
SOMA 55
Starting Up a Project (SU) phase 248
state attribute 217
state date attribute 217
statefulness, service 71, 72
storeData operation 84

stovepiped 127
Straight-Through Processing 104
Successor attribute 217
supply side 242
supporting processes 9
system 20
system by system, roadmap 195
System Center Operations Manager (SCOM) 169
System Development Methodology (SDM) 250

T

technical and software faults 67, 69
technical artifacts attribute 217
technical layer 95
technical risk 9
technical service identification 59, 60
test-driven development (TDD) 250
Test suite attribute 217
test tooling, IBM 163
test tooling, Microsoft 168
test tooling, Oracle
  about 155
  from console 156
  SCA testing framework 156
  transformations 155
test tools 146
The Open Group Architecture Framework. See TOGAF
TMap 250
TM Forum Frameworx and eTOM for telecommunications
  URL 28
TMS (Too Many Systems) company 182
TOGAF
  about 22
  Architecture Capability Framework 27
  Architecture Development Method (ADM) 26
  content framework 26
  enterprise continuum and tools 27
  reference models 27

tooling
  registry 213
  repository 213
top-down development 113
top-down identification 191
top-down service identification
  about 59
  business service identification 59
  information service identification 59
  technical service identification 60
top-down service identification
  about 56
  business service identification 57
  business service identification, example 57
  information service identification 57
  information service identification, example 57
  technical service identification 57
  technical service identification, example 57
TPIR (The Price Is Right) company 180-182
type attribute 217

U

UDDI 214, 215
Universal Description Discovery and Integration. See UDDI
user interface, IBM 161
user interface, Microsoft 167
user interface, Oracle 153
user interface, SOA platform
  about 127
  capabilities 128
  information mismatch 130
  integrated user interface, benefits 129, 130

V

Validate-Enrich-Transform-Route-Operate (VETRO) 121
Vecoz company 178
version attribute 217
version control 205
versioning schemes
  about 205, 208, 209
  for service consumers 210-212
  versioning and life cycle stages 209

W

WATB (We Are The Best) company 177
waterfall methodologies 250
web content management systems 11
WebLogic Scripting Tool (WLST) 157
Web Service Description Language
      (WSDL) 41, 116
web services
  about 115
  RESTful services 117
  SOAP-based services 116
WebSphere ESB Registry edition 162
WebSphere Operational Decision
      Management 159
WebSphere Registry and Repository
      (WSRR) 162
whiteboards 136
Windows Server AppFabric 166
Windows Workflow Foundation (WF) 167
World Wide Web Consortium (W3C) 116
WS-* 116

X

XML Process Definition Language
      (XPDL) 123
XML Schema (XSD) 41

Z

Zachman
  URL 20

Thank you for buying
SOA Made Simple

About Packt Publishing

Packt, pronounced 'packed', published its first book "Mastering phpMyAdmin for Effective MySQL Management" in April 2004 and subsequently continued to specialize in publishing highly focused books on specific technologies and solutions.

Our books and publications share the experiences of your fellow IT professionals in adapting and customizing today's systems, applications, and frameworks. Our solution based books give you the knowledge and power to customize the software and technologies you're using to get the job done. Packt books are more specific and less general than the IT books you have seen in the past. Our unique business model allows us to bring you more focused information, giving you more of what you need to know, and less of what you don't.

Packt is a modern, yet unique publishing company, which focuses on producing quality, cutting-edge books for communities of developers, administrators, and newbies alike. For more information, please visit our website: www.packtpub.com.

About Packt Enterprise

In 2010, Packt launched two new brands, Packt Enterprise and Packt Open Source, in order to continue its focus on specialization. This book is part of the Packt Enterprise brand, home to books published on enterprise software – software created by major vendors, including (but not limited to) IBM, Microsoft and Oracle, often for use in other corporations. Its titles will offer information relevant to a range of users of this software, including administrators, developers, architects, and end users.

Writing for Packt

We welcome all inquiries from people who are interested in authoring. Book proposals should be sent to author@packtpub.com. If your book idea is still at an early stage and you would like to discuss it first before writing a formal book proposal, contact us; one of our commissioning editors will get in touch with you.

We're not just looking for published authors; if you have strong technical skills but no writing experience, our experienced editors can help you develop a writing career, or simply get some additional reward for your expertise.

Oracle SOA Suite 11g R1 Developer's Guide

ISBN: 978-1-849680-18-9   Paperback: 720 pages

Develop Service-Oriented Architecture Solutions with the Oracle SOA Suite

1. A hands-on, best-practice guide to using and applying the Oracle SOA Suite in the delivery of real-world SOA applications

2. Detailed coverage of the Oracle Service Bus, BPEL PM, Rules, Human Workflow, Event Delivery Network, and Business Activity Monitoring

3. Master the best way to use and combine each of these different components in the implementation of an SOA solution

Oracle BPM Suite 11g Developer's cookbook

ISBN: 978-1-849684-22-4   Paperback: 512 pages

Over 80 advanced recipes to develop rich, interactive business processes using the Oracle Business Process Management Suite

1. Dive into lessons on Fault ,Performance and Rum Time Management

2. Explore User Interaction ,Deployment and Monitoring

3. Dive into BPM Process Implementation as process developer while conglomerating BPMN elements

Please check www.PacktPub.com for information on our titles

Do more with SOA Integration: Best of Packt

ISBN: 978-1-849685-72-6 Paperback: 702 pages

Integrate, automate, and regulate your business processes with the best of Packt's SOA books

1. Get to grips with SOA integration in this comprehensive guide which draws on the value of eight separate Packt SOA books!

2. Learn about SOA integration through both step-by-step tutorial and cookbook chapters

3. A mash-up book from a range of expert SOA professionals, and a total of eight Packt titles - professional expertise distilled in a true sense

Oracle SOA Suite 11g Administrator's Handbook

ISBN: 978-1-849686-08-2 Paperback: 380 pages

Create a reliable, secure, and flexible environment for your Oracle SOA Suite 11g Service Infrastructure and SOA composite applications

1. Monitor your Oracle SOA Suite environment and fine tune the performance of your Oracle SOA Suite services and applications

2. Manage the underlying WebLogic server, threads and timeouts, file systems, and composite applications

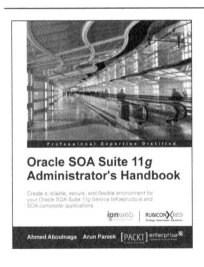

Please check www.PacktPub.com for information on our titles

CPSIA information can be obtained at www.ICGtesting.com
Printed in the USA
LVOW02s2326230713

344267LV00020B/1244/P